Pragmatic Ajax

A Web 2.0 Primer

Pragmatic Ajax
A Web 2.0 Primer

Justin Gehtland

Ben Galbraith

Dion Almaer

The Pragmatic Bookshelf

Raleigh, North Carolina   Dallas, Texas

Many of the designations used by manufacturers and sellers to distinguish their products are claimed as trademarks. Where those designations appear in this book, and The Pragmatic Programmers, LLC was aware of a trademark claim, the designations have been printed in initial capital letters or in all capitals. The Pragmatic Starter Kit, The Pragmatic Programmer, Pragmatic Programming, Pragmatic Bookshelf and the linking *g* device are trademarks of The Pragmatic Programmers, LLC.

Every precaution was taken in the preparation of this book. However, the publisher assumes no responsibility for errors or omissions, or for damages that may result from the use of information (including program listings) contained herein.

Our Pragmatic courses, workshops, and other products can help you and your team create better software and have more fun. For more information, as well as the latest Pragmatic titles, please visit us at

http://www.pragmaticprogrammer.com

ISBN 0-9766940-8-5

Printed on acid-free paper with 85% recycled, 30% post-consumer content.

First printing, March 2006

Version: 2006-3-13

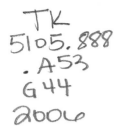
Contents

Acknowledgments

Writing a book is a lot like (we imagine) flying a spaceship too close to a black hole. One second you're thinking "Hey, there's something interesting over there" and a picosecond later, everything you know and love has been sucked inside and crushed.

OK, that's hyperbole, but the point is that books don't write themselves. More to the point, books aren't even just written by the authors. It takes the combined efforts of a lot of people to extract information from the chaos. We'd like to hereby issue the following thanks.

To every single beta purchaser of the book and especially the ones who sent in *all those errata posts*. You are a fantastic bunch, and we can't thank you enough for your belief in the project and your help in making it a better book.

To the team at the Pragmatic Programmers (especially you, Dave): you exhibited endless patience, forbearance, and wisdom during the process.

Finally, to the authors of all the wonderful frameworks and tools we highlight in this book: your work is inspiring and we hope that this book helps shed just a little more light on the work you've done.

From Justin Gehtland

To my coauthors: thanks for thinking of me.

My colleagues are an endless font of inspiration and vexation, both of which help with the creative process. So, thanks to Stu Halloway, Glenn Vanderburg, Neal Ford, and Ted Neward, all of whom provided various amounts of both.

I keep telling my family that one day I'll write a book they'd like to read. At least this one has an interesting cover. Lisa, Zoe, and Gabe: thanks for putting up with my office hours.

From Ben Galbraith

Thank you to my family, for all your patience while I spent late nights and early mornings working on this project. I love you.

My sincere gratitude also goes to my publisher Dave Thomas (who patiently and gracefully watched this project go from early arrival to, well, somewhat less than early arrival) and my fellow authors, Justin Gehtland and Dion Almaer, who made many personal sacrifices to get across the finish line.

Finally, I thank all of my peers and colleagues who have taught me throughout the years. The patience and kindness of nearly everyone in our industry has always been an inspiration to me.

From Dion Almaer

Ah, acknowledgments. This is the moment where you feel like you are at the podium and don't want to forget anyone.

Firstly, I would like to thank my fellow Ajaxians: Ben Galbraith, Justin Gehtland, Stu Halloway, Rob Sanheim, Michael Mahemoff, and the entire community that visits and contributes to ajaxian.com. This book is really for you, the readers.

Secondly, I would like to thank all of the great technical folk who I have had the pleasure of working with. This includes buddies from Adigio, the No Fluff Just Stuff tour, and the general blogosphere. You know who you are.

Finally, I would like to thank my family, especially my wife, Emily, who lets me work crazy hours without putting me through guilt trips. You are my best friend, Em.

Chapter 1

Building Rich Internet Applications with Ajax

This is a book about developing effective web applications. We're not going to dance around this issue. Underneath everything else, this book is about XHTML, JavaScript, CSS, and standards that have been around for almost a decade now. Not only do we admit this truth, we embrace it. Just because these standards have been around for a while doesn't mean we can't build something new and exciting out of them. Technology, like Jello, takes a while to solidify into something tasty and satisfying.

Ajax (and Web 2.0) represents the maturation of Internet standards into a viable application development platform. The combination of stable standards, better understanding, and a unifying vision amount to a whole that is greater, by far, than the sum of its parts. With Ajax, you'll be able to achieve the double Holy Grail: feature-filled user interfaces *and* a no-hassle, no-install deployment story.

It wasn't long ago that Jesse James Garrett coined the term *Ajax*. When he first released the term onto the public consciousness, it stood for *Asynchronous JavaScript And XML*. It has since, like SOAP before it, lost its acronym status and is just a word. However, it is an enormously powerful word. With this single word, Jesse James was able to harness an industry-wide trend toward richer, install-free web applications and give it focus.

Naming a thing is powerful. In this case, it's not powerful enough to become a movement, though. A spark was still lacking. It was to be provided by an entirely unlikely entity. What follows is the story of one development team, that spark, and how it changed the way we approach web software.

1.1 A Tale in Three Acts

Hector is a project manager for a web application development shop. With a long history of Perl, CGI, ASP, Servlet, and JSP development under his belt, Hector's been around the block. For the last year his team has been building a CRM application for a large Fortune 500 company with offices all over the world. The application used to be a green-screen mainframe application; the company wants to take advantage of the great reach of the Internet to deploy the application to every office.

Hector and his team focus a lot of their energy on the server side of the application. They have been using one of the modern MVC frameworks from the Java community to implement the business logic, a high-performance persistence framework to access the database, and messaging-based infrastructure to connect to other existing systems.

Yesterday

On the client side, Hector and his team have become masters of CSS. The look of the pages bends to their will; when the customer wants rounded corners, they get rounded corners. Rollover colors? That's easy. Multiple color schemes? No problem. In fact, Hector and his team long ago reached a point where they weren't really worried about the user interface. See, the Web operates one way: it essentially distributes static documents. When users want more data, they incur a complete interface refresh. It isn't optimal from an efficiency perspective, but it's how the Web works, and users have just learned to live with it.

Then, sometime a couple of weeks ago, Hector's customer came to a meeting. The customer was usually a polite, accommodating fellow. He understood the Web, and he understood the restrictions he had to live with to get the reach of the Internet. In fact, Hector had never seen him get really angry. Until this meeting.

As soon as he walked in, the team knew something was up. He had his laptop with him, and he never carried it. As he stormed into the room, the team glanced around the table: what have we done? The customer sat down at the table, fired up the laptop, and hammered away at the keyboard for a minute. While he pounded the keys, he told the team,

"Last night, my wife and I were invited to a party at the CEO's house."
"Uh oh," thought the team, "this can't be good."

"Well, I certainly jumped at the chance," he continued. "I've never been before. This project got me on his radar." ("Double uh-oh," thought Hector.) "When I couldn't figure out how to get there with my city map, I went to the Internet. I found THIS!" He hissed the last word with venom and scorn. He flipped the laptop around so the table could see it. There, quietly couched in his browser window, was Google Maps. "Why," he said, through clenched teeth, "can't I have this?"

Today

Since that meeting, Hector and his team have been rethinking the user interface. Hector went out to learn how Google could have completely ignored conventional wisdom and generated such a thing. He came across an article by Jesse James Garrett describing this thing called Ajax. He has been digging since then, learning everything he can about this new way of making Internet applications.

The team has begun reimplementing the UI. They're using JavaScript and DHTML techniques to provide a more dynamic experience. Most of all, they've begun taking advantage of a useful object available in modern browsers called XMLHttpRequest (XHR for short). This handy little guy lets Hector and his team request and receive fresh data from the server without reloading everything in the page.

In other words, Hector spearheaded a move from Web 1.0 to Web 2.0. And his customer is happy again.

Tomorrow

So what comes next for Hector? His team is learning a bunch about JavaScript, XHTML, and even more about CSS than it ever knew before. The team is really excited about the results: the user experience is just like any other application now, except the team doesn't have to manage an installer as well as the application itself. But they've realized that there's a downside to all this.

Now, they are writing a ton of code in JavaScript. It turns out that all this page manipulation and XHR access requires a lot of real, honest-to-goodness code. And even though JavaScript looks a lot like Java, they've discovered that it really is a different beast. And now they have two codebases to manage, test, and maintain.

So Hector is off to find out how to solve these problems. And what he will see is that most web application development frameworks are rapidly incorporating Ajax tools into their own suites. Soon, Hector and his team will be able to leverage Tapestry components, Spring tag libraries, ASP.NET widgets, Rails helpers, and PHP libraries to take advantage of Ajax without having to incorporate a second way of working. The (near) future of Ajax development is total, invisible integration. And this is exactly what Hector needs.

1.2 Google Maps: The Missing Spark

Google Maps (http://maps.google.com) really ignited the Ajax fire. And Google was just about the most unlikely candidate to do it. Think about what made Google an overnight sensation in the first place: better search results and the world's most minimal UI. It was a white page, with a text box and a button in the middle of it. It doesn't get any more minimal than that. If Google had had a soundtrack, it would have been written by Philip Glass.

When it became obvious that Google was going to enter the online mapping space, we all expected something similar: a straightforward, unintrusive approach to viewing maps. And this is what we got; just not the way we expected. Google, through the clever use of XHR callbacks, provided the first in-page scrollable map. If you wanted to look at the next grid of map panels, Google went off and retrieved them and just slid the old ones out of the way. No messy page refresh; no reloading of a bunch of unchanged text. Particularly, no waiting around for a bunch of ads to refresh. It was just a map, the way a map ought to work.

Then we clicked on a push pin and got the info bubble. With live text in it. And a drop shadow. And that was the end of an era. We've been told the same story that you just lived through with Hector again and again. Somebody's boss or customer or colleague sees Google Maps and says, "Why not me?"

As programmers, too, there's another reaction: "I wish I could work on that kind of application." There's an impression out there that Google Maps, and applications like it, are rocket science and that it takes a special kind of team, and a special kind of developer, to make them happen. This book, if nothing else, will lay to rest that idea. As we'll demonstrate in Chapter 2, *Creating Google Maps*, on page 9, making web pages sing and dance isn't all that challenging once you know what tools are available. It becomes even more impressive once you discover that Google Maps isn't really proper Ajax; it doesn't take advantage of any of the modern asynchronous callback technology and is really just dynamic HTML trickery.

1.3 What Is Ajax?

Ajax is a hard beast to distill into a one-liner. The reason it is so hard is because it has two sides to it:

- Ajax can be viewed as a set of technologies.
- Ajax can be viewed as an architecture.

Ajax: Asynchronous JavaScript and XML

The name Ajax came from the bundling of its enabling technologies: an asynchronous communication channel between the browser and server, JavaScript, and XML. When it was defined, it was envisioned as the following:

- Standards-based presentation using XHTML and CSS
- Dynamic display and interaction using the browser's Document Object Model (DOM)
- Data interchange and manipulation using XML and XSLT
- Asynchronous data retrieval using XMLHttpRequest or XMLHTTP (from Microsoft)
- JavaScript binding everything together

Although it is common to develop using these enabling technologies, it can quickly become more trouble than reward. As we go through the book, we will show you how you can do the following:

- Incorporate Ajaxian techniques that do not use formal XML for data transport
- Bypass the DOM APIs themselves for manipulating the in-memory page model
- Use synchronous calls to the server, which can be powerful but is also dangerous
- Abstract away the complexity of XMLHttpRequest

It is for these reasons that the more important definition for Ajax is...

Ajax: The Architecture

The exciting evolution that is Ajax is in how you architect web applications. Let's look first at the conventional web architecture:

1. Define a page for every event in the application: view items, purchase items, check out, and so on.

2. Each event, or action, returns a *full* page back to the browser.

3. That page is rendered to the user.

This seems natural to us now. It made sense at the beginning of the Web, as the Web wasn't really about applications. The Web started off as more of a document repository; it was a world in which you could simply link between documents in an ad hoc way. It was about document and data sharing, not interactivity in any meaningful sense.

Picture a rich desktop application for a moment. Imagine what you would think if, on every click, all of the components on the application screen redrew from scratch. Seems a little nuts, doesn't it? On the Web, that was the world we inhabited until Ajax came along.

Ajax is a new architecture. The important parts of this architecture are:

- *Small server-side events*: Now components in a web application can make small requests back to a server, get some information, and tweak the page that is viewed by changing the DOM. No full page refresh.

- *Asynchronous*: Requests posted back to the server don't cause the browser to block. The user can continue to use other parts of the application, and the UI can be updated to alert the user that a request is taking place.

- *onAnything*: We can interact with the server based on almost anything the user does. Modern browsers trap most of the same user events as the operating system: mouseovers, mouse clicks, keypresses, etc. Any user event can cause an asynchronous request.

In Figure 1.1, on the next page, we illustrate the new life cycle of an Ajax page.

1. The user makes an initial request against a given URL.

2. The server returns the original HTML page.

3. The browser renders the page as in-memory DOM tree.

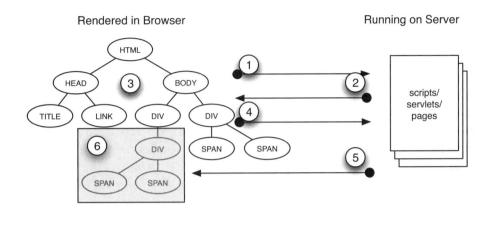

Figure 1.1: AJAX PAGE LIFECYCLE

4. Some user activity causes an asynchronous request to another URL, leaving the existing DOM tree untouched.

5. The browser returns data to a callback function inside the existing page.

6. The browser parses the result and updates the in-memory DOM with the new data. This is reflected on the screen to the user (the page is redrawn but not "refreshed").

This all sounds great, doesn't it? With this change we have to be careful, though. One of the greatest things about the Web is that anybody can use it. Having simple semantics helps that happen. If we go overboard, we might begin surprising the users with new UI abstractions. This is a common complaint with Flash UIs, where users are confronted with new symbols, metaphors, and required actions to achieve useful results. Usability is an important topic that we will delve into in Chapter 7, *Ajax UI, Part II*, on page 125.

Ajax: The Future

Where is Ajax going? What is the future going to hold? This is a vital question, because Ajax is one of those amorphous terms that seems to change with the context. Ajax itself is a unifying term for describing a collection of technologies. We believe that the term itself, as unifying and rallying as it has been, is likely to disappear from the public consciousness within the next couple of years.

That's because the technologies you will learn about in this book will eventually become the substrate of your favorite web application development platform. Instead of representing this brave new world of shiny gadgets and nifty tricks, it will just be *how web apps work*. Does this mean that this book is unimportant? Far from it. You need to understand how this works now to get it done, and you'll need to understand it in the future to debug your applications. But you probably won't think of those apps as Ajax, just as Web apps. And that's a good thing.

1.4 Whither Now?

The rest of this book will introduce you to the breadth of the Ajax movement. We'll walk through the conversion of an application to this new style and provide deep coverage of the enabling technologies behind Ajax. We'll introduce you to commonly available toolsets and frameworks that make seemingly advanced effects as simple as a single line of code. You'll get to see what your favorite development platforms are doing to take advantage of, and integrate with, this new style of development.

Most important, we'll talk a lot about how to use Ajax effectively, pragmatically, even. That's because the only thing worse than being left behind when the train leaves the station is getting on the wrong train. We intend this book to be a guide through a new and rapidly evolving landscape. We want to help you find out how, and even if, Ajax can help your projects. We're not trying to sell you anything (except this book). But we believe that Ajax represents a major event, and we want to be there to help you make the best of it.

But let's start with the spark that ignited the fire: Google Maps.

Chapter 2

Creating Google Maps

For many of us, Google Maps (http://maps.google.com) ignited the Ajax revolution. While Ajaxian techniques had been creeping into mainstream websites long before Google Maps, nothing in recent memory presented commodity browsers with such a visually impressive experience. Google Maps showed the world that a wide world of potential lay hidden in the technologies we thought we understood so well.

As we said in Chapter 1, Ajax was initially defined as the intersection of the XMLHttpRequest object and the usage of XML to update a DOM tree. However, the current definition of Ajax (and Web 2.0) spans much more. This chapter demonstrates the underpinnings of Google Maps and how modern browser-based applications can use nothing but standard HTML and JavaScript to achieve entirely new kinds of web apps.

The purpose of this chapter is to lay bare the techniques that Google used to wow us all with Google Maps. What we'll discover here is fascinating and important; it also might be more than you want to bite off right now. If so, don't worry about skipping ahead to the rest of the book and coming back here later; we won't mind.

This chapter contains a lot of code. It's all available online, so you can download the archives containing all the book's source.[1] Alternatively, if you're reading the PDF version of this book, just click a link to get to the file. However, if the file you're fetching contains HTML, it'll probably get rendered by your browser. This is good if you want to see the running application. If instead you want to see the code, use your browser's View Source option.

---

[1]From http://pragmaticprogrammer.com/titles/ajax/code.html

2.1 Rocket Scientists?

Shortly after Google Maps launched, entrenched commercial interests who relied upon the staidness of standard HTML-based web interfaces to make money were quick to claim that mainstream HTML developers need not attempt to create web interfaces like Google Maps. The CEO of Macromedia, maker of the popular Flash browser plug-in, stated in at least one interview that such non-Flash web interfaces required the skills of "rocket scientists." (Ironically, when Macromedia finally produced a clone of Google Maps in Flash four or five months later, it failed to function on the two Mac laptops we used to try it out—actually locking up the browser. Google Maps works just fine on both machines. We're actually not anti-Flash; we just found it ironic, that's all.)

Such statements have added to the general impression many developers have that creating something like Google Maps is just, well, hard. In fact, some developers have even felt a little fear and intimidation—fear that someday soon, they'll be asked to create something like Google Maps!

Certainly many of us who have been writing HTML for years might like to believe that it took a team of rocket scientists to produce a litany of innovations supporting the technologies behind the Google Maps interface, if nothing else to provide an excuse as to why we haven't been writing apps like that all this time. However, we believe all this business about rocket science and intimidation is a bit exaggerated.

In fact, after spending ten minutes examining Google Maps a bit deeper, we realized that, far from being the product of rocket scientists, the Google Maps interface is actually fairly straightforward to implement. Perhaps, some might say, easy. Not "same-amount-of-effort-as-a-PHP-web-form" easy, but we were able to implement something a great deal like it in about two hours. And this wasn't just any two hours, mind you; it was two hours of sitting in a crowded convention center during a technical conference whilst being interrupted by our friends every few minutes.

So while there's no doubt Google has recently hired some of the most visible computer scientists—perhaps the closest examples of rocket scientist—like brainpower in our industry, such as Adam Bosworth (famed Microsoft innovator), Joshua Bloch (famed Java innovator at Sun Microsystems), and Vint Cerf (famed Internet innovator)—we're pretty sure they weren't involved in the creation of the Google Maps

The Real Rocket Science

OK, OK we admit—it isn't easy to create something like Google Maps. The geocoding features behind the scenes that map addresses to locations on a map, that normalize a maps features against satellite imagery to such an amazing degree that they can be overlaid on top of each other and look relatively accurate, and the plotting of routes from Point A to Point B are all incredibly nontrivial.

However, we maintain that it's not the geocoding features of Google Maps that is particularly innovative or impressive. MapQuest and other software packages have been doing this kind of work for years. No, what's impressive about Google Maps is the *web interface* on top of the geocoding engine. And it's that interface that we find easy, not the geocoding under the covers.

As our good friend Glenn Vanderburg says, though: "*Technically* it's easy, but the *conception* of this kind of interface is the really amazing part, just having the idea and then realizing that it could be done. So many things are simple once you've seen that they're possible." The take-home lesson is that Google Maps shows that once you have conceived of your next great UI idea, you can take comfort in knowing that the technical solution to implementing it might not be so daunting.

interface. (We should say, though, that we stand in awe of Lars Rasmussen and his team for being the brains and fingers behind Google Maps.) The reality is if we can create an interface like Google Maps in a couple of hours, imagine what a few capable web developers could do in a few weeks or a month.

2.2 Your Own Google Maps

In fact, we'll spare you from putting your imagination to the test. Let us show you firsthand how you can create your own version of Google Maps. In the next few pages, we'll walk you through the creation of Ajaxian Maps, our own derivative of the big GM. We'll start out by explaining how the Google Maps user interface works.

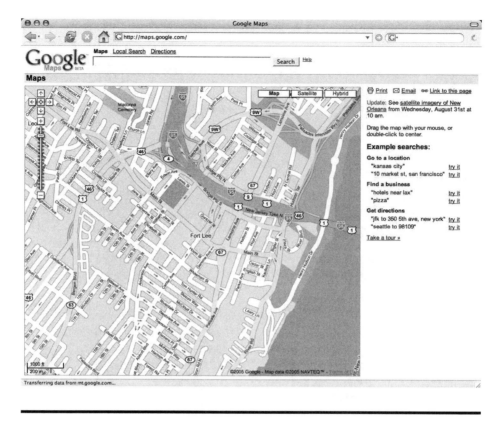

Figure 2.1: GOOGLE MAPS

Google Maps Deconstructed

We're going to break down the elements of Google Maps one by one. Let's start out with the most dramatic feature: the big scrolling map, the heart of the application.

The Map

As you know, the map works by allowing you to interactively move the map by dragging the map using the mouse. We've seen mouse dragging in browsers for years, but the impressive bit is that the scrolling map is massive in size, can have the zoom level changed and so forth. How do they do that?

Of course, the browser could never fit such a large map in memory at once. For example, a street-level map of the entire world would prob-

More Than A Million Pixels

We say in "The Map" section that a street-level map of the world would be about a million square pixels. Actually, that number's a wild underestimate. At Google's highest level of magnification, a square mile consumes about 7,700,000 pixels. The Earth is estimated to contain 200,000,000 square miles, but only 30% of that is land, so let's reduce the number to 60,000,000 square miles.

Multiplying the number of pixels by the number of square miles in the Earth produces the mind boggling number of 462 million million pixels, which at 16.7 million colors (the color depth of any modern home computer) would consume at least three times that amount of memory in bytes. Of course, most image viewing programs have some sort of paged memory subsystem that views a portion of the image at any one time, but you get the idea....

ably be about a million pixels square. How much memory would it take to display that map? For the sake of conversation, let's assume that the map is displayed with just 256 colors, meaning each pixel would consume just 1 byte of memory. Such a map would require 1,000,000,000,000 bytes of memory, or roughly 1 terabyte (1000 gigabytes) of RAM. So, simply displaying an *<img>* element just isn't going to work.

What the Googlers do to work around the paltry amount of memory our desktop PCs have is split up the map into various tiles. These tiles are laid out contiguously to form one cohesive image. Figure 2.2, on the next page, shows an example of these tiles. While the size of these tiles has changed, the current size is 250 pixels square.

The tiles themselves are all laid out within a single HTML div element, and this div element is contained within another div; we'll call these two divs the *inner* and *outer* divs, respectively.

We mentioned just a moment ago that the browser couldn't fit the entire map image in memory. Of course, dividing a single map into an arbitrary number of tiles and then displaying all those tiles at once would consume an equal amount of memory as the entire image. To compensate for memory limitations, Google Maps virtualizes the grid of tiles

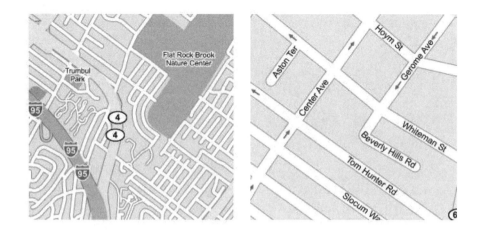

Figure 2.2: GOOGLE MAPS TILES

in memory and displays only the set of tiles that the user can see, in addition to a few additional tiles outside of the viewing area to keep the scrolling smooth.

If this whole grid virtualization mishmash sounds a little complex, don't worry; it's fairly straightforward, though it is the most complicated bit of the UI.

Zoom Level

Another key feature of Google Maps is the ability to zoom in and out, enlarging or reducing the size of the map, which lets you get a view of the entire world at one moment and a view of your street the next. This is actually the simplest of the features to implement. Changing the zoom level just changes the size of the tile grid in memory as well as the URLs of the tile images that are requested.

For example, the URL to one of the tiles in Figure 2.2 is as follows:

```
http://mt.google.com/mt?v=w2.5&n=404&x=4825&y=6150&zoom=3
```

By changing the value of the zoom parameter to another value, such as 1, you can retrieve a tile at a different zoom level. In practice, it's not quite that simple because the grid coordinates change rather a great deal with each zoom level and they often become invalid.

Figure 2.3: The Google Maps Push Pin and Dialog

How do they get the zoom level to constantly hover over the map in a constant position? The zoom level widget is an image embedded in the outer div, and makes use of transparency to blend in with the map image.

Push Pins and Dialogs

Other neat-o features are the push pins and dialogs that appear after a search. Figure 2.3 shows these elements. These are especially cool because they both include rounded edges and shadows that make them blend in with the background map in a sophisticated fashion.

We said the zoom level was the easiest feature, and frankly, we were probably wrong. This is ridiculously easy. The push pins and dialogs are simply a PNG image. The PNG image format is supported by the major browsers and supports a nice feature called *alpha transparency.* *alpha transparency* Alpha transparency allows for more than just the simple transparency that GIF images support; it allows a pixel to be one of 254 different values between fully transparent and fully opaque, and it's this gradient transparency support that allows the push pins and dialog to use a shadow that blends in with the map.

Showing these features is simply a matter of positioning images in the inner div at an absolute position.

Feature Review

There are other features, of course. But we'll stick to the set of features we've enumerated; we think these represent the vast majority of the "ooh, ahh" factors. In review, they were as follows:

- *The scrolling map*: This is implemented as an outer div containing an inner div. Mouse listeners allow the inner div to be moved within the confines of the outer div. Tiles are displayed as img elements inside the inner div, but only those tiles necessary to display the viewing area and a buffer area around it are present in the inner div.

- *The zoom level*: This is an image embedded in the outer div. When clicked, it changes the size of the grid representing the tiles and changes the URL used to request the tiles.

- *The push pins and dialogs*: These are PNG images with alpha transparency, placed in absolute positions within the inner div.

Now that we've deconstructed Google Maps a bit, let's set about implementing it.

2.3   Creating Ajaxian Maps

Because Ajaxian Maps won't bother with all of that geocoding mumbo jumbo, all of our heavy lifting will be in JavaScript. However, we will use Java to provide some server features and a few image manipulation tasks.

IE 6, Firefox 1.*x*, and Safari 2.*x* Only

We've tested this version of Ajaxian Maps in the three major browsers but haven't bothered with older versions and more obscure browsers (sorry, Opera users). It should work on older platforms, but without testing, we can't be sure we've caught everything.

Step 1: Create a Map

The first step in displaying a map is, err, creating it. While we could simply steal the wonderful map that Google Maps uses, Google might not appreciate that. So, we'll go ahead and use a map that is explicitly open source. The Batik project (http://xml.apache.org/batik), an open-source Java-based SVG renderer, comes with an SVG map of Spain. We'll use that.

Because most browsers don't provide native support for SVG, we'll need to convert the map to a bitmap-based format. Fortunately, Batik can do that for us. One of the nice features of SVG is that it can scale to arbitrary sizes, so we could conceivably create a huge image for our map. However, creating truly huge images is a little tricky; because of memory limitations, we'd have to render portions of the SVG image, generate our tiles over the portions, and have some sort of scheme for unifying everything together. To keep this chapter simple, we'll just limit our map to 2,000 pixels in width and 1,400 pixels in height. In order to implement zooming, we'll also generate a smaller image that represents a view of the map in a zoomed-out mode.

The following code excerpt shows how to use Batik to convert the map of Spain into both a 2000x1400 pixel JPG file and a 1500x1050 pixel JPG file:

File 31

```
package com.ajaxian.amaps;

import org.apache.batik.apps.rasterizer.DestinationType;
import org.apache.batik.apps.rasterizer.SVGConverter;

import java.io.File;

public class SVGSlicer {
    private static final String BASE_DIR = "resources/";

    public static void main(String[] args) throws Exception {
        SVGConverter converter = new SVGConverter();

        // width in pixels; height auto-calculated
        converter.setWidth(2000);
        converter.setSources(new String[] { BASE_DIR + "svg/mapSpain.svg" });
        converter.setDst(new File(BASE_DIR + "tiles/mapSpain.jpg"));
        converter.setDestinationType(DestinationType.JPEG);
        converter.execute();

        converter.setWidth(1500);
        converter.setDst(new File(BASE_DIR + "tiles/mapSpain-smaller.jpg"));
        converter.execute();
    }
}
```

To compile the code, you'll need to put the Batik JARs in your classpath

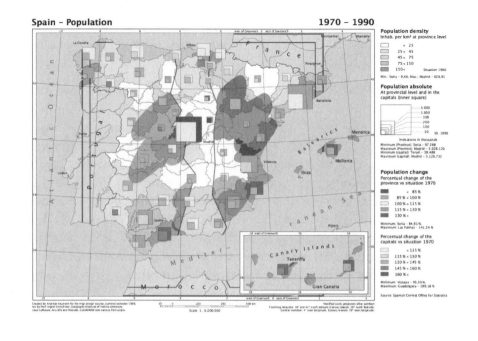

Figure 2.4: BATIK'S SVG SPAIN MAP

(everything in BATIK_HOME and BATIK_HOME/lib) and place the source code in the following directory hierarchy: com/ajaxian/amaps. Figure 2.4 shows what either map JPG file should look like. You can also replace the value of the BASE_DIR variable with whatever is most convenient for you.

Step 2: Create the Tiles

Now that we have a map at two different zoom levels, we need to slice it up into tiles. This is pretty easy with the nice image manipulation libraries available in many programming languages. We'll demonstrate how to do that with Java here:

File 30

```
package com.ajaxian.amaps;

import org.apache.batik.apps.rasterizer.DestinationType;
import org.apache.batik.apps.rasterizer.SVGConverter;

import javax.imageio.ImageIO;
import java.io.File;
import java.awt.*;
```

```java
import java.awt.image.BufferedImage;

public class ImageTiler {
    private static final String BASE_DIR = "resources/";
    private static final int TILE_WIDTH = 100;
    private static final int TILE_HEIGHT = 100;

    public static void main(String[] args) throws Exception {
        // create the tiles
        String[][] sources = { { "tiles/mapSpain.jpg", "0" },
                {"tiles/mapSpain-smaller.jpg", "1"} };
        for (int i = 0; i < sources.length; i++) {
            String[] source = sources[i];
            BufferedImage bi = ImageIO.read(new File(BASE_DIR + source[0]));
            int columns = bi.getWidth() / TILE_WIDTH;
            int rows = bi.getHeight() / TILE_HEIGHT;
            for (int x = 0; x < columns; x++) {
                for (int y = 0; y < rows; y++) {
                    BufferedImage img = new BufferedImage(TILE_WIDTH, TILE_HEIGHT,
                            bi.getType());
                    Graphics2D newGraphics = (Graphics2D) img.getGraphics();
                    newGraphics.drawImage(bi, 0, 0, TILE_WIDTH, TILE_HEIGHT,
                            TILE_WIDTH * x, TILE_HEIGHT * y,
                            TILE_WIDTH * x + TILE_WIDTH,
                            TILE_HEIGHT * y + TILE_HEIGHT,
                            null);
                    ImageIO.write(img, "JPG", new File(BASE_DIR + "tiles/" +
                            "x" + x + "y" + y + "z" + source[1] + ".jpg"));
                }
            }
        }
    }
}
```

Note that to make things interesting, we made our tile size a bit smaller than Google Maps: 100 pixels square. We chose x0y0z0.jpg as the naming convention for the tiles, where the zeros are replaced with the *x* and *y* grid coordinates (0-based) and the zoom level (0 or 1; 0 is for the bigger of the two maps).

Step 3: Creating the Inner and Outer Divs

Now that we have the image tiles, we can start building our map UI. We'll start with a simple web page, shown here:

File 32

```html
Line 1    <html>
     -        <head>
     -            <title>Ajaxian Maps</title>
     -            <style type="text/css">
     5                h1 {
```

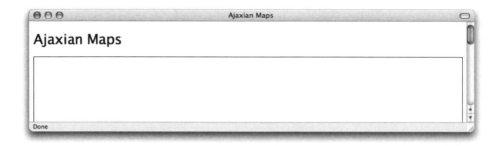

Figure 2.5: HUMBLE BEGINNINGS

```
   -                    font: 20pt sans-serif;
   -                }
   -                #outerDiv {
   -                    height: 600px;
  10                    width: 800px;
   -                    border: 1px solid black;
   -                    position: relative;
   -                    overflow: hidden;
   -                }
  15            </style>
   -        </head>
   -        <body>
   -            <p>
   -                <h1>Ajaxian Maps</h1>
  20            </p>
   -            <div id="outerDiv">
   -            </div>
   -        </body>
   -    </html>
```

Figure 2.5 show this page. Pretty simple so far. Let's get to the good stuff. The div on line 21 will become what we've called the outer div. The outer div is the visible window into the tiles and will be entirely contained in the visible space within the browser. The inner div, on the other hand, will contain all the tiles and be much larger than the available visible space. Let's start out by giving it an inner div with some simple content:

File 33

```
<html>
    <head>
        <title>Ajaxian Maps</title>
        <style type="text/css">
            h1 {
                font: 20pt sans-serif;
            }
```

```
            #outerDiv {
                height: 600px;
                width: 800px;
                border: 1px solid black;
                position: relative;
                overflow: hidden;
            }

            #innerDiv {
                position: relative;
                left: 0px;
                top: 0px;
            }
        </style>
    </head>
    <body>
        <p>
            <h1>Ajaxian Maps</h1>
        </p>
        <div id="outerDiv">
            <div id="innerDiv">
                The rain in Spain falls mainly in the plains.
            </div>
        </div>
    </body>
</html>
```

Now we need to make the inner div large enough to contain all of the image tiles. We could just set a style on the inner div to make it some arbitrary size, as in <div style="width: 2000px; height: 1400px">, but we'll do this via JavaScript. Why? Well, because we'll implement the ability to change zoom levels a little later, we know we'll have to change the size of the inner div dynamically anyway, so we might as well start out that way. We'll use an onload JavaScript handler to initialize the size of the inner div once we load the page. Check out the code:

File 34

```
<html>
    <head>
        <title>Ajaxian Maps</title>
        <style type="text/css">
            h1 {
                font: 20pt sans-serif;
            }
            #outerDiv {
                height: 600px;
                width: 800px;
                border: 1px solid black;
                position: relative;
                overflow: hidden;
            }
```

```
        #innerDiv {
            position: relative;
            left: 0px;
            top: 0px;
        }
    </style>
    <script type="text/javascript">
        function init() {
            setInnerDivSize('2000px', '1400px')
        }

        function setInnerDivSize(width, height) {
            var innerDiv = document.getElementById("innerDiv")
            innerDiv.style.width = width
            innerDiv.style.height = height
        }
    </script>
</head>
<body onload="init()">
    <p>
        <h1>Ajaxian Maps</h1>
    </p>
    <div id="outerDiv">
        <div id="innerDiv">
            The rain in Spain falls mainly in the plains.
        </div>
    </div>
</body>
</html>
```

OK, now we've got an inner div big enough to display the tiles for the largest of our two maps. Now we need to add the dragging functionality.

Step 4: Dragging the Map

We'll implement dragging using three different mouse event listeners. When the user clicks the mouse in the map area, we'll use a listener to indicate that a drag operation has started. Now, if the user moves the mouse, we'll use a listener to move the inner div along with the user's mouse movements to create the dragging effect. Finally, we'll use a listener to turn off the dragging operation when the mouse is released. The following code demonstrates how we implemented the listeners:

File 35
```
// used to control moving the map div
var dragging = false;
var top;
var left;
var dragStartTop;
var dragStartLeft;
```

```
function init() {
    // make inner div big enough to display the map
    setInnerDivSize('2000px', '1400px');

    // wire up the mouse listeners to do dragging
    var outerDiv = document.getElementById("outerDiv");
    outerDiv.onmousedown = startMove;
    outerDiv.onmousemove = processMove;
    outerDiv.onmouseup = stopMove;

    // necessary to enable dragging on IE
    outerDiv.ondragstart = function() { return false; }
}

function startMove(event) {
    // necessary for IE
    if (!event) event = window.event;

    dragStartLeft = event.clientX;
    dragStartTop = event.clientY;
    var innerDiv = document.getElementById("innerDiv");
    innerDiv.style.cursor = "-moz-grab";

    top = stripPx(innerDiv.style.top);
    left = stripPx(innerDiv.style.left);

    dragging = true;
    return false;
}

function processMove(event) {
    if (!event) event = window.event;  // for IE
    var innerDiv = document.getElementById("innerDiv");
    if (dragging) {
        innerDiv.style.top = top + (event.clientY - dragStartTop);
        innerDiv.style.left = left + (event.clientX - dragStartLeft);
    }
}

function stopMove() {
    var innerDiv = document.getElementById("innerDiv");
    innerDiv.style.cursor = "";
    dragging = false;
}

function stripPx(value) {
    if (value == "") return 0;
    return parseFloat(value.substring(0, value.length - 2));
}
```

If you run the code at this point, you'll now be able to drag that inner
<div> around.

Step 5: Displaying the Map Tiles

The next step requires us to populate our inner div with the map tiles.
Our approach to this will be fairly simple. The scrolling map effect
is achieved by moving an inner div inside of an outer div; therefore,
the tiles we need to display are calculated by determining the current
position of the inner div relative to the outer div and then working out
which tiles are visible in the portion of the inner div that is visible. We'll
then add those tiles to the inner div.

It turns out implementing this behavior is not terribly difficult. We'll
create the function checkTiles() to do all this and call it from within the
processMove() function. processMove() is called when the user drags the
map, so by calling it from within, we'll be able to load our tiles as the
map moves. The following code excerpt shows how we've added these
elements to our JavaScript code; for now, checkTiles() is just stubbed
out with comments:

File 39

```
function processMove(event) {
    if (!event) event = window.event;  // for IE
    var innerDiv = document.getElementById("innerDiv");
    if (dragging) {
        innerDiv.style.top = top + (event.clientY - dragStartTop);
        innerDiv.style.left = left + (event.clientX - dragStartLeft);
    }

    checkTiles();
}

function checkTiles() {
    // check which tiles should be visible in the inner div

    // add each tile to the inner div, checking first to see
    // if it has already been added
}
```

Now, let's implement our stubbed-out checkTiles() function.

Calculating the Visible Tiles

Calculating the set of tiles that the user can see in the inner <div> is
fairly straightforward. To understand how this works, it will help to
visualize the inner div as a grid where each grid cell is a placeholder of
the tiles that we'll load. Figure 2.6 illustrates this concept.

Inner Div

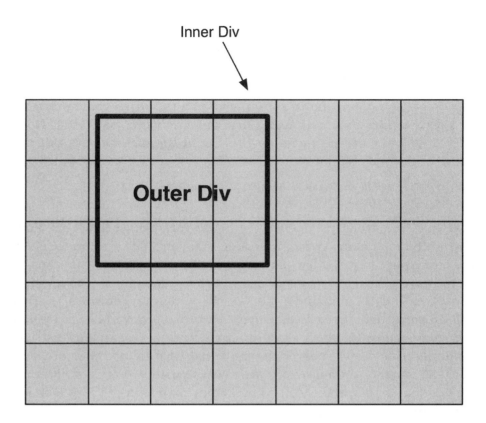

Outer Div

Figure 2.6: THE TILE GRID

Because we can't load *all* the tiles in the grid up front, we'll need to calculate which of these grid cells are visible and load the tiles needed to fit into these cells. As Figure 2.6 shows, this is accomplished by calculating which grid cells are visible within the viewport created by the size of the outer div. In the figure, we see that nine cells are visible across three rows. Note that those cells that are only partially visible still count as being visible.

Let's see how to implement all this behavior we just described. To make things simple, we'll encapsulate all of the code to figure out which tiles are visible in a particular method, which we'll call getVisibleTiles(). The first thing we need to figure out in getVisibleTiles() is the position of the inner div relative to the outer div. This is fairly easy:

```
function getVisibleTiles() {
    var innerDiv = document.getElementById("innerDiv");
    var mapX = stripPx(innerDiv.style.left);
    var mapY = stripPx(innerDiv.style.top);
}
```

The stripPx() function, shown earlier, converts the string value returned by innerDiv.style.left (such as 100px) to a numeric value (say, 100). Now, we can divide these positions by the size of the tiles to work out the starting row and column of the tiles. This is just two lines of code:

```
var startX = Math.abs(Math.floor(mapX / tileSize)) - 1;
var startY = Math.abs(Math.floor(mapY / tileSize)) - 1;
```

Note that we haven't yet defined the tileSize variable; we'll do that globally (at the top of our JavaScript code), and you'll see it when we show the entire page in just a few paragraphs. (Or, you can see it now on the facing page.) The call to Math.floor() will round the quotient to an integer, discarding the remainder (so 1.4 will be rounded down to 1). This will cause partial tiles to be displayed. Math.abs() converts negative values to a positive number, which in our case is necessary because the inner div position will nearly always be negative to the outer div, and because our tile columns/rows are always positive numbers. Finally, we subtract 1 from the result to make our map load the tiles a touch early for a smoother effect.

The final bit of calculation is to determine the number of rows and columns visible in the viewport:

```
var tilesX = Math.ceil(viewportWidth / tileSize) + 1;
var tilesY = Math.ceil(viewportHeight / tileSize) + 1;
```

As with tileSize(), we'll declare both viewportWidth and viewportHeight as global variables and show that in just a bit. We use Math.ceil(), the opposite of Math.floor() (so it rounds the quotient up regardless of the size of the remainder), to ensure that if any portion of a column or row is visible, we'll display it. And, just as we subtracted 1 from the index of the tiles in the previous lines, we'll add 1 to the number of columns and rows to make the scroll effect smooth.

We now have all the data we need to calculate all of the visible tiles in the viewport plus, as we've discussed, a few around the edges that aren't immediately visible but will be shortly. Now we'll build an array that contains all of the tiles that need to be loaded. To build this array, we'll write two for loops, one nested inside the other, that each perform an iteration for each column and row that is currently visible. Inside each loop iteration, we'll add the column and row number of each tile to display:

```
var visibleTileArray = [];
var counter = 0;
for (x = startX; x < (tilesX + startX); x++) {
    for (y = startY; y < (tilesY + startY); y++) {
        visibleTileArray[counter++] = [x, y];
    }
}
return visibleTileArray;
```

Note that we're actually creating a two-dimensional array; the value of each item in our array is another array. We did this because we need to pass back two values: the column and row index. And now, we're done calculating the tiles that are visible in the inner div, and we can move on and work on the code to actually display them. But first, let's review all of the code we've written so far:

File 36

```
function checkTiles() {
    // check which tiles should be visible in the inner div
    var visibleTiles = getVisibleTiles();

    // add each tile to the inner div, checking first to see
    // if it has already been added
}

function getVisibleTiles() {
    var innerDiv = document.getElementById("innerDiv");

    var mapX = stripPx(innerDiv.style.left);
    var mapY = stripPx(innerDiv.style.top);

    var startX = Math.abs(Math.floor(mapX / tileSize)) - 1;
    var startY = Math.abs(Math.floor(mapY / tileSize)) - 1;

    var tilesX = Math.ceil(viewportWidth / tileSize) + 1;
    var tilesY = Math.ceil(viewportHeight / tileSize) + 1;

    var visibleTileArray = [];
    var counter = 0;
    for (x = startX; x < (tilesX + startX); x++) {
        for (y = startY; y < (tilesY + startY); y++) {
            visibleTileArray[counter++] = [x, y];
        }
    }
    return visibleTileArray;
}
```

Displaying the Visible Tiles

We've now coded half of the checkTiles() function, which as you may recall is the function responsible for both calculating the visible tiles and displaying them. Now, let's implement the other half of that function: displaying the tiles.

All we need to do here is iterate through each element of the array of visible tiles we returned from the getVisibleTiles() function and for each array element add a tile image to the inner div. Here's the new code for our checkTiles() function:

File 37

```
Line 1  function checkTiles() {
    -       // check which tiles should be visible in the inner div
    -       var visibleTiles = getVisibleTiles();
    -
    5       // add each tile to the inner div, checking first to see
    -       // if it has already been added
    -       var innerDiv = document.getElementById("innerDiv");
    -       var visibleTilesMap = {};
    -       for (i = 0; i < visibleTiles.length; i++) {
   10           var tileArray = visibleTiles[i];
    -           var tileName = "x" + tileArray[0] + "y" + tileArray[1] + "z0";
    -           visibleTilesMap[tileName] = true;
    -           var img = document.getElementById(tileName);
    -           if (!img) {
   15               img = document.createElement("img");
    -               img.src = "resources/tiles/" + tileName + ".jpg";
    -               img.style.position = "absolute";
    -               img.style.left = (tileArray[0] * tileSize) + "px";
    -               img.style.top = (tileArray[1] * tileSize) + "px";
   20               img.setAttribute("id", tileName);
    -               innerDiv.appendChild(img);
    -           }
    -       }
    -   }
```

We start out on line 8 by creating an empty map (*map* in the JavaScript sense; a hash that contains key-to-value mappings). We're going to add an entry to this map for each visible image; we'll discuss why we're doing this a little later.

On line 9, we start looping through each element in the array we sent back from getVisibleTiles(). For each element, we build the name of the image file that will be loaded in. (If you recall, the file-naming convention we chose in Step 2 was x0y0z0, where the numbers are replaced with the index of the tile in the tile grid.) We also use this name as the key in the visibleTilesMap variable, and on lines 13 and 20 you can see that we also use it as the id attribute for each img element that we add to the inner div. This is so on lines 13 and 14, we can check to see we've already added a given tile to the inner div and, if we have, avoid adding it again.

Finally, in lines 15 through line 21, we create the <*img*> element and add it to the inner div. Note that on line 16 we have to specify the URL of the image tile. If you have Java installed and executed the code from Steps 1 and 2 to create your own image tiles, great! Reference them on line 16, setting the URI to wherever you put them. If not, you can reference our tiles online.[2]

You can now enjoy a scrolling map of Spain in your browser! We've placed a copy online at GoogleMaps/step5-3.html. Here's all the code we've written so far:

File 37

```html
<html>
    <head>
        <title>Ajaxian Maps</title>
        <style type="text/css">
            h1 {
                font: 20pt sans-serif;
            }
            #outerDiv {
                height: 600px;
                width: 800px;
                border: 1px solid black;
                position: relative;
                overflow: hidden;
            }

            #innerDiv {
                position: relative;
                left: 0px;
                top: 0px;
            }
        </style>
        <script type="text/javascript">
            // constants
            var viewportWidth = 800;
            var viewportHeight = 600;
            var tileSize = 100;

            // used to control moving the map div
            var dragging = false;
```

---

[2]GoogleMaps/resources/tiles/x0y0z0.jpg, where x0y0z0 should be replaced with the tile you want to load

OUACHITA TECHNICAL COLLEGE

```javascript
var top;
var left;
var dragStartTop;
var dragStartLeft;

function init() {
    // make inner div big enough to display the map
    setInnerDivSize('2000px', '1400px');

    // wire up the mouse listeners to do dragging
    var outerDiv = document.getElementById("outerDiv");
    outerDiv.onmousedown = startMove;
    outerDiv.onmousemove = processMove;
    outerDiv.onmouseup = stopMove;

    // necessary to enable dragging on IE
    outerDiv.ondragstart = function() { return false; }

    checkTiles();
}

function startMove(event) {
    // necessary for IE
    if (!event) event = window.event;

    dragStartLeft = event.clientX;
    dragStartTop = event.clientY;
    var innerDiv = document.getElementById("innerDiv");
    innerDiv.style.cursor = "-moz-grab";

    top = stripPx(innerDiv.style.top);
    left = stripPx(innerDiv.style.left);

    dragging = true;
    return false;
}

function processMove(event) {
    if (!event) event = window.event;  // for IE
    var innerDiv = document.getElementById("innerDiv");
    if (dragging) {
        innerDiv.style.top = top + (event.clientY - dragStartTop);
        innerDiv.style.left = left + (event.clientX - dragStartLeft);
    }

    checkTiles();
}
function checkTiles() {
    // check which tiles should be visible in the inner div
    var visibleTiles = getVisibleTiles();
```

```
        // add each tile to the inner div, checking first to see
        // if it has already been added
        var innerDiv = document.getElementById("innerDiv");
        var visibleTilesMap = {};
        for (i = 0; i < visibleTiles.length; i++) {
            var tileArray = visibleTiles[i];
            var tileName = "x" + tileArray[0] + "y" + tileArray[1] + "z0";
            visibleTilesMap[tileName] = true;
            var img = document.getElementById(tileName);
            if (!img) {
                img = document.createElement("img");
                img.src = "resources/tiles/" + tileName + ".jpg";
                img.style.position = "absolute";
                img.style.left = (tileArray[0] * tileSize) + "px";
                img.style.top = (tileArray[1] * tileSize) + "px";
                img.setAttribute("id", tileName);
                innerDiv.appendChild(img);
            }
        }
    }

    function getVisibleTiles() {
        var innerDiv = document.getElementById("innerDiv");

        var mapX = stripPx(innerDiv.style.left);
        var mapY = stripPx(innerDiv.style.top);

        var startX = Math.abs(Math.floor(mapX / tileSize)) - 1;
        var startY = Math.abs(Math.floor(mapY / tileSize)) - 1;

        var tilesX = Math.ceil(viewportWidth / tileSize) + 1;
        var tilesY = Math.ceil(viewportHeight / tileSize) + 1;

        var visibleTileArray = [];
        var counter = 0;
        for (x = startX; x < (tilesX + startX); x++) {
            for (y = startY; y < (tilesY + startY); y++) {
                visibleTileArray[counter++] = [x, y];
            }
        }
        return visibleTileArray;
    }

    function stopMove() {
        var innerDiv = document.getElementById("innerDiv");
        innerDiv.style.cursor = "";
        dragging = false;
    }
```

```
        function stripPx(value) {
            if (value == "") return 0;
            return parseFloat(value.substring(0, value.length - 2));
        }

        function setInnerDivSize(width, height) {
            var innerDiv = document.getElementById("innerDiv");
            innerDiv.style.width = width;
            innerDiv.style.height = height;
        }
    </script>
</head>
<body onload="init()">
    <p>
        <h1>Ajaxian Maps</h1>
    </p>
    <div id="outerDiv">
        <div id="innerDiv">
            The rain in Spain falls mainly in the plains.
        </div>
    </div>
</body>
</html>
```

Cleaning Up Unused Tiles

We've got some neat scrolling, but this has one glaring inefficiency. We add tiles to the inner div on demand, but we never remove the tiles that are no longer visible. Fortunately, we've already done some of the work to accommodate this feature. If you recall, we created a JavaScript map named visibleTilesMap in the checkTiles() function but never did anything with it. Now, we're going to do something.

After we add the image tiles to the inner div, we'll select all of the img elements that are present in the inner div, and for each img element, we'll check to see whether its id attribute is present in the visibleTilesMap variable. If so, we know that it's a currently visible tile and should be left in the inner div. If not, the <img> is no longer visible and can be removed. Here's the additional code in checkTiles() to implement this functionality:

File 38

```
function checkTiles() {
    // check which tiles should be visible in the inner div
    var visibleTiles = getVisibleTiles();

    // add each tile to the inner div, checking first to see
    // if it has already been added
    var innerDiv = document.getElementById("innerDiv");
```

```
var visibleTilesMap = {};
for (i = 0; i < visibleTiles.length; i++) {
    var tileArray = visibleTiles[i];
    var tileName = "x" + tileArray[0] + "y" + tileArray[1] + "z0";
    visibleTilesMap[tileName] = true;
    var img = document.getElementById(tileName);
    if (!img) {
        img = document.createElement("img");
        img.src = "resources/tiles/" + tileName + ".jpg";
        img.style.position = "absolute";
        img.style.left = (tileArray[0] * tileSize) + "px";
        img.style.top = (tileArray[1] * tileSize) + "px";
        img.setAttribute("id", tileName);
        innerDiv.appendChild(img);
    }
}

var imgs = innerDiv.getElementsByTagName("img");
for (i = 0; i < imgs.length; i++) {
    var id = imgs[i].getAttribute("id");
    if (!visibleTilesMap[id]) {
        innerDiv.removeChild(imgs[i]);
        i--;  // compensate for live nodelist
    }
}
}
```

Figure 2.7, on the next page, shows what this looks like.

Step 6: Zooming

Zooming is wicked easy; in fact, the hardest bit is just getting a zoom widget to appear floating above the map. First, we need to create some kind of image that the user can click on to enable zooming. In Google Maps, it's a slider (shown in the margin here); for us, we'll just create a simple image that toggles between our two zoom levels. You can use any image you like; ours is at GoogleMaps/resources/images/zoom.png.

Second, to float the image above the map, we have to properly set the z-index of our inner div. Browsers support layering elements on top of each other; the z-index CSS property is used to determine how the layering occurs. The lower the value, the lower in the layer the element will appear. Because we want to put our zoom widget above the tile images, we'll need to set the z-index of the inner div to 0. The z-index of the zoom widget then needs to be any value greater than 0 (we use 1).

Now, let's add the zoom widget. We'll enclose it in a div, place it inside the outer div as a peer of the inner div, and we'll set the z-index properties appropriately:

Figure 2.7: AJAXIAN MAPS!

File 40

```
Line 1    <body onload="init()">
   -        <p>
   -          <h1>Ajaxian Maps</h1>
   -        </p>
   5      <div id="outerDiv">
   -          <div style="position: absolute; top: 10px; left: 10px; z-index: 1">
   -            <img src="resources/images/zoom.png"
   -                 onclick="toggleZoom()"/>
   -          </div>
   10       <div id="innerDiv" style="z-index: 0">
   -            The rain in Spain falls mainly in the plains.
   -          </div>
   -        </div>
   -      </body>
```

That will give us our floating zoom widget; now we need to create the
toggleZoom() function that we referenced on line 8. This will require a

few minor changes to our code. First, we need to create some sort of global state that tracks the current zoom level of our map. Second, we need to reference this state in the various relevant places in our code (just one, actually).

Let's start with the global state. We'll create a variable zoom to track the current zoom level and while we're at it add a constant (in the form of a two-dimensional array) for declaring the two different sizes of the inner div:

File 40
```
var zoom = 0;
var zoomSizes = [ [ "2000px", "1400px" ], [ "1500px", "1050px" ] ];
```

Now, in the name of cleanliness, we'll change the first line of our init method from this:

File 38
```
setInnerDivSize('2000px', '1400px');
```

to this:

File 40
```
setInnerDivSize(zoomSizes[zoom][0], zoomSizes[zoom][1]);
```

There's just one other place we need to wire in the zoom support: our checkTiles() function, which creates the img elements for the tiles and gives them their URL. We need to change this hard-coded zoom-level code:

File 38
```
var tileName = "x" + tileArray[0] + "y" + tileArray[1] + "z0";
```

to this:

File 40
```
var tileName = "x" + tileArray[0] + "y" + tileArray[1] + "z" + zoom;
```

All that remains is implementing the toggleZoom() function, which we've done here:

File 40
```
function toggleZoom() {
    zoom = (zoom == 0) ? 1 : 0;

    var innerDiv = document.getElementById("innerDiv");
    var imgs = innerDiv.getElementsByTagName("img");
    while (imgs.length > 0) innerDiv.removeChild(imgs[0]);

    setInnerDivSize(zoomSizes[zoom][0], zoomSizes[zoom][1]);

    checkTiles();
}
```

Nothing too tricky; we swap the value of the zoom variable from 0 to 1, delete all the <img> elements from the inner div, change the size of the

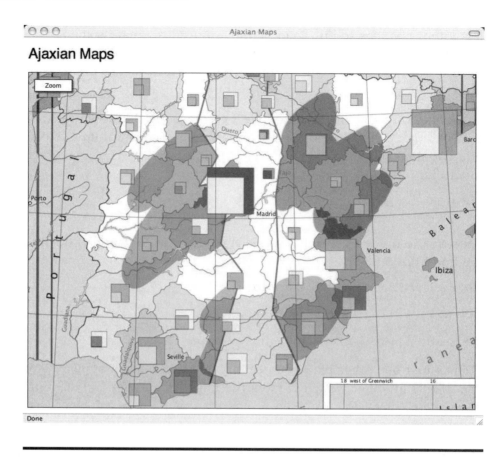

Figure 2.8: AJAXIAN MAPS ZOOMED OUT

inner div based on the zoom level, and invoke checkTiles() to rebuild the map with the new zoom level's tiles.

And now, we have zooming in our map application! Cool. The code for this version is on-line if you need it.[3] Figure 2.8 shows the zoom feature in action, with our map zoomed to the smaller size.

Step 7: Push Pins and Dialogs

The final feature is adding push pins with alpha transparency. When clicked, these show a dialog that also has alpha transparency. The

---

[3]http://media.pragprog.com/titles/ajax/code/GoogleMaps/step6.html

hardest part is creating the images.[4] These images will not render properly in IE 6, but see the end of this section for a workaround.

We're not going to implement a server back end that does searching, and so on, so just as with zooming we implemented a toggle, we'll implement a toggle for our push pin. The graphic for the toggle is available at GoogleMaps/resources/images/pushpin.png.

We'll place the push pin toggle right next to the zoom toggle by adding a new div for it:

File 42

```
<body onload="init()">
    <p>
        <h1>Ajaxian Maps</h1>
    </p>
    <div id="outerDiv">
        <div style="position: absolute; top: 10px; left: 10px; z-index: 1">
            <img src="resources/images/zoom.png" onclick="toggleZoom()"/>
        </div>
        <div style="position: absolute; top: 10px; left: 87px; z-index: 1">
            <img src="resources/images/pushpin.png" onclick="togglePushPin()"/>
        </div>
        <div id="innerDiv" style="z-index: 0">
            The rain in Spain falls mainly in the plains.
        </div>
    </div>
</body>
```

Now we need to implement togglePushPin(), which, frankly, is a piece of cake. We'll just add an absolutely positioned image with a z-index of 1 to the inner div, add an onclick handler to it, and wire that handler to display the dialog at an absolute position just above the push pin:

File 42

```
function togglePushPin() {
    var pinImage = document.getElementById("pushPin");
    if (pinImage) {
        pinImage.parentNode.removeChild(pinImage);
        var dialog = document.getElementById("pinDialog");
        dialog.parentNode.removeChild(dialog);
        return;
    }

    var innerDiv = document.getElementById("innerDiv");
    pinImage = document.createElement("img");
    pinImage.src = "resources/images/pin.png";
    pinImage.style.position = "absolute";
    pinImage.style.left = (zoom == 0) ? "850px" : "630px";
    pinImage.style.top = (zoom == 0) ? "570px" : "420px";
```

---

[4]GoogleMaps/resources/images/pin.png and GoogleMaps/resources/images/dialog.png.

```
        pinImage.style.zIndex = 1;
        pinImage.setAttribute("id", "pushPin");
        innerDiv.appendChild(pinImage);

        var dialog = document.createElement("div");
        dialog.style.position = "absolute";
        dialog.style.left = (stripPx(pinImage.style.left) - 90) + "px";
        dialog.style.top = (stripPx(pinImage.style.top) - 210) + "px";
        dialog.style.width = "309px";
        dialog.style.height = "229px";
        dialog.style.backgroundImage = "url(resources/images/dialog.png)";
        dialog.style.zIndex = 2;
        dialog.setAttribute("id", "pinDialog");
        dialog.innerHTML = "<table height=' 80%' width=' 100%' >" +
            "<tr><td align=' center' >The capital of Spain</td></tr></table>";
        innerDiv.appendChild(dialog);
}
```

There's just one little problem with this new behavior. Do you remember the image remover code in checkTiles()? It removes any img element child of the inner div that has been explicitly added to that function. Of course, it will clobber our push pin as well, since it is an img child of the inner div, so we need to modify the function to ignore the push pin:

File 42

```
var imgs = innerDiv.getElementsByTagName("img");
for (i = 0; i < imgs.length; i++) {
    var id = imgs[i].getAttribute("id");
    if (!visibleTilesMap[id]) {
        if (id != "pushPin") {
            innerDiv.removeChild(imgs[i]);
            i--;   // compensate for live nodelist
        }
    }
}
```

We're done! We've implemented all of the features we discussed in the introduction of this chapter. Let's wrap up by...err, wait a second. While Firefox, Safari, and other browsers provide native support for PNGs with alpha transparency, IE 6 does not. If you've been using that browser to try this sample code, the zoom and push pin buttons as well as the push pin and dialog itself have looked really awful.

Fortunately, this has an easy (but annoying) fix. Despite not supporting PNGs out of the box, IE can use some (IE-specific) JavaScript magic to parse out the alpha channel from a PNG at runtime and display it correctly. A number of websites document this workaround; in order to avoid sidetracking our Google Maps story, we'll just use a JavaScript library provided by one of these websites, www.alistapart.com,[5] to solve our problem.

First, we need to include these new JavaScripts in our webpage, which we'll do at the top:

File 41
```
<script language="javascript"
        src="resources/js/browserdetect_lite.js"
        type="text/javascript">
</script>
<script language="javascript"
        src="resources/js/opacity.js"
        type="text/javascript">
</script>
```

Then, because this library requires that the PNGs it fixes be background images in a div, we need to change our push pin from an img element to a div, as well as our two toggle buttons, and then finally use this library to fix all of these divs. We'll change the toggle button images to div background images first:

File 41
```
<body onload="init()">
    <p>
        <h1>Ajaxian Maps</h1>
    </p>
    <div id="outerDiv">
        <div id="toggleZoomDiv" onclick="toggleZoom()">
        </div>
        <div id="togglePushPinDiv" onclick="togglePushPin()">
        </div>
        <div id="innerDiv" style="z-index: 0">
            The rain in Spain falls mainly in the plains.
        </div>
    </div>
</body>
```

As part of this change, we moved the style attribute settings on the toggle divs into the style sheet we defined at the top of the file (something we probably should have done anyway):

File 41
```
#toggleZoomDiv {
    position: absolute;
    top: 10px;
    left: 10px;
    z-index: 1;
    width: 72px;
    height: 30px;
}
```

---

[5]http://www.alistapart.com/articles/pngopacity

```
#togglePushPinDiv {
    position: absolute;
    top: 10px;
    left: 87px;
    z-index: 1;
    width: 72px;
    height: 30px;
}
```

We now need to add two lines to our init() method to use our new IE transparency library with the toggle divs:

File 41

```
// fix the toggle divs to be transparent in IE
new OpacityObject('toggleZoomDiv','resources/images/zoom')
                        .setBackground();
new OpacityObject('togglePushPinDiv','resources/images/pushpin')
                        .setBackground();
```

And finally, we need to reformat the togglePushPin() function to use this new technique:

File 41

```
function togglePushPin() {
    var pinImage = document.getElementById("pushPin");
    if (pinImage) {
        pinImage.parentNode.removeChild(pinImage);
        var dialog = document.getElementById("pinDialog");
        dialog.parentNode.removeChild(dialog);
        return;
    }

    var innerDiv = document.getElementById("innerDiv");
    pinImage = document.createElement("div");
    pinImage.style.position = "absolute";
    pinImage.style.left = (zoom == 0) ? "850px" : "630px";
    pinImage.style.top = (zoom == 0) ? "570px" : "420px";
    pinImage.style.width = "37px";
    pinImage.style.height = "34px";
    pinImage.style.zIndex = 1;
    pinImage.setAttribute("id", "pushPin");
    innerDiv.appendChild(pinImage);
    new OpacityObject('pushPin','resources/images/pin')
                        .setBackground();

    var dialog = document.createElement("div");
    dialog.style.position = "absolute";
    dialog.style.left = (stripPx(pinImage.style.left) - 90) + "px";
    dialog.style.top = (stripPx(pinImage.style.top) - 210) + "px";
    dialog.style.width = "309px";
    dialog.style.height = "229px";
    dialog.style.zIndex = 2;
    dialog.setAttribute("id", "pinDialog");
    dialog.innerHTML = "<table height='80%' width='100%'><tr>" +
```

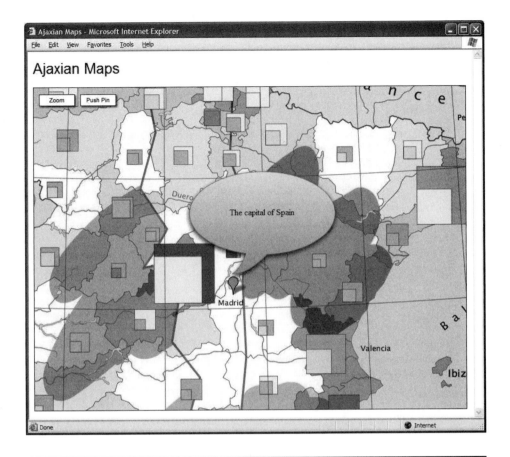

Figure 2.9: AJAXIAN MAPS PUSH PIN AND DIALOG ON IE 6

```
    "<td align=' center' >The capital of Spain</td></tr></table>";
innerDiv.appendChild(dialog);
new OpacityObject(' pinDialog' ,' resources/images/dialog' )
                        .setBackground();
}
```

And now, finally, we are done. Up until the image transparency bit, our code was really quite clean and had very little in the way of cross-browser hacks. Now, unfortunately, it has had to undergo a bit of an IE makeover, but the consolation prize is that IE 7 natively supports PNG so all of this may someday be unnecessary.

For review, let's take a look at our entire page:

File 41

```html
<html>
    <head>
        <title>Ajaxian Maps</title>
        <style type="text/css">
            h1 {
                font: 20pt sans-serif;
            }
            #outerDiv {
                height: 600px;
                width: 800px;
                border: 1px solid black;
                position: relative;
                overflow: hidden;
            }
            #innerDiv {
                position: relative;
                left: 0px;
                top: 0px;
            }
            #toggleZoomDiv {
                position: absolute;
                top: 10px;
                left: 10px;
                z-index: 1;
                width: 72px;
                height: 30px;
            }
            #togglePushPinDiv {
                position: absolute;
                top: 10px;
                left: 87px;
                z-index: 1;
                width: 72px;
                height: 30px;
            }
        </style>
        <script language="javascript"
                src="resources/js/browserdetect_lite.js"
                type="text/javascript">
        </script>
        <script language="javascript"
                src="resources/js/opacity.js"
                type="text/javascript">
        </script>
        <script type="text/javascript">
            // constants
            var viewportWidth = 800;
            var viewportHeight = 600;
            var tileSize = 100;
            var zoom = 0;
            var zoomSizes = [["2000px","1400px"], ["1500px","1050px"]];
```

```javascript
// used to control moving the map div
var dragging = false;
var top;
var left;
var dragStartTop;
var dragStartLeft;

function init() {
    // make inner div big enough to display the map
    setInnerDivSize(zoomSizes[zoom][0], zoomSizes[zoom][1]);

    // wire up the mouse listeners to do dragging
    var outerDiv = document.getElementById("outerDiv");
    outerDiv.onmousedown = startMove;
    outerDiv.onmousemove = processMove;
    outerDiv.onmouseup = stopMove;

    // necessary to enable dragging on IE
    outerDiv.ondragstart = function() { return false; }

    // fix the toggle divs to be transparent in IE
    new OpacityObject('toggleZoomDiv','resources/images/zoom')
                        .setBackground();
    new OpacityObject('togglePushPinDiv','resources/images/pushpin')
                        .setBackground();

    checkTiles();
}

function startMove(event) {
    // necessary for IE
    if (!event) event = window.event;

    dragStartLeft = event.clientX;
    dragStartTop = event.clientY;
    var innerDiv = document.getElementById("innerDiv");
    innerDiv.style.cursor = "-moz-grab";

    top = stripPx(innerDiv.style.top);
    left = stripPx(innerDiv.style.left);

    dragging = true;
    return false;
}

function processMove(event) {
    if (!event) event = window.event;  // for IE
    var innerDiv = document.getElementById("innerDiv");
    if (dragging) {
        innerDiv.style.top = parseFloat(top) +
```

```
                                    (event.clientY - dragStartTop);
            innerDiv.style.left = parseFloat(left) +
                                    (event.clientX - dragStartLeft);
        }

        checkTiles();
    }
    function checkTiles() {
        // check which tiles should be visible in the inner div
        var visibleTiles = getVisibleTiles();

        // add each tile to the inner div, checking first to see
        // if it has already been added
        var innerDiv = document.getElementById("innerDiv");
        var visibleTilesMap = {};
        for (i = 0; i < visibleTiles.length; i++) {
            var tileArray = visibleTiles[i];
            var tileName = "x" + tileArray[0] + "y" +
                                    tileArray[1] + "z" + zoom;
            visibleTilesMap[tileName] = true;
            var img = document.getElementById(tileName);
            if (!img) {
                img = document.createElement("img");
                img.src = "resources/tiles/" + tileName + ".jpg";
                img.style.position = "absolute";
                img.style.left = (tileArray[0] * tileSize) + "px";
                img.style.top = (tileArray[1] * tileSize) + "px";
                img.style.zIndex = 0;
                img.setAttribute("id", tileName);
                innerDiv.appendChild(img);
            }
        }

        var imgs = innerDiv.getElementsByTagName("img");
        for (i = 0; i < imgs.length; i++) {
            var id = imgs[i].getAttribute("id");
            if (!visibleTilesMap[id]) {
                innerDiv.removeChild(imgs[i]);
                i--;   // compensate for live nodelist
            }
        }
    }

    function getVisibleTiles() {
        var innerDiv = document.getElementById("innerDiv");

        var mapX = stripPx(innerDiv.style.left);
        var mapY = stripPx(innerDiv.style.top);

        var startX = Math.abs(Math.floor(mapX / tileSize)) - 1;
        var startY = Math.abs(Math.floor(mapY / tileSize)) - 1;
```

```
    var tilesX = Math.ceil(viewportWidth / tileSize) + 1;
    var tilesY = Math.ceil(viewportHeight / tileSize) + 1;

    var visibleTileArray = [];
    var counter = 0;
    for (x = startX; x < (tilesX + startX); x++) {
        for (y = startY; y < (tilesY + startY); y++) {
            visibleTileArray[counter++] = [x, y];
        }
    }
    return visibleTileArray;
}


function stopMove() {
    var innerDiv = document.getElementById("innerDiv");
    innerDiv.style.cursor = "";
    dragging = false;
}

function stripPx(value) {
    if (value == "") return 0;
    return parseFloat(value.substring(0, value.length - 2));
}

function setInnerDivSize(width, height) {
    var innerDiv = document.getElementById("innerDiv");
    innerDiv.style.width = width;
    innerDiv.style.height = height;
}

function toggleZoom() {
    zoom = (zoom == 0) ? 1 : 0;

    var innerDiv = document.getElementById("innerDiv");
    var imgs = innerDiv.getElementsByTagName("img");
    while (imgs.length > 0) innerDiv.removeChild(imgs[0]);

    setInnerDivSize(zoomSizes[zoom][0], zoomSizes[zoom][1]);

    if (document.getElementById("pushPin")) togglePushPin();

    checkTiles();
}

function togglePushPin() {
    var pinImage = document.getElementById("pushPin");
    if (pinImage) {
        pinImage.parentNode.removeChild(pinImage);
        var dialog = document.getElementById("pinDialog");
```

```
                          dialog.parentNode.removeChild(dialog);
                          return;
                    }

                    var innerDiv = document.getElementById("innerDiv");
                    pinImage = document.createElement("div");
                    pinImage.style.position = "absolute";
                    pinImage.style.left = (zoom == 0) ? "850px" : "630px";
                    pinImage.style.top = (zoom == 0) ? "570px" : "420px";
                    pinImage.style.width = "37px";
                    pinImage.style.height = "34px";
                    pinImage.style.zIndex = 1;
                    pinImage.setAttribute("id", "pushPin");
                    innerDiv.appendChild(pinImage);
                    new OpacityObject('pushPin','resources/images/pin')
                                        .setBackground();

                    var dialog = document.createElement("div");
                    dialog.style.position = "absolute";
                    dialog.style.left = (stripPx(pinImage.style.left) - 90) + "px";
                    dialog.style.top = (stripPx(pinImage.style.top) - 210) + "px";
                    dialog.style.width = "309px";
                    dialog.style.height = "229px";
                    dialog.style.zIndex = 2;
                    dialog.setAttribute("id", "pinDialog");
                    dialog.innerHTML = "<table height='80%' width='100%'><tr>" +
                      "<td align='center'>The capital of Spain</td></tr></table>";
                    innerDiv.appendChild(dialog);
                    new OpacityObject('pinDialog','resources/images/dialog')
                                        .setBackground();
              }
        </script>
    </head>
    <body onload="init()">
        <p>
            <h1>Ajaxian Maps</h1>
        </p>
        <div id="outerDiv">
            <div id="toggleZoomDiv" onclick="toggleZoom()">
            </div>
            <div id="togglePushPinDiv" onclick="togglePushPin()">
            </div>
            <div id="innerDiv" style="z-index: 0">
            The rain in Spain falls mainly in the plains.
            </div>
        </div>
    </body>
</html>
```

2.4 Conclusion

The Ajaxian Maps code we showed you in this chapter has changed little from our initial seat-of-the-pants version coded in two hours. We spent another two hours polishing things up, fixing a few bugs, and introducing compatibility for Internet Explorer 6.0 (which required two minor changes that we commented in the source code as well as the transparency issues we just finished discussing).

Imagine how far you could take this code if you had two or three full-time developers working on it for a few months! Certainly all of the remaining interface features in Google Maps you could easily accommodate in that time period.

Feel free to use the code from this chapter to implement your own Google Maps interface. Such an application can ultimately be generalized for any time you need to display an image too large for the screen (or available memory) and enable annotations to appear on top of that image.

And the next time someone tells you Ajax is hard? Tell them you know better.

Chapter 3

Ajax in Action

In Chapter 1, Hector and his team went on a voyage of discovery about the possibilities for web applications. They learned that Ajaxian techniques can transform conventional web pages into dynamic web interfaces. This chapter is about lifting the veil and showing you how Ajax really works. To do this, we'll transform a traditional web page into an Ajax application right before your eyes.

3.1 Ajaxifying a Web Application

Hector released the first version of their application a few months ago. As he reviewed the user feedback, he found that some users expressed frustration with a customer data entry screen. Figure 3.1, on the next page, shows the current version of the page.

So what's the problem with this screen? It turns out that the users of Hector's application are used to the behavior of the "green-screen" application it replaced. In the old application, all the users had to do was enter the customer's Zip code, and the City and State fields would autopopulate with the correct values; the users of Hector's new web application are frustrated that they now have to enter this data manually.

3.2 Ajax to the Rescue

With Ajaxian techniques, it is possible for Hector to faithfully re-create the autopopulation of data enjoyed by users of the old green-screen application. Let's look at how this feature can be added to Hector's code.

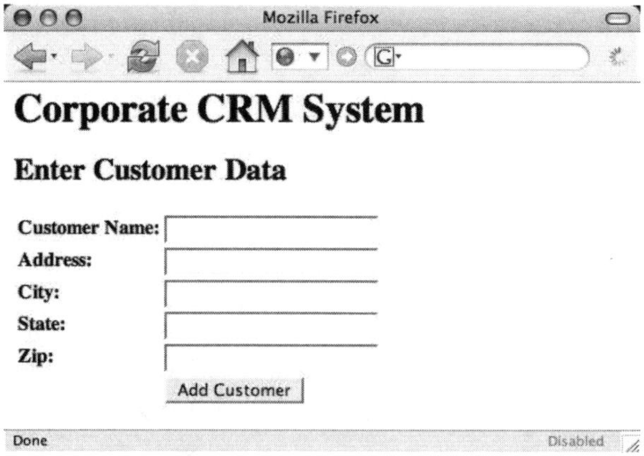

Figure 3.1: HECTOR'S PROBLEM ENTRY SCREEN

Ajaxifying the CRM Screen

To start, let's look at the source code for the CRM screen:

File 1

```html
<html>
    <head>
        <title>Customer Data Screen</title>
    </head>
    <body>
        <h1>Corporate CRM System</h1>
        <h2>Enter Customer Data</h2>
        <table>
            <tr>
                <th>Customer Name:</th>
                <td><input type="text" name="name"/></td>
            </tr>
            <tr>
                <th>Address:</th>
                <td><input type="text" name="address"/></td>
            </tr>
            <tr>
                <th>City:</th>
                <td><input type="text" name="city"/></td>
            </tr>
            <tr>
                <th>State:</th>
                <td><input type="text" name="state"/></td>
            </tr>
            <tr>
                <th>Zip:</th>
                <td><input type="text" name="zip"/></td>
```

```
            </tr>
            <tr>
                <th></th>
                <td><input type="Submit" value="Add Customer"/></td>
            </tr>
        </table>
    </body>
</html>
```

We want to add behavior so that when the user enters a value in the Zip field, we'll send the ZIP code to the server, receive a response containing the city and state that correspond to the ZIP, and populate the City and State fields with those values.

Preparing the HTML

The first step toward this end will be to add an *event handler* to the Zip *<input>* tag. Chances are, if you've done any HTML development before, you've dealt with event handlers; they allow you to execute script code in the web page when certain user interactivity or browser tasks occur. The second step will be to add id= attributes to the City and State *<input>* elements. You may not have had experience with id attributes; we'll talk more about those in a bit.

event handler

Our revised *<input>* elements look like this (with the surrounding table rows shown for context):

File 2

```
<tr>
    <th>Zip:</th>
    <td><input onblur="getZipData(this.value)"
               type="text" name="zip"/></td>
</tr>
<tr>
    <th>City:</th>
    <td><input id="city" type="text" name="city"/></td>
</tr>
<tr>
    <th>State:</th>
    <td><input id="state" type="text" name="state"/></td>
</tr>
```

The event handler is registered via the onblur= attribute. This causes the JavaScript function named getZipData() to be invoked when the focus leaves this element. The parameter passed to this function, this.value, specifies that the value property of the *<input>* element will be passed; the this is a reference to the element on which the event handler has been registered.

The Back End

We demonstrated how to request city/state data from the server, but we never showed you how the server processed the request and generated the response. Unfortunately, this can be somewhat tricky to do; what programming language should we use to demonstrate the server process? Later in the book, starting with Chapter 11, *Server-side Framework Integration*, on page 197, we talk fairly extensively about different programming language frameworks for creating server processes that can interact with Ajax web pages; for now, just take it on faith that a server is providing data to the page.

We've also changed the ordering of the table rows; now the Zip input comes first. While this new layout is atypical for American addresses, it reflects a more natural flow for the Ajaxified version of the screen, since entering the ZIP code will autopopulate the other two fields beneath it.

Communicating with the Server

We're now done with the first half of our task: wiring the HTML to a script that will perform our Ajax behavior. Now we need to tackle the slightly trickier second bit: writing the script.

The key to Ajax is a JavaScript object called XMLHttpRequest, the engine that can send HTTP requests, receive responses, and parse them as XML. We'll use this object in our getZipData() function, which will create an instance of XMLHttpRequest and use it to send the ZIP code to the server. Remember, this function will be invoked whenever the Zip input loses focus, that is, whenever the user enters the field and then leaves it, either with the mouse, with the Tab key, or with some other mechanism. Here's what it looks like so far:

```
Line 1   <script type="text/JavaScript">
    -        var xhr;
    -        function getZipData(zipCode) {
    -            xhr = new XMLHttpRequest();
    5            xhr.open("GET",
    -                    "/getCityStateFromZip.request?" + zipCode);
    -            xhr.send(null);
    -        }
    -    </script>
```

XMLHttpRequest

The syntax we have used so far to create an instance of XML-HttpRequest is browser-specific. Microsoft Internet Explorer, the first browser to offer this feature, uses an ActiveX component to accomplish the same tasks. Creating one requires a different syntax, which we will cover later in the book. There is talk right now that the next major release of IE (as of this writing, IE is on version 6 with Service Pack 1) will use the syntax described previously, thus (eventually) eliminating the confusion.

So far, pretty simple, right? On line 4, we create our XMLHttpRequest instance. On the next line, we configure it using the open() function; the first parameter indicates the HTTP method to use for the request, and the second indicates the URL we'll be requesting. Finally, we invoke the send() function, which predictably enough sends the request.

Parsing the Response

Now that we've demonstrated how to send a request to the server, we need to add some code that will process the response that the server sends back. We'll do that by creating the function processZipData():

```
Line 1    function processZipData() {
   -          var data = xhr.responseText;
   -          var cityState = data.split(',');
   -          document.getElementById("city").value = cityState[0];
   5          document.getElementById("state").value = cityState[1];
   -      }
```

The first few lines of this function are fairly intuitive; we retrieve the data sent back from the server—the city and state, formatted as City, State—and split the string into a two-element string array so that we can access the city and state values separately.

Lines 4 and 5 demonstrate why we gave id attributes to the City and State input elements earlier. Web browsers model every web page they display as XML documents (regardless of how ugly the page's HTML markup is). In JavaScript code, we can access this XML document using the document variable. document has a handy getElementById() function that can return a reference to any XML element based on the id attribute. Once we have a reference to the element, we can manipulate it. In this case, we set the value attribute of the elements to the city and state values returned by the server.

Tying It All Together

We've created two JavaScript functions: getZipData() sends a request to the server, and processZipData() processes the response. However, we haven't yet connected them. As our code currently stands, processZipData() will never be invoked.

You might think that we should invoke processZipData() as we do on line 6 of the following example:

```
Line 1   function getZipData(zipCode) {
    -         xhr = new XMLHttpRequest();
    -         xhr.open("GET",
    -                 "/getCityStateFromZip.request?" + zipCode);
    5         xhr.send(null);
    -         processZipData();
    -     }
```

Unfortunately, this just doesn't work. The *A* in Ajax stands for *asynchronous*, and asynchronous behavior is exactly what we're seeing here.

asynchronous

It turns out that when we invoke the send() function on line 5, the invocation returns immediately, and the XMLHttpRequest will make the request and receive the response on a separate thread. Thus, if we were to try to process the response from the server on the following line, we couldn't—we would not yet have received the response.

callback handler

The solution is to register a *callback handler*—a function that will be invoked when the XMLHttpRequest has received the response from the server. Line 3 in the following example demonstrates how to register processZipData() as a callback handler:

```
Line 1   function getZipData(zipCode) {
    -         xhr = new XMLHttpRequest();
    -         xhr.onreadystatechange=processZipData;
    -         xhr.open("GET",
    5                 "/getCityStateFromZip.request?" + zipCode);
    -         xhr.send(null);
    -     }
```

By simply passing the name of the function to the onreadystatechange() method, we are almost ready. Why is the method named onreadystatechange() and not, say, onresponsereceived()? It turns out that XMLHttpRequest calls back into the function we registered multiple times as

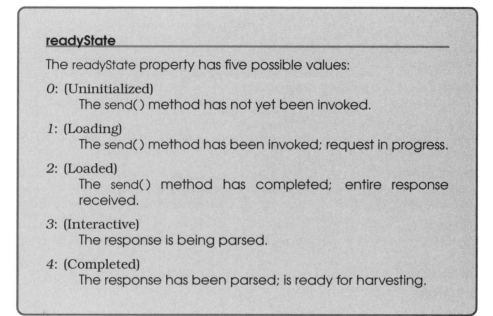

it sends the request and receives the response, each time indicating that it has made progress. We're interested in parsing the data only once the entire process has finished, so we need to check the current status of the XMLHttpRequest before we attempt to get the response data in processZipData():

```
Line 1    function processZipData() {
    -         if (xhr.readyState == 4) {
    -             var data = xhr.responseText;
    -             var cityState = data.split(',');
    5             document.getElementById("city").value = cityState[0];
    -             document.getElementById("state").value = cityState[1];
    -         }
    -     }
```

XMLHttpRequest provides a readyState property that indicates its current status; a state of 4 indicates that the response has been received.

The Big Picture

That's it, we're done. Let's look at the entire web page source code to see how all these pieces fit together:

File 2
```
<html>
    <head>
        <title>Customer Data Screen</title>
```

```html
<script type="text/javascript">
    var xhr;
    function getZipData(zipCode) {
        xhr = new XMLHttpRequest();    //<label id="code.xhr"/>
        xhr.onreadystatechange=processZipData;
        xhr.open("GET",
                "/getCityStateFromZip.request?" + zipCode);
        xhr.send(null);
    }
    function processZipData() {
        if (xhr.readyState == 4) {
            var data = xhr.responseText;
            var cityState = data.split(',');
            document.getElementById("city").value = cityState[0];
            document.getElementById("state").value = cityState[1];
        }
    }
</script>
</head>
<body>
    <h1>Corporate CRM System</h1>
    <h2>Enter Customer Data</h2>
    <table>
        <tr>
            <th>Customer Name:</th>
            <td><input type="text" name="name"/></td>
        </tr>
        <tr>
            <th>Address:</th>
            <td><input type="text" name="address"/></td>
        </tr>
        <tr>
            <th>Zip:</th>
            <td><input onblur="getZipData(this.value)"
                    type="text" name="zip"/></td>
        </tr>
        <tr>
            <th>City:</th>
            <td><input id="city" type="text" name="city"/></td>
        </tr>
        <tr>
            <th>State:</th>
            <td><input id="state" type="text" name="state"/></td>
        </tr>
        <tr>
            <th></th>
            <td><input type="Submit" value="Add Customer"/></td>
        </tr>
    </table>
</body>
</html>
```

Of course, Ajax is all about interactivity; seeing a code listing doesn't quite capture the drama of having the fields autopopulate. If you visit AjaxInAction/screenAjax1.html you'll find an online version of this code.

3.3 The Grubby Details

Ajax doesn't seem that hard, does it? If you have much experience with HTML and JavaScript, you probably already knew how to do 90% of what we just explained. Despite what some industry figures have claimed, Ajax really isn't rocket science. However, it isn't quite as simple as we've just demonstrated, either. Before we move on, we really should stop to explain a few more things.

Cross-browser Issues

The Ajaxified web page we just looked at has at least one rather severe cross-browser limitation. The way it initializes the XMLHttpRequest object will function only on Mozilla 1.0+ and Safari 1.2+; it does not function on Internet Explorer. On IE 5.0+, the way to create it is as follows:

```
var xhr = new ActiveXObject("Microsoft.XMLHTTP");
```

On earlier versions of Internet Explorer, the library had a different name, and the code should read as follows:

```
var xhr = new ActiveXObject("MSXML2.XMLHTTP");
```

A common idiom for supporting all major browsers fairly easily is to use a JavaScript try/catch block to attempt to create the object in different ways:

File 3
```
function createXHR() {
    var xhr;
    try {
        xhr = new ActiveXObject("Msxml2.XMLHTTP");
    } catch (e) {
        try {
            xhr = new ActiveXObject("Microsoft.XMLHTTP");
        } catch (E) {
            xhr = false;
        }
    }

    if (!xhr && typeof XMLHttpRequest != 'undefined') {
        xhr = new XMLHttpRequest();
    }
    return xhr;
}
```

Fortunately, these days a multitude of libraries encapsulate all of this complexity into a simple, single line of code. We'll discuss some of these libraries in Chapter 5, *Ajax Frameworks*, on page 79.[1]

Handling Errors

Recall the processZipData() function:

File 2

```
function processZipData() {
    if (xhr.readyState == 4) {
        var data = xhr.responseText;
        var cityState = data.split(',');
        document.getElementById("city").value = cityState[0];
        document.getElementById("state").value = cityState[1];
    }
}
```

This implementation works fairly well—until the server responds with an error. Because XMLHttpRequest uses the familiar HTTP transport to make its requests, it uses the same scheme of status codes that web developers have learned over the ages. For example, a status code of 200 indicates that the request was successfully processed, 404 indicates that the resource could not be found, and so forth.

To make our function a bit more robust, we ought to do something like this:

File 3

```
function processZipData() {
    if (xhr.readyState == 4) {
        if (xhr.status == 200) {
            var data = xhr.responseText;
            var cityState = data.split(',');
            document.getElementById("city").value = cityState[0];
            document.getElementById("state").value = cityState[1];
            document.getElementById("zipError").innerHTML = "";
        } else {
            document.getElementById("zipError").innerHTML = "Error";
        }
    }
}
```

Note the addition of a new element to the page: zipError. This is an element with an id= attribute set to zipError. When our XMLHttpRequest fails, the element will display the Zen-like message "Error."

---

[1]The file AjaxInAction/screenAjax2.html contains code that's compatible with Internet Explorer 5.0+.

Synchronous Ajax?

We've misled you a little bit. It turns out that you don't have to use XMLHttpRequest asynchronously. When you call the open function, if you pass a third argument of false, XMLHttpRequest will make its request without spawning a background thread—thus allowing you to work with it in a synchronous fashion, such as in this example:

```
xhr.open("GET", "/myURL", false);
xhr.send(null);
processZipData();
```

This seems so much simpler than all of that asynchronous callback mumbo jumbo; why not use XMLHttpRequest this way?

It turns out that when you use XMLHttpRequest in this fashion, the browser's user interface becomes nonresponsive for the duration of the request. If the request takes a few milliseconds, as some do, that's really not a big deal. However, when it comes to networks, one should *never* make assumptions about latency; if the request takes a second or two, the user is sure to notice. If it takes five or ten seconds, the user is sure to become rather annoyed and will perhaps even terminate the browser.

In short, you should probably never do synchronous Ajax (err, Synjax).

Network Latency

When utilizing the synchronous version of XMLHttpRequest.open, one of the biggest worries you have is *latency*. You have to be concerned with the length of time it takes the response to arrive from the server, since the browser will be blocked and the user will be sitting idle while they wait.

latency

Less obvious, but just as important, is the effect latency can have on asynchronous requests. Take, for example, an asynchronous Ajax request that should autopopulate several form fields. If the background request takes too long to return, the user might begin populating the fields by hand, expecting that some kind of error has occurred. When the results arrive from the server, what should the page do? Overwrite the user-provided values, or drop the server-returned values? If it has to drop the server values, should it do so silently or with a warning?

It really doesn't matter what style of network call you utilize in your application. Network speed is always an issue on the UI, and it benefits your users when the code takes possible delays into account. We cover some ways to handle this in Chapter 7, *Ajax UI, Part II*, on page 125.

3.4 Wrapping Up

And so, armed with his new Ajax version of the customer screen, Hector is ready to satisfy his users by giving them the rich interaction they demanded. There are some ridiculously fancy Ajax websites out there, to be sure, but what you've seen in this chapter forms the foundation of all Ajaxian techniques: asynchronous JavaScript requesting data dynamically from the server and doing DOM manipulation of the page to dynamically update it with the new data.

As this book progresses, we'll build on this foundation to show you how to create much more advanced effects and functionality and to do it more simply with JavaScript helper libraries and sophisticated toolkits in various programming languages.

Chapter 4

Ajax Explained

As we discussed in previous chapters, Ajax is the technique of using JavaScript (specifically, the XMLHttpRequest object) to request data asynchronously and then dynamically update a web page with the requested data. We demonstrated this technique by revamping Hector's CRM application to retrieve the city/state values for a ZIP code.

In this chapter, we will provide a crash course in the basic techniques you'll need to master in order to implement Ajax effects of all shapes and sizes in your own applications. Though we will cover the foundational technologies in this chapter, you will likely leverage frameworks with higher-level abstractions. In future chapters, we will discuss how third-party frameworks can give you complex effects.

In the following sections, we'll help you build a foundation of JavaScript understanding that will help you comprehend the technical portions of the remainder of this book. Our approach is to assume some programming experience on your part. In fact, we're betting that you're already a capable programmer in your language(s) of choice.

Our agenda for the chapter is as follows:

- Reviewing client-side JavaScript
- Manipulating the web page
- Sending and retrieving data
- Debugging techniques

4.1 A Review of Client-Side JavaScript

Do you hate programming JavaScript? Do you consider JavaScript code inherently ugly? Do you find any nontrivial JavaScript codebase to be a maintenance nightmare? You're certainly not alone. JavaScript is widely hated and feared by many web developers, especially those with backgrounds in statically typed languages such as Java and C#.

Why do so many have it in for JavaScript? We believe that JavaScript's poor general reputation is not at all because of the syntax or capabilities of JavaScript itself. In fact, the truth of the matter is that modern JavaScript is actually a very advanced programming language. It supports continuations, closures, aspect-oriented programming, on-the-fly type modification, and a host of other features found in languages such as Python, Ruby, and Lisp. We think that its poor reputation stems more from its historical misuse in early web applications for cramming business logic into the view. This chapter, and this book, is about using JavaScript for its natural purpose: creating a rich user interface.

The Basics of JavaScript

Depending on your background, you may find variables in JavaScript surprising. Specifically, you don't need to declare them or define their type. Instead, you simply reference them, as in this:

```
myVariable = "What am I? Who made me?"
```

In this example, the variable myVariable is automatically conjured into existence for us on the spot. This flexible manner of creating variables is neat but also a bit confusing. Consider this next example:

```
Line 1    myVariable = 10
   -      myOtherVariable = 20
   -      mySumTotal = myVariable + myOtherVariable
   -      myVariable = 5
   5      myOtherVarable = 10
   -      mySumTotal = myVariable + myOtherVariable
```

What do you suppose the value of mySumTotal is at the end of the example? If you guessed 15, you're wrong; it's actually 25. You see, on line 5, myOtherVariable was misspelled. In a language such as Java or C#, this would produce some kind of error. In JavaScript, it's not an error at all—we've simply created a new variable on the fly named myOther-Varable. Fortunately, JavaScript does consider it an error if you reference an undefined variable in an expression. If the typo had occurred

JavaScript, booleans, and You

JavaScript can evaluate numbers and strings as booleans, too; any nonempty string and any nonzero number evaluate to true.

in line 3 or 6, as in mySumTotal = myVariable + myOtherVarable, an error would be thrown.

For this reason, we consider it good style to use the optional var keyword when declaring variables; this makes it explicit whether a variable was intended to be declared or whether a declaration is a probable typo. With var, the example looks as follows:

```
Line 1    var myVariable = 10
    -     var myOtherVariable = 20
    -     var mySumTotal = myVariable + myOtherVariable
    -     myVariable = 5
    5     myOtherVarable = 10
    -     mySumTotal = myVariable + myOtherVariable
```

JavaScript supports four basic types of values: object, number, string, and boolean (there are some others, like functions and arrays, but they aren't important just now). Unlike most other languages, JavaScript variable declarations do not declare the type of data they store. Rather, the type is determined automatically based both on what has been assigned to the variable and the type of expression in which the variable is used. What's more, JavaScript variables change their type automatically as necessary. Consider the following examples:

```
myVariable = "What am I? Who made me?"   // a string
myVariable = 42                          // now a number
myVariable = 42 + "The answer"           // a string ("42The answer")
myVariable = true                        // a boolean
```

Functions

On the surface, functions in JavaScript work much as they do in any other language. They are declared with the keyword function(), they can take zero or more parameters, and they can return values:

```
function addNumbers(one, two) {
  return one + two;
}
```

Undefined

The undefined value is a first-class type in JavaScript. Most commonly, it is the value provided by JavaScript for a variable that has been declared but whose value has never been assigned. Some JavaScript implementations also use it for the value of variables that have never been declared, though this is less common, since most JavaScript interpreters allow for in-line variable declaration.

It is important to note that it isn't merely a value. Though it has a string representation (undefined), it is actually a first-class type. This means that the typeof() operator, when applied to a variable with this value, will return Undefined.

Java and C# developers may find it odd that no return type need be declared; if a function returns a value, it simply uses the return() keyword at some point. It is perfectly legal to create functions that branch and return a value in one path but don't in another. Variables that are assigned the result of a nonreturning function contain the special JavaScript value undefined.

Consider this next example snippet:

```
Line 1    function myFunction(a) {
   -          return "Hello";
   -       }
   -
   5      function myFunction() {
   -          return "World";
   -       }
   -
   -      var myResult = myFunction("aValue");
```

What do you suppose the value of myResult on line 9 is? If you are used to a language that supports method overloading, you'd probably expect the value to be Hello. It's not. JavaScript doesn't support overloading; that is, it doesn't match function invocations to function definitions based on both the name and parameters of the function, just the name.

Therefore, there can be only one function with a given name at runtime. If two or more functions are defined with the same name, the version that was last processed by JavaScript is invoked. In our example, that turns out to be the one defined on line 5.

Because a function's parameters play no role in defining it, their presence is entirely optional. In fact, there's even a way to reference an invocation's parameters without declaring them—but we'll return to that in just a bit.

The Function Type

Earlier, we talked about the four types of values in JavaScript (object, number, string, and boolean) and hinted that more existed. Functions are in fact a type in JavaScript.: In fact, once you define a function using the traditional syntax we saw earlier, a variable exists that references the function; the variable takes on the same name as the function name itself.

Consider this next example:

```
function myFunction() {
  // imagine that this function does something useful
}

alert(typeof myFunction)
```

If you execute this code in your browser, JavaScript's built-in alert() function will cause a dialog to appear that displays the type of the myFunction variable; the contents of the dialog will be function.

This particular property of JavaScript—having functions as a type—leads to some pretty interesting behaviors. Consider the following:

```
function myFunction() {  // we've created a variable myFunction
  return "Hello";        // of the type "function"
}

var myFunction = 10;     // we've now reassigned myFunction to be a number

var myResult = myFunction();  // an error -- we can't invoke a number
```

Yikes! In many languages, code like this would work just fine; variables and functions are entirely different entities, and their names don't collide. In JavaScript, because functions are variables, code like this is nonsense.

In addition to the conventional syntax for defining functions that we've used up to now, there's another way to define a function:

```
var a = 10;
var b = 12;
```

```
var myFunction = function() {
  return a + b;
}

var result = myFunction();   // result is 22;
```

In this example, we've created a new function named myFunction(). The cool bit is that the function is able to access the state of its enclosing block. We can reference the a and b variables from within the func-

closure

tion. This feature is known as a *closure*, and it's a powerful feature. Normally, values in the enclosing scope are lost when the scope terminates. A closure retains access to the state of the enclosing block; when used later, that state is still available to the closure.

JavaScript Events: Binding to the Web Page

Up to now, nothing of what we've considered about JavaScript is specific to web browsers. In fact, many people actually use JavaScript outside of web browsers. From here on out, however, we will start to consider properties unique to the JavaScript environment hosted in modern web browsers.

The first consideration is how web pages interact with JavaScript. If you've ever written JavaScript before, you probably know that most JavaScript in the web page must be included inside a <*script*> tag. By convention, this is typically included in the web page's <*head*> section, as in the following:

```
<html>
  <head>
    <script type="text/javascript">
      /* javascript code here */
    </script>
  </head>
  <body>
    // the web page contents here
  </body>
</html>
```

Actually, you can include <*script*> elements anywhere in the web page; their contents will be executed in top-to-bottom order. It is generally considered bad form to include them anywhere but in the <*head*>, however.

JavaScript in a Web Page

We said that most JavaScript in a page should be included in a *<script>* tag. The exception is that JavaScript can be embedded inline as the value of attributes on a tag. Specifically, instead of referencing JavaScript functions in event handler attributes, you can embed JavaScript directly. There is no functional difference between the following:

```
<div id="myDiv" onclick="clickIt();"/>
<script type="text/javascript">
  function clickIt() {
    alert("You clicked me!");
    alert("That tickles!")
  }
</script>
```

and this:

```
<div id="myDiv" onclick="alert('You clicked me!');
                         alert('That tickles!');"/>
```

Defining Events

The most common way to launch JavaScript code from a web page is to use *HTML events*. These events provide hooks for web pages to execute arbitrary JavaScript code when the user interacts in certain ways with the web page. For example, in the previous chapter, you saw an example of the onblur event registered on an *<input>* tag:

HTML events

```
<input onblur="getZipData(this.value)" type="text" name="zip"/>
```

As we explained back then, the onblur event is fired (that is, its contents are executed) when the user moves the cursor from the input component to some other place on the web page. In this example, the contents of the event attribute is a function invocation. As we've shown, you can place any arbitrary JavaScript code you like here, but it is a good idea to limit yourself to function invocations to keep your code a bit easier to maintain.

There are a large number of events available in a web page. These range from the so-called classic events defined many years ago in the official HTML 4 specification to some additional de facto events that have emerged in various browsers in more recent years. There are numerous resources on the Web for discovering the various types of events possible in browsers; our favorite website is QuirksMode.org.[1] QuirksMode offers a very detailed discussion of events and browsers and offers fairly recent compatibility tables for different browser types.

4.2 Manipulating the Web Page

So far, we've covered the basics of JavaScript and discussed how to get a web page to call JavaScript functions in response to user events. This covers a third of what you need to know to create an Ajax application. The next major piece is knowing how to actually change web page content from JavaScript.

XML under the Covers

Modern browsers store a copy of every web page you visit in memory as an XML document, regardless of whether you're visiting a modern XHTML site or an old crufty HTML 2.0-era site. (When a web page isn't well-formed XML, the browser follows an internal algorithm for promoting the HTML to XML.) This in-memory XML representation of the web page can be accessed by JavaScript code to programmatically determine all kinds of information about the page.

More important, the XML document can be modified, and such modifications are instantly reflected by the browser's rendering of that page. Thus, to achieve animation, dynamic modification, and other effects, all one has to do is modify the web page's underlying XML document. We'll now consider how to go about making such modifications.

Modifying the XML: The DOM API

The major browsers all implement the same API for exposing the XML document to JavaScript code; it's known as the DOM API. Short for Document Object Model, DOM represents XML elements, attributes, and other components as objects in memory. The DOM API models an XML document in memory as a document object.

You can obtain a reference to the document object that represents the current web page by simply referencing a variable named document. From this instance, you can retrieve references to individual XML elements in the web page, which are modeled as Element objects. You can also modify the attributes of an XML element via an Element object.

---

[1] http://www.quirksmode.org

Defining Events Outside of HTML

We have so far shown that JavaScript event handler functions can be wired up to node events through HTML attributes. This is a fairly common practice, though there is a class of programmer (we'll call them "purists") who frown upon this usage. Even though JavaScript is embedded within the web page itself, many developers like to consider the JavaScript and the HTML as separate artifacts. Specifically, web designers will want to work on the HTML and styles, while programmers will want to focus on the scripting. Directly embedding the JavaScript into the HTML is too much coupling.

The main alternative is to use JavaScript's object properties. A reference to a node of an HTML document exposes its events as a series of properties. Functions can be directly attached to those properties. The following:

```
<div id="mydiv" onclick="myfunc()"/>
```

is functionally equivalent to this:

```
<div id="mydiv"/>
<script type="text/javascript">
  document.getElementById('mydiv').onclick = myfunc;
</script>
```

The value to this technique is that the designer can worry about HTML, and only HTML. Programmers can hook events transparently. However, the downside is that the scripts that reference those events must be parsed after the HTML they reference. Otherwise, the element cannot be found by getElementById(), and the result is that no event is actually handled. There is a relatively new library out called Behaviour (http://bennolan.com/behaviour/) that helps programmers by allowing you to assign behaviors to CSS classes, adding an extra layer of indirection.

Modern browsers support a new kind of binding. The new attachEventListener() function takes the name of the event to handle (minus the "on" part), the function pointer, and a boolean value called *capture mode.* The beauty of the new attachEventListener() method is that it can wire up multiple handlers to the same event, creating a chain of handlers. Using the direct property access, any subsequent assignments to a property just override the last assignment. Before using attachEventListener(), make sure your browser is supported. At last look, IE5+ for Windows, Firefox 1.0+, and Safari 1.2+ were all supported, but not IE for the Mac.

It's time for an example. This next code excerpt contains a simple web page that will modify itself when its button is clicked:

```html
<html>
  <head>
    <script type="text/javascript">
      function modifyPage() {
        var htmlElement = document.documentElement
        var children = htmlElement.childNodes
        var bodyElement
        for (i = 0; i < children.length; i++) {
          if (children[i].nodeName == "BODY") {
            bodyElement = children[i]
            break;
          }
        }
        children = bodyElement.childNodes
        var divElement
        for (i = 0; i < children.length; i++) {
          if (children[i].nodeName == "DIV") {
            divElement = children[i]
            break;
          }
        }
        divElement.replaceChild(document.createTextNode("Goodbye, world!"),
                                divElement.childNodes[0])
      }
    </script>
  </head>
  <body>
    <div>Hello, world.</div>
    <button onclick="modifyPage()">Click Me</button>
  </body>
</html>
```

As you can see, the DOM API is a pleasure to use. Actually, no, it's not. The DOM API is actually quite obtuse. You might be expecting something that models XML in an intuitive and easy fashion. For example, you might expect to be able to get a reference to the root element in your web page, the *<html>* element, and from there say something like:

```
htmlElement.getElement("BODY");
```

No such luck, my friend. You see, the DOM API models all of the different types of content in an XML file (elements, attributes, text, comments, and processing instructions) as nodes, and inexplicably, the API doesn't provide a way for you to retrieve just the element children from a parent element. This means navigating through the web page as XML is excruciating, as you can see for yourself.

Further, matters get a touch worse. Earlier we explained that browsers canonicalize all web pages—that is, convert all HTML to XML in a standard way. As part of this process, certain elements are added. For example, consider the case of an HTML table:

```
<table>
  <tr>
    <td>A table</td>
  </tr>
</table>
```

When the browser converts this HTML to XML, it automatically adds a *<tbody>* element as a child of the *<table>* element. Unexpected things happen to your HTML when the browser parses it; for this reason, you should steer clear of literally walking your page using the DOM, as things may not be where you expect them.

DOM Shortcuts

Fortunately, the DOM API includes a few shortcuts. Document objects have a method, getElementsByTagName(), that could have come in handy in our example. Consider this alternate JavaScript function:

```
function modifyPage() {
  var divElements = document.getElementsByTagName("DIV");
  var divElement = divElements[0];
  divElement.replaceChild(document.createTextNode("Goodbye, world!"),
  divElement.childNodes[0])
}
```

That's much more palatable. Sure, but we still have the brittle ordering problem. We're assuming that the *<div>* element that we're interested in will always occur in the same location relative to other *<div>* elements. In our trivial example, this is a safe assumption, but in the real world, this won't work at all.

What we really need is a way to easily reference a specific element in the web page. Fortunately, there is just such an easy and convenient mechanism. If you give an element an id= attribute, you can then retrieve that element using the getElementById() function on the document object. Consider this further revised version of the earlier example:

```
Line 1    <html>
   -        <head>
   -          <script type="text/javascript">
   -            function modifyPage() {
   5              var divElement = document.getElementById("toReplace")
```

```
-              divElement.replaceChild(document.createTextNode("Goodbye, world!"),
-                                      divElement.childNodes[0])
-          }
-      </script>
10   </head>
-    <body>
-      <div id="toReplace">Hello, world.</div>
-      <button onclick="modifyPage()">Click Me</button>
-    </body>
15   </html>
```

Hey, that's not looking too bad. Line 5 seems to be a fairly clean way to get the div we're looking for. Now, if only we could clean up the next two lines; they still seem a bit complex. And actually, we can.

The official DOM API requires that developers manually manipulate all of an element's child nodes and add new ones, in order to change their contents. Some time ago, Internet Explorer introduced an alternative mechanism for changing the contents of an element—one that is dramatically easier to use. In recent years, Mozilla and Safari have both implemented support for this feature. Take a look at the revised modifyPage() function:

```
function modifyPage() {
  var divElement = document.getElementById("toReplace")
  divElement.innerHTML = "Goodbye, world!"
}
```

Ahh, finally—something that is easy to write! The innerHTML property allows you to change the contents of an element by passing it a string that it will parse as XML and use to replace the current contents of the element. Nice and easy.

While the prose of these previous few sections has been biased against the more traditional DOM API methods, you can choose for yourself which mechanism seems most natural to you. Some folks prefer dealing with nodes directly and actually enjoy writing code like some of the previous iterations of our example. In our experience, however, most people prefer these shortcut mechanisms for retrieving elements and modifying their contents.

Attributes

So far we've talked about dealing with XML elements using JavaScript. What about attributes? Just as with elements, changes to attributes take effect immediately in the browser's view of a web page, so manipulating them can be pretty handy.

Inner and Outer

The innerHTML() property that we've just demonstrated is useful, but it has a rather storied history. It was introduced as a proprietary addition to Internet Explorer; other browsers have decided to support it because it has proved fairly useful, for obvious reasons. There are, though, two related properties: innerText() and outerHTML().

innerText() accomplishes almost the same thing as innerHTML(). The internal representation of the referenced node is replaced with the text passed into the method. However, unlike innerHTML(), the new text is not parsed as XML. It is, rather, rendered directly as a textual child node of the containing node. This performs better than parsing the text as XML and is preferable for just adding data rather than new elements to the tree.

outerHTML() is a different beast. innerHTML() detaches any and all existing child nodes of the target node, parses the new text, and adds the new nodes as children of the target (essentially replacing everything between the opening and closing tags of the target node). outerHTML(), on the other hand, replaces the target node itself. All children of the existing node are lost as a byproduct of destroying the target node. The node is replaced with whatever new nodes are created by parsing the input to the method.

This latter approach is actually much more useful when writing web pages that are dumb shells that aggregate components. The server-side code that renders the component can return the full entity (top-level node and its children), which can be placed anywhere on the page. Using innerHTML(), the containing page has to have full control over the layout of the components, with specifically designed container nodes to use as targets. The server endpoints that render the components output the contents of a node only; if the containing page puts them in the wrong kind of node, or at the root of the document, the rendering will most likely be wrong.

Using outerHTML(), however, the server target renders the containing node and its contents, thus ensuring that no matter where the containing page puts the results, it will be fully contained as designed. That means a real component, not just component contents. This sounds like an excellent thing—and it is—except it's still a proprietary IE addition. Firefox, for example, has not yet adopted it and has no public plans to do so.

The DOM API has a generic mechanism for manipulating attributes. Once you have a reference to an element, you can use the getAttribute() and setAttribute() functions to access and change attribute values, such as in this example:

```
var div = document.getElementById("someDiv")
div.setAttribute("style", "background: red") // make the div red
```

Surprisingly, this is fairly easy stuff. After seeing how the DOM API treats elements, you might have expected to have to navigate through some obtuse list of attributes in order to change them. In fact, changing attribute values can be even easier than this.

Cast your mind back to the CRM application we enhanced for Hector in the previous chapter. Specifically, let's review a particular JavaScript excerpt that powered that application:

```
Line 1   function processZipData() {
    -        if (xhr.readyState == 4) {
    -          var data = xhr.responseText;
    -          var cityState = data.split(',');
    5          document.getElementById("city").value = cityState[0];
    -          document.getElementById("state").value = cityState[1];
    -        }
    -      }
```

Take a look at lines 5 and 6. What's that .value bit? What that's actually doing is changing the value attribute for the City input element. Given what we just talked about a few paragraphs ago, we ought to accomplish that using the setAttribute() function, as in setAttribute("value", "city"). What's that value property all about?

It turns out that the DOM API also defines a standard for mapping specific attributes from the HTML grammar directly into a special extended version of the DOM API that browsers supply. Using these special extensions, you can set an attribute's new value by modifying a property of the element itself. Thus, when getElementByID("city") returns an input element, we can change its value attribute just by setting the value property on the object. Nifty!

4.3 Retrieving Data

We've talked about JavaScript and we've talked about how to manipulate the web page with the DOM API, so we're just missing one key element to explain Ajax: retrieving data. The heart of data retrieval is the XMLHttpRequest object (XHR for short) that we introduced in the previous chapter. In this section, we'll discuss more details about XHR.

XMLHttpRequest

In the previous chapter, we saw the basics of how to create an instance of an XHR and use it to retrieve data. Let's review that again here, briefly, in the context of a different example. The following code listing shows how a simple web page can retrieve a message from a server and display it:

```
Line 1    <html>
  -         <head>
  -           <script type="text/javascript">
  -             var xhr;
  5
  -             function modifyPage() {
  -               try {
  -                 xhr = new ActiveXObject("Msxml2.XMLHTTP");
  -               } catch (e) {
  10                try {
  -                   xhr = new ActiveXObject("Microsoft.XMLHTTP");
  -                 } catch (e) {
  -                   xhr = false;
  -                 }
  15              }
  -
  -               if (!xhr && typeof XMLHttpRequest != 'undefined') {
  -                 xhr = new XMLHttpRequest();
  -               }
  20
  -               xhr.open("GET", "/message");
  -               xhr.onreadystatechange=function() {
  -                 if (xhr.readyState != 4) return;
  -
  25                document.getElementById("message").innerHTML = xhr.responseText;
  -               }
  -               xhr.send(null);
  -             }
  -           </script>
  30        </head>
  -         <body>
  -           <div id="message"></div>
  -           <button onclick="modifyPage()">Click Me</button>
  -         </body>
  35      </html>
```

This HTML will render a very simple web page that presents a button to the user. Once clicked, the page will display the results of a query to the server in the page above the button. Line 21 shows the requested URL as "/message"; you could implement this URL using any web-enabled language. A Java Servlet implementation would look something like this:

```
import javax.servlet.http.*;
import javax.servlet.ServletException;
import java.io.IOException;
import java.util.Date;

public class MessageServlet extends HttpServlet {
  protected void doGet(HttpServletRequest request,
                       HttpServletResponse response)
  throws ServletException, IOException {
    response.getWriter().println("Hello; the current time is " + new Date());
  }
}
```

But really, you could also implement the message URL as a flat file containing plain text or an HTML snippet; it really doesn't matter. XHR requests the URL just like the browser would and returns the results just as though you entered the URL in the browser URL field.

XHR in Detail

Let's talk about some of the other features of XHR that we haven't covered thus far.

States

The onreadystatechange property is a key feature of XHR. It lets you register an asynchronous callback handler that will be invoked as the state of XHR changes during a request/response communication with a server. In the previous chapter, we looked at the five possible states of the readyState property. Generally speaking, the important state is 4 (Completed). The other four states are all different shades of "incomplete." They are described in more detail in Chapter 3, *Ajax in Action*, on page 49.

Headers

In addition to exposing somewhat granular information about its current state, XHR also lets you modify or add HTTP headers in the request and view headers in the response. This is accomplished using the setRequestHeader(), getResponseHeader(), and getAllResponseHeaders() functions. In this example, we spoof the browser used to send the XHR:

GET Requests and the Browser Cache

A common gotcha for developers new to the XHR object is because of the way that IE, and now Firefox 1.5, handles caching XHR requests. If you use the GET method, then in IE and FF 1.5, it will dip into the browser cache unless the server side returned the cache-busting headers (e.g. Pragma: no-cache, Cache-Control: no-cache, etc.). What does this mean to you? As you fire off XHR requests, you lose hair wondering why the same item keeps coming back, and you see only one hit on the server side.

The solution is to do one of the following:

- Server side: Set the cache control headers to force the browser to go back.

- Client side: Build a URL that has a changing attribute such as /message?date=20050101002311 or /message?numreq=5

```
xhr.setRequestHeader("User-Agent", "My Custom Browser");
```

Response Data

In the examples, we've used the responseText() property to retrieve the response body from the server. Another property, responseXML(), that returns the response from the server as a DOM instance. This can be useful if you want to send structured data back to the web page from the server; you can use the DOM API to navigate through the data as XML and update the web page as appropriate based on that data.

4.4 Summary

This chapter dove into the underpinnings of Ajax. You've seen the JavaScript language and DOM model up close and personal. Though it is certainly possible to write applications using only the constructs you've seen here, programmers generally tend to appreciate tools that give them more leverage. After we tackle implementing Google Maps, the next several chapters will look at the frameworks that have sprouted lately to make the gory details of DOM manipulation, event binding, and node traversal disappear.

Chapter 5

Ajax Frameworks

Until now, we've looked at Ajax either at an abstract architectural level or from down in the tunnels underneath the structure. The DOM API and JavaScript's sometimes tortured interactions with it form the basis of all other Ajaxian techniques. Though it is vital to understand these things for when you run into trouble, it is also likely that you've been left scratching your head from time to time. Maybe you wondered who decided to use magic numbers for all the readyState() values. Or why the industry-standard way to create an XHR instance is in a try/catch block that will encounter an exception ~70% of the time. In fact, if you are anything like us, it probably occurred to you that you could write a fairly simple wrapper around this stuff to make it more usable in production code. These wrappers are fairly common; the Internet is littered with their corpses.

A few library wrappers have survived and flourished to become full-fledged toolkits. They provide us with much better leverage for using these Ajaxian techniques to make real applications. In this chapter, we will look at several of these frameworks at our disposal and will rewrite Hector's CRM application using the most mature and popular versions.

5.1 Frameworks, Toolkits, and Libraries

As Ajax has taken off, we've been inundated with projects claiming to have Ajax support. Since the term itself has such a broad meaning in the popular consciousness, it's often hard to know exactly what this means. Does the site perform asynchronous callbacks to the server? Does it re-render fresh data in-page? Or does it just manipulate the properties of existing DOM nodes? Figure 5.1, on the following page, clarifies the distinct layers of Ajax proper.

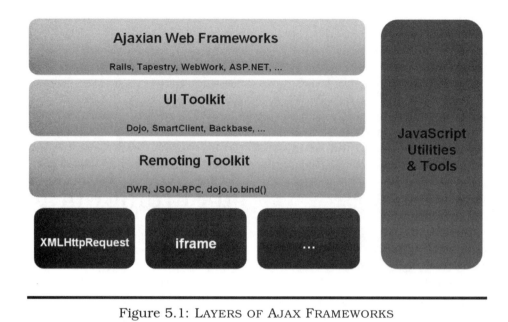

Figure 5.1: LAYERS OF AJAX FRAMEWORKS

Remoting Toolkit

The lowest level of Ajax helpers is a remoting toolkit. If you were to create your own toolkit, this would probably be where you'd start out: wrapping XMLHttpRequest with your own API to make life easier. A really good remoting toolkit should be able to do much more than simply hide our ugly try/catch XHR instantiation code. What should happen if your Ajaxian page is loaded into a browser that does not support XMLHttpRequest? It ought to find a way, if possible, to provide all (or at least some) of the page's functionality by other means. For example, some remoting toolkits will use a hidden iframe to provide fake XHR support to the page.

Figure 5.1 lists a handful of such frameworks, and shows what each attempts to provide to developers. The Dojo Toolkit, JSON-RPC, and Prototype are all pure JavaScript frameworks that are agnostic about the world of the server side (although Prototype was built with Ruby on Rails in mind).

Others, such as DWR (Direct Web Remoting), couple a JavaScript client library with a server-side listener piece written for the Java platform. JSON-RPC itself has various bindings for many back-end languages.

iframes

Prior to the broad adoption of the XMLHttpRequest object, many web applications were using a hidden iframe to accomplish in-page round-trips back to the server. An iframe is just like a normal HTML frame (a container that can be targeted at a URL and render the results) except that it is embedded in another page. These applications simply created an iframe of 0px by 0px and then caused it to refresh against a given URL in order to pull more data back from the server.

While the technique is valid and worked for many, there were two inherent problems. The first is, if you wanted multiple asynchronous requests, you had to have multiple iframes. This became a game of guessing how many you would need and embedding that many in the page, which is not a tremendous burden, just somewhat ungainly.

More important is the question of *coding intentionally*: the use of iframe is a quintessential kludge. By that, we mean it's the repurposing of a technology to do something it wasn't quite meant to do. Though it works, it always feels a little like cheating. XMLHttpRequest, however poorly named, is an object specifically designed for initiating, monitoring, and harvesting the results of in-page postbacks. Programming against it feels natural, and lends itself to more readable (and therefore maintainable) code.

A third issue, which affects IE, is that the iframe issues audio feedback to the user whenever it makes a request. This comes in the form of a "click" sound, which can be jarring for the user since they usually have no other indication of ongoing asynchronous behavior.

Toolkit Resources

- Dojo: http://dojotoolkit.com
- Prototype: http://prototype.conio.net/
- Script.aculo.us: http://script.aculo.us
- DWR: https://dwr.dev.java.net/
- Backbase: http://www.backbase.com
- SmartClient: http://www.isomorphic.com
- Ajax.NET: http://ajax.schwarz-interactive.de/
- SAJAX: http://www.modernmethod.com/sajax/
- JSON-RPC: http://json-rpc.org/

DWR, JSON-RPC, Ajax.NET, and SAJAX are all examples of ORB-based Ajax frameworks. They allow you to map JavaScript methods to back-end services, treating the client-side JavaScript as though it could directly access your server-side objects.

UI Toolkit

Above, or potentially alongside, remoting toolkits we find JavaScript UI libraries. These give us the ability to use rich UI components and effects out of the box, but they differ in many ways.

Richer UI Components

Toolkits such as Dojo give us rich widgets like trees, tabbed panes and menus. These are self-contained, instantiable UI components that can be used to compose a rich, though still very "webish," application. The result is still unmistakably an HTML UI.

Web Application Toolkit

Toolkits such as SmartClient aim to give you widgets that build a UI that looks and feels the same as a native application on Windows or Mac OS X.These are useful if you are building an application that happens to be on the Web versus a website that uses a couple of UI effects and components. SmartClient, for example, features widgets that make the page look and feel exactly like a Windows NT application.

Markup Based

Backbase allows you to add rich components through a markup programming API. Your traditional HTML becomes something like this:

File 4

```
<xmp b:backbase="true" style="display:none;"
    xmlns:nav="http://www.backbase.com/site/nav">
  <s:event b:on="construct" b:action="show"/>

  <!-- everything that is never shown - in here -->
  <div style="display:none;">
    <s:include b:url="/chrome/bb3/skin.xml"/>
    <s:include b:url="/data/navigation.xml"/>
    <s:include b:url="/data/forms.xml"/>

    <!-- listeners for links to non-BDOC documents... -->
    <div id="forum">
      <s:event b:on="nav:show-page"
               b:action="select"
               b:target="id('forumBuffer')" />
    </div>
    <div id="/shop/">
      <s:event b:on="nav:show-page"
               b:action="select"
               b:target="id('shop_main_panel')" />
    </div>

    <!-- Contains references to protected buffers -->
    <!-- Trigger 'command' event to issue bufferdirty on them all -->
    <div id="clear_protected_trigger">
      <s:event b:on="command">
        <s:task b:action="trigger"
                b:event="command"
                b:target="*" b:test="*" />
      </s:event>
    </div>
  </div>

  <!-- Include shop -->
  <s:include b:url="/shop/shopIndex.html?cmd=index" />
  <!-- ... -->
</xmp>
```

Such a system could potentially enable a new generation of visual development tools. Part of the problem with such tools is the conflict between markup and code. Traditional JavaScript-based pages have caused problems for such tools because it is difficult to provide visual representations of code resources. An all-markup framework, on the other hand, would provide the right abstractions for these kinds of development environments. See, for example, the markup-based components in ASP.NET, Tapestry, and JavaServer Faces.

Simple JavaScript-Driven Effects

In Chapter 6, *Ajax UI, Part I*, on page 95, and Chapter 7, *Ajax UI, Part II*, on page 125, we'll look at several frameworks that use pure JavaScript and HTML to create extremely complex UI effects. These kinds of frameworks provide high-level abstractions on top of some meaty JavaScript, making the effects simple to implement in your application. The results are often completely cross-browser compatible and fail gracefully to static HTML in legacy browsers.

Ajaxian Web Frameworks

At the top of the tower are the web frameworks that are aware of Ajax. This is a growing group and covers all of the platforms. All the major players are represented: Java, .NET, Ruby, PHP, Python, Perl, etc.

Once again, the various frameworks offer different models for how you can work with them in an Ajaxian world.

Code Generation

The Ruby on Rails community jumped on Ajax like nobody else. They offer high-level Ruby helper functions that generate Prototype-based JavaScript code. WebWork2 is doing the same thing on the Java platform, utilizing the Dojo Toolkit as the base JavaScript framework. Many other frameworks are following suit, from Spring to CherryPy to PHP.

Component-Based

ASP.NET had Ajaxian components before there was Ajax. Other frameworks such as JavaServer Faces and Tapestry on the Java platform join ASP.NET by letting you use components that may happen to use Ajaxian techniques. In this world, you drag your DataTableComponent onto your designer view and start tweaking the property sheet for that component. Here you may see a checkbox for *autoupdate*. Simply checking that box will put this component in Ajax mode, and the rest is history.

5.2 Remoting with the Dojo Toolkit

Now that we've examined the landscape of available helper toolkits, we'll port Hector's CRM application to several of them to see how they work. Hector's CRM system is working OK with our low-level XMLHttpRequest example from the previous chapter, but we want to move up the stack and utilize a remoting toolkit to abstract away browser compatibility issues and give us more options for controlling the remoting calls.

We will first port our application to use the Dojo Toolkit,[1] explaining choices that you have along the way and finally discussing more advanced features.

What Is the Dojo Toolkit?

Dojo is a *browser toolkit*. It is an open-source project that (to quote its marketing text) aims to "allow you to easily build dynamic capabilities into web pages and any other environment that supports JavaScript. Dojo provides components that let you make your sites more useable, responsive, and functional. With Dojo you can build degradable user interfaces more easily, prototype interactive widgets quickly, animate transitions, and build Ajax-based requests simply."

It is a full-featured toolkit that has many packages, including the following:

- dojo.io: The core package that we will look at in this chapter, which makes Ajax requests easy

- dojo.event: Browser-compatible event system

- dojo.lang: Support for mixins and object extension

- dojo.graphics: Support for nifty HTML effects such as fadeIn/Out, slideTo/By, explode/implode, etc)

- dojo.dnd: Drag-and-drop support

- dojo.animation: Animation effects

- dojo.hostenv: Support for JavaScript packages (think imports and includes instead of having to create script src="...")

Porting CRM to dojo.io.bind()

This chapter is all about the remoting layer, and in Dojo that means the dojo.io package. We are going to go from where we left off with the CRM application and replace the raw XMLHttpRequest object with a call to dojo.io.bind().

---

[1]http://dojotoolkit.org

<u>**autocomplete="off"**</u>

As part of cleanup, we added the HTML attribute autocomplete="off" on the city and state input values. This stops your browser from trying to do its own completion, which gets in the way when the value is being set by a return from Ajax.

Cleaning Up the JavaScript

Before we even get into Dojo, we should clean up the JavaScript a little and encapsulate the acts of assigning the city and state in the form and announcing errors. Until now these acts were hidden in the callback function used by XMLHttpRequest.

First, we create a function that assigns the city and state:

File 11

```
function assignCityAndState(data) {
  var cityState = data.split(',');
  document.getElementById("city").value = cityState[0];
  document.getElementById("state").value = cityState[1];
  document.getElementById("zipError").innerHTML = "";
}
```

Then we have a simple error assignment procedure:

File 11

```
function assignError(error) {
  document.getElementById("zipError").innerHTML = "Error: " + error;
}
```

With this simple abstraction, we will be able to use any remoting solution and reuse these functions.

Migrating to dojo.io.bind()

Now we get to the dojo.io package and in particular, a dojo.io.bind() function that encapsulates remoting. Everything you need to do with remoting can be done with this simple function. dojo.io.bind() takes a hash as input, using the values to initialize the underlying XHR object and register callbacks to other JavaScript functions.

We have to include Dojo in our HTML head element:

```
<script language="JavaScript" type="text/javascript"
        src="../scripts/dojo/dojo.js">
</script>
```

Let's look at the code that now does the Ajax request for the Zip data:

File 11

```
function getZipData(zipCode) {
  dojo.io.bind({
    url: url + "?zip=" + zipCode,
    load: function(type, data, evt){ assignCityAndState(data); },
    error: function(type, error){ assignError(error); },
    mimetype: "text/plain"
  });
}
```

The must-have element in the dojo.io.bind() parameter is the url key. In our example it will become /ajaxian-book-crm/zipService?zip=53711 if you are looking up a Wisconsin city.

The load key takes a function object as a callback. After the Ajax request has loaded a response, this function will be called (think of this as being the callback when the status from an XMLHttpRequest is the magic 4). In your callback you get access to the following:

- type, which tells you whether the response returned normally (load) or from an error condition (error).

- data, the response (harvested from XHR.responseText). This is the payload of the request.

- evt, a DOM event.

The error key handles errors, whereas load handles successful requests. The function callback gets access to the error message itself in its second function parameter.

The mimetype key is important. We have discussed how there are various styles of remoting and how you can choose to return HTML, JavaScript, or your own text. Here, we decided to use text/plain, get back the city/state information as the string Madison,WI, and split up for our usage.

Changing dojo.io.bind() to Use a Return Type of JavaScript

Now we have our Ajax request encapsulated in one simple dojo.io.bind() function call. This is a lot more elegant than using the raw XMLHttpRequest API, and we will soon see how we have access to features above and beyond the simple requesting and retrieving of data.

What if we wanted to talk to a service that responded directly with JavaScript for us to evaluate, instead of a proprietary string that we

---

Generic Handle

Rather than separating the load and error handlers, in theory you can use one handler named handle. This is when you would use the type parameter and would probably check against it to see how you were called. We could have written the same example as follows:

```
handle: function(type, data, evt){
        if (type == "load") {
            assignCityAndState(data);
        } else if (type == "error") {
            assignError(error);
        } else {
            // could potentially handle other types!
        }
    },
```

---

needed to parse? For example, instead of returning Madison,WI, the service could return this:

```
document.getElementById('city').value = 'Boulder';
document.getElementById('state').value = 'CO';
```

Making this change is quite trivial with Dojo, and it will simplify our code even more. We can get rid of the assignCityState() call itself, and there is no need for a load() function, because Dojo will automatically load a JavaScript result from the server if we tell it via the MIME type text/javascript:

File 10

```
function getZipData(zipCode) {
        dojo.io.bind({
                url: url + "?zip=" + zipCode + "&type=eval",
                error: function(type, error){ assignError(error); },
                mimetype: "text/javascript"
        });
}
```

Notice that we added &type=eval to the URL to make sure that the server sent us back JavaScript this time.

Advanced Features of dojo.io.bind()

We hope at this point you have seen that it makes little sense to use the low-level API when you have a nice, clean, simple interface that Dojo gives you. It turns out that dojo.io.bind() can do a lot more for you. For one, it is able to do browser detection and makes sure that it finds the

---

Transport Enforcement

Sometimes, we don't want graceful, transparent failover. If, for some reason, we must mandate that only certain kinds of postback transport mechanisms be used, we can pass in our rule on the dojo.io.bind() call. If we want to enforce one transport only, we can do so by setting the following

```
transport: 'XMLHTTPTransport'
```

in the hash that we pass in.

---

right XMLHttpRequest object for your browser. If it can't find one, it can drop back to iframes to do the deed. All of this happens transparently to the developer.

Submitting Forms

Dojo can submit a form asynchronously for you as well as access a given URL. All you need to do to submit your form is tell Dojo about the form element in your HTML via the following:

```
dojo.io.bind({
  url: "http://your.formsub.url",
  load: function(type, obj) { /* use the response */ },
  formNode:  document.getElementById('yourForm')
})
```

What if your form has a file upload as part of it? XMLHttpRequest can't do the job here, because it can't get the file from disk in a reliable way. Dojo has a solution, though, thanks to the pluggable I/O layer.

Browsers know how to send files, and we piggyback on that by selecting the IframeIO transport.

So, the simple solution is to place the following piece of code before you have forms with file uploads:

```
dojo.require("dojo.io.IframeIO");
```

Support for Browser Back/Forward Buttons

This feature is a gem. One of the issues with using XMLHttpRequest versus an iframe is that iframe events are placed in the browser history,

> ### Uploading a File without a File!
>
> You can actually upload content as though it is a file using the XMLHttpRequest transport.
>
> In your dojo.io.bind(..) call, pass in a file object to the argument object itself:
>
> ```
> file: {
>   name: "upload.txt",
>   contentType: "plain/text",
>   content: "look ma! no form node!"
> }
> ```

while XHR events are not. This can cause an issue if a user clicks something that causes an Ajax request that changes the page, and then they hit the back button assuming that it will take them to the state they were in before that request. Instead, they are taken to the page before the Ajax code (which could be away from your website!).

Dojo allows you to tie into the browser buttons, passing in the work that you want to do when a user clicks back or forward. In our CRM example, you could save the current city and state information and clean it out in the form when the user clicks back. Then, if the user clicks forward you could reset it into the form without having to go back to the server.

```
backButton: function() {
  saveCityState();
  cleanCityState();
},

forwardButton: function() {
  setupCityState();
},
```

How does Dojo do this? Is there a nice API that Firefox and IE give you to hook in? No. The actual implementation differs depending on the browser, but at a high level Dojo creates a hidden iframe, makes it go forward two requests, and then one back. Now, it is set up ready to do your bidding. If you click back, the onload event will call into your backButton callback. Ditto for the forward button.

Bookmarkability

Another UI issue with Ajax applications is making sure that the book-mark paradigm still works. We have all seen Ajax applications that are just one page, and hence you can't bookmark anything (Google's Gmail is sometimes bad like this).

Dojo gives you a simple hook to change the URL and hence potentially allow for bookmarking events that happen within an Ajax world.

To turn on this feature, you have to set the changeURL parameter in your calls to dojo.io.bind(). You can set it to either of the following:

- true: Changes the URL to the form:

```
http://yoursite.com/yoururl.html#12345678
```

  where the content after the hash mark is a time stamp.

```
dojo.io.bind({
  url: "http://your.sub.url",
  load: function(type, obj) { /* use the response */ },
  changeURL: true
})
```

- yourownvalue: The given string will be added to the URL. If you set the following:

```
dojo.io.bind({
  url: "http://your.sub.url",
  load: function(type, obj) { /* use the response */ },
  changeURL: "ajaxian"
})
```

  the URL will be changed to http://yoursite.com/yoururl.html#ajaxian.

Miscellaneous Options: method, content, postContent, sync, and cache

You can pass other (rarely mentioned) options to dojo.io.bind():

- method: You can set the HTTP method to use for the request (get or post, for example).

- content and postContent: You can think of these options as the request parameters that you want to post to the server in a hash form:

```
content: { key1: 'value1', key2: 'value2' }
```

postContent is sent only if the method is POST, allowing you to selectively push certain values on post requests only.

- sync: By default your requests are asynchronous (which is good), but you can change that with the following setting:

```
sync: true
```

- useCache: Dojo can use a cache that you can dip into, allowing Dojo to manage the XHR objects. To turn this on, you must set the following:

```
useCache: true
```

5.3   Remoting with the Prototype Library

Prototype jumped onto the scene with the rise of the popular Ruby on Rails web framework. The Prototype library is another open-source JavaScript toolkit that provides a straightforward wrapper around XHR and some foundational UI effects. We'll port Hector's app to use the Prototype remoting capabilities in order to contrast it with Dojo.

Porting to Prototype

Since you've already seen the port to a remoting framework, this will probably look familiar. Start with the Prototype library:

```
<script language="JavaScript" type="text/javascript"
        src="../scripts/prototype/prototype-1.3.1.js"/>
```

Ajax.Request()

The dojo.io.bind() equivalent in Prototype is Ajax.Request(). It works in a similar way to Dojo in that you pass in most of the information as an object with callbacks. The CRM example is as follows:

File 14
```
function getZipData(zipCode) {
        new Ajax.Request(url, {
                asynchronous: true,
                method: "get",
                parameters: "zip=" + zipCode,
                onSuccess: function(request) {
                        assignCityAndState(request.responseText);
                },
                onFailure: function(request) {
                        assignError(request.responseText);
                }
        });
}
```

The differences are subtle. First, you pass the URL as the first parameter to Ajax.Request() rather than in the object hash itself. You can also choose between a synchronous or asynchronous request. You will want to use asynchronous 99.99% of the time, because you don't want to freeze the browser while the request happens. You also get to choose the HTTP method (GET, POST, and so on) and the parameters that we want to add to the URL itself. Finally, the callback functions get the XMLHttpRequest object itself, so you can grab responseText, responseXML, or anything else you need from that object.

Evaluating the Return as JavaScript

If you want to use the model of having the server return JavaScript for you to run, you can implement this by doing eval() yourself in the onSuccess callback function:

File 12

```
function getZipData(zipCode) {
        new Ajax.Request(url, {
                asynchronous: true,
                method: "get",
                parameters: "zip=" + zipCode + "&type=eval",
                onSuccess: function(request) {
                        eval(request.responseText);
                }
        });
}
```

Returning HTML to the Client

Ruby on Rails favors returning HTML from the server and putting that HTML into the DOM via the innerHTML property. Since Prototype is a good sister to Rails, it makes this simple on the JavaScript side.

The trick is that you need to make sure the content that you want to change has been given an id= attribute. Then, you can use an Ajax.Updater() that makes the XHR request, gets the output, and writes it to the element with the given ID.

In our CRM example this is a two-step process. First we tag the city and state HTML content that we want to replace:

File 13

```
<tr id="rewrite">
  <th>City:</th>
  <td><input id="city" type="text" name="city"/></td>
  <th>State:</th>
  <td><input id="state" type="text" name="state" size='3' maxlength='2' /></td>
</tr>
```

Then we associate an updater with the element that has an id of rewrite by wiring up the Ajax.Updater():

File 13

```
function getZipData(zipCode) {
  new Ajax.Updater("rewrite", url, {
    asynchronous: true,
    method: "get",
    parameters: "zip=" + zipCode + "&type=html",
    onFailure: function(request) {
      assignError(request.responseText);
    }
  });
}
```

5.4 Wrapping Up

We took the raw XMLHttpRequest version of the CRM application and showed you how quality JavaScript libraries such as Dojo and Prototype can lift up your level of abstraction. There are no more magic state numbers, odd try/catch blocks, or the like. Dojo even offers advanced features like back/forward button support, which have largely been unavailable to JavaScript programmers until now.

Next, we'll look at the frameworks that provide support for UI manipulation and see how they combine with these techniques to give us real power over the user experience.

Ajax UI, Part I

In the previous several chapters, we gave you an earful about what Ajax is, what it isn't, and where it came from. By now, you've seen the "asynchronous" and "XML" parts. In this chapter and the next, we'll introduce you to the "JavaScript" and flashy UI parts of the framework. You'll get to see the CRM application grow into a full-fledged rich client application and learn some of the emerging standard patterns for Ajaxifying the UI. Perhaps most important, we'll walk you through a cautionary tale about going too far and knowing when to say "when."

6.1 Ajax and JavaScript for the UI

Dynamic HTML. The words roll around your brain and make you think of Nirvana, Lewinski, and Razorfish. DHTML was so '97. Most readers may now be wondering "What's Ajax got that DHTML didn't have?" The answer, it turns out, is fairly complex. But it starts with maturity.

When we did DHTML apps back in the '90s, browsers were still duking it out over the best way to render tables. Heck, we didn't even have *<div>* tags until the late '90s. Cascading Style Sheets were just coming out, and the language hadn't settled yet. There were browser-specific extensions to the DOM and CSS, and browsers couldn't even be trusted to render their own extensions properly on a consistent basis.

Fast-forward to 2006. Browsers are still disagreeing about the best way to render certain tags, and there are still browser-specific extensions to worry about. But the amount of commonality between modern browsers has grown immensely in the intervening years, leaving a much greater common ground. Gone are the days when you had to have browser-specific rendering of simple CSS styles. We have a much broader scope of acceptable UI techniques that will work anywhere now. This kind of common ground, which eliminates the need for vast tracts of browser-specific JavaScript and CSS, makes the development of rich client apps much more straightforward and accessible.

Further, when we were developing DHTML applications back then, we didn't have the benefit of universal XMLHttpRequest support. Sure, IE 4 had it built in as an ActiveX component, but that can hardly be considered universal. We remember teaching die-hard Windows web developers about it in '99 and getting a lot of odd stares in response, so even for those developers to whom it was available, it wasn't widely used. And without an asynchronous, embedded channel back to the server, DHTML applications were just about pop and flash. They added only marginal usability improvements in and of themselves, and if we wanted to make them talk back to the server, we ended up jumping through major hoops.

Think of that most ubiquitous of DHTML widgets, the tree nav. It was easy to write DHTML-based trees. It involved a couple of CSS styles, some onclick handlers, and some crossed fingers, but it didn't amount to much effort. And, in return, we got collapsible, expandable tree navigation. What we didn't get, unless we put in endless hours of effort, was a way to update portions of the tree from the server without reloading the whole thing. So we ended up putting the tree in a frame, all by its lonesome self, and refreshing it *en toto* whenever the app demanded. This made for tortured JavaScript and a less than ideal user experience.

We even went so far as to invent the iframe to allow us to execute background threads of operation. As we saw previously, the iframe was a convenient, if nonstandard, way to cause a secondary request to be sent to the server. JavaScript can modify the src= attribute to cause a new request to be spawned. This seems, at first glance, to provide everything XHR provides. Dig down, though, and you'll see some problems. First, iframes provide no graceful method for checking on the state of a request; once fired, either the iframe renders its results or it doesn't. Second, the iframe automatically renders the response sent back from the server. If the response isn't HTML, the iframe must be navigated, DOM-style, to retrieve the results. All this is effective but hardly efficient and certainly not elegant.

The ability to exert fine-grained control over pieces of the UI becomes profound only when we also exert similar fine-grained control over the data we are retrieving from the server. Being able to flash the background color of a *<div>* tag as the user mouses over it is pretty; being able to autoupdate a text search box as the user types into it is an actual usability improvement. The code to control the UI of the latter is not appreciably harder than for the former; it is the access to an asynchronous trip to the server to fetch more information that makes it special.

Ajax Encourages OO Over DOM

The biggest change from DHTML to Ajax has to do with the way we think about JavaScript code in the browser. In good old DHTML, we wrote JavaScript to manipulate the DOM; we treated the DOM as a giant repository of dumb entities, each with a collection of styles appended to it. We walked the DOM using nightmarish code like this:

```
element.parent.parent.sibling.child
```

and when we got there, we set text properties to be interpreted as style changes in the rendering engine. We wrote our common code as a series of functions, devoid of organizing classes or conventions. None of this looked like the server-side code we were writing; it certainly didn't feel modern in any way. JavaScript was an adjunct to our "real work," and it showed.

Ajax strives to treat JavaScript in the browser as the first-class programming environment it can be. Instead of writing procedural programs, we write class libraries to encapsulate our behavior. Instead of treating the DOM as a collection of dumb elements, we treat it as a hierarchy of types. Instead of thinking of styles as strings to be constructed and parsed, we think of them as properties of objects, to be modified individually. We write modern OO code, complete with error handling, instance methods static methods and type hierarchies.

Even better, though, we write this modern OO code using a language more expressive than the statically typed languages we use on the server. With JavaScript, we can extend types without modifying the base code. If we want to add functionality to the document object, we can declare a new function name and supply it with an anonymous definition. This new function has full access to the instance data of document, and can be called by any other type contained in our JavaScript. Functions can be sent around like data objects, invoked without knowing the originating instance. In other words, this is metaprogramming without extraneous reflection syntax.

We say that Ajax *encourages* this style of programming. There is nothing inherent about Ajax that mandates this, however. You can happily write the same old style of procedural, DOM-oriented JavaScript code and achieve Ajax effects. The frameworks that have sprouted up around Ajax, though, all eagerly pursue the more modern, object-oriented style of programming. They supply common APIs and types through which to modify the look and behavior of elements in the DOM, and they provide better ways to navigate the DOM to look for for specific items. Typically, these frameworks use object-oriented libraries and metaprogramming to achieve this. For example, the Script.aculo.us library adds a new method, getElementsByClass(), to the document object at the root of the DOM model. By injecting this method into the existing class, we get the more convenient method for navigating our DOM tree through OO methods.

Common UI Frameworks

With the creation of the Ajax moniker, there has been a concomitant explosion of JavaScript libraries to help users take better advantage of the technology shift. Instead of making users find their own paths through the desert to the OOasis, these libraries drastically shorten the learning and adoption curves for Ajax. We've already talked about them at some length in the previous chapter; there, we focused on the libraries' efforts to encapsulate the remoting features of JavaScript. Here, we'll discover what they do for our UI code.

The first area is DOM navigation. The DOM model is a beast to get around in; as much as it seems like navigating an XML infoset should be a highly standard operation, there can be interesting differences between navigation commands and their results as you move from browser to browser and from version to version. Even if there weren't, though, navigating the DOM requires too much intimacy with the overall hierarchy of the current page. Puttering around the DOM tree using .parent references and .children collections often leads to finding the wrong element, or finding no element at all.

The major UI frameworks find ways to help you around this problem. In addition to the standard getElementByID() method, these frameworks allow you to discover elements by class, by style, by tag, and by a variety of other options. They give you ways to treat elements and their names interchangeably so that you can pass either to a function and get the correct result. Mostly, they provide handy shortcuts to tedious navigation commands usually with more predictable results.

Affecting the look and style of DOM nodes is a painful exercise in string-based CSS styles, element property modulation, and general mucking about trying to get the element to look or act the way you want. Do you use the visible or hidden property? How do you increase the size: in pixels or percent? What's the best way to move an element around the page? The answers are usually an ungainly mix of techniques that seem to feel more like guesswork than solid programming.

Good Ajax libraries take the guesswork and pain out of manipulating element styles. Instead of having to guess what mix of properties you have to modify to get the desired behavior, certain typical and canonical effects are canned and supplied to you through a single method call. Users can modify the default behavior of the effects or combine them in unique ways to achieve tailored results.

In this chapter, we'll cover three major frameworks in heavy use today: Prototype, by Sam Stephenson; Script.aculo.us, by Thomas Fuchs; and Dojo, by the Dojo Foundation. There are other libraries out there worth keeping on eye on as well, such as Rico (http://openrico.org/rico/home. page), which grew out of the development for Sabre Airline Solutions. We're sure that between now and when you read this more frameworks will have popped up, so keep on the lookout.

Remember the figure back in Chapter 5, *Ajax Frameworks*? That chapter looked at the frameworks that live at the lowest level, the remoting toolkits. This chapter moves up one layer on the chart to examine the toolkits that deal directly with UI issues. It turns out there's plenty of overlap.

Prototype

The Prototype library is the grandaddy of them all. Other JavaScript libraries (notably, Script.aculo.us) are built on top of the basic functionality provided here. Prototype is a relatively simple JavaScript file; clocking in at 1,041 lines of code as of version 1.4.0_pre2, it manages to pack an enormous punch for dealing with UI issues in the browser. We've already covered what Prototype does for remoting in earlier chapters. Now we'll examine how it replaces the standard DOM and CSS idioms for manipulating UI elements.

Extensions to Common Types

Prototype adds a series of helpful utility methods to our lexicon, either by providing globally accessible functions or, in some cases, by extending existing types in JavaScript or the DOM. Since JavaScript types can be extended at runtime without modifying the original source (the very definition of a *dynamic language*), this is relatively straightforward to do. The result is that Prototype can provide extremely useful shortcuts to common functionality but present them in the most natural way possible: as properties and methods of the types where we would expect such features to appear.

Prior to the Ajax libraries, the two most common lines of JavaScript found in DHTML applications were the following:

```
var myElem = document.getElementById('some_element');
var myValue = document.getElementById('some_other_element').value;
```

Though this code is not particularly glaring, it is difficult to read and can make even the simplest of functions difficult to scan and understand. Bear in mind, also, that bandwidth is (even today) an expensive resource. For evidence, we present the current crop of JavaScript compressors with which you can eliminate all the whitespace from your scripts to provide for quicker downloading. Given that the previous code is ubiquitous and oft repeated, it would make sense to find a way to minimize the surface area of these statements. Prototype replaces them with the following lines:

```
var myElem = $('some_element');
var myValue = $F('some_other_element');
```

Even better, $() can take an arbitrary number of IDs and return an array of elements to match them.

```
var elems = $('element_one', 'element_two', 'element_three');
for(var i=0;i<elems.length;i++) {
   elems[i].value = "changed";
}
```

There is a major caveat to this technique, though. Prototype doesn't bother to check whether the ID you passed is valid within the document. In the previous case, if there's no element with ID element_two, the call still returns an array of length 3. The second element, however, is null instead of a reference to a DOM node. Also bear in mind that $F() works only for input elements. If you are looking for the text contained within an arbitrary DOM node, $F() is useless.

Prototype also extends the document object to include the new getElementsByClassName() method. You pass in the string name of a CSS class and the function will collect all the elements in the DOM that contain that class in their class list. It doesn't matter whether the class name is the first or only entry in the element's list, Prototype will still find it.

```
<div id="one" class="class1"/>
<div id="two" class="class2"/>
<div id="three" class="class1"/>
<div id="four" class="class2, class1"/>

<script type="text/javascript">
    var classOnes   = document.getElementsByClassName('class1').length; // 3
    var classTwos   = document.getElementsByClassName('class2').length; // 2
    var classThrees = document.getElementsByClassName('class3').length; // 0
</script>
```

This method takes only a single class name, though. It is up to you to make any sort of union if you are looking for elements implementing one of a list of classes.

Once you can successfully retrieve nodes from the DOM, the next step is manipulating them. Among the most common things to do is to simply change the content of a node by resetting the value of its innerHTML property. innerHTML is just a string representation of the contents of the node. If you fill it in with properly formatted HTML, the browser will render it as such. When you retrieve it, the HTML tags will be embedded in the returned value. Sometimes, you will want to maintain the tag structure in its original format. Other times, you'll want to actually display the tags as strings rather than have them rendered as HTML. Prototype extends the JavaScript String class with some new methods. escapeHTML() returns the innerHTML but with any HTML tags escaped so they can be displayed as text. unescapeHTML() does the exact opposite. This is useful for displaying HTML source within an HTML page.

A final case is when you want to eliminate the tags altogether. Imagine a div that contains a bibliography entry, rendered so that the title of the book is underlined and the author's name is boldfaced. You want to retrieve that value as data; any embedded style notation (or, Heaven help us, <b> tags) are extraneous. String now has the stripTags() method, which eliminates any angle brackets (and what's inside them) from the output. Whitespace is otherwise maintained, allowing you to treat HTML as raw data.

---

innerHTML Limitations

According to the IE documentation, the innerHTML property is read-only for this list of enclosing tags: COL, COLGROUP, FRAMESET, HTML, STYLE, TABLE, TBODY, TFOOT, THEAD, TITLE, TR. This means that, in IE, you cannot use the innerHTML property to set the contents of a table row. This works fine in all other browsers but can be a serious limitation to cross-browser effects.

The final set of extensions to cover are Prototype's extensions to the collection classes. The Prototype library was written by Sam Stephenson, a Rails committer and general Ruby aficionado. Ruby provides a suite of useful convenience methods on collection types that make it easier and more direct to manipulate, search, collect, and delete items from collections. Prototype adds very Rubyesque collection methods to JavaScript by creating a mixin called Enumerable.

Enumerable adds a bunch of methods that interact with a type's iterator to provide a more elegant way to achieve standard collection-based functionality. For example, the mixin adds an each() method to the target type. Thus, accessing the members of an array could be written using standard for loop notation:

```
var prices = [19.99, 29.99. 14.50];
var sum = 0;

for (i=0; i < prices.length(); i++) {
  sum += prices[i];
}
```

With Enumerable, you can now use the arguably more elegant each():

```
var prices = [19.99, 29.99, 14.50];
var sum = 0;

prices.each(function(price) {
  sum += price;
})
```

The each() method uses the array's iterator to grab each element in turn and pass it as the argument to the supplied anonymous function (the function need not be anonymous, obviously). If you need the current index of the current item, the function takes an optional second parameter, which is the index:

> ### Mixin
>
> A mixin is just a collection of methods that can be added to any existing type. In statically typed languages such as Java and C#, the way to do this is to make a base class with the set of functionality and then extend it. With a dynamically typed language such as JavaScript, we can apply this kind of functionality after the type has been defined (and even after it has been instantiated).

```
var prices = [19.99, 29.99, 14.50];
var sum = 0;

prices.each(function(price, index) {
  sum += price;
  alert("Price " + index + ": " + price);
})
```

each() provides the underpinnings of a variety of other useful methods.

- all(): Takes a comparison function and returns true if all of the members of the collection pass the comparison.

- any(): Takes a comparison function and returns true if any of the members of the collection pass the comparison.

- collect(): Allows you to use each element of a collection in turn to build a new collection. For each iteration, you return a value; those values are *collected* into the new result array.

- detect(): Takes a comparison function and returns the first item in the collection that matches (returns true).

- findAll(): Takes a comparison function and returns the collection of all items that match it.

- grep(): Takes a regular expression, applies it to each element of the collection and adds any match to the results array.

- include(): Takes an input object and returns true if the collection contains that object.

- inject(): Useful for creating sums across numerical collections. inject() takes an initial value and a function for calculating results and applies the function across all members of the collection, treating the first input as the first item of the collection. An example should help:

```
var prices = [19.99, 29.99, 14.50];
var sum = prices.inject(0, function(sum, price) {
  return sum + price;
})
// sum == 64.48
```

- invoke(): Takes a function name and invokes it on the collection object.

- max(): Takes a comparison function and applies it to each item of the collection, returning the one that is greater than all the rest (as defined by the comparison function).

- min(): Same as max but returns the item that evaluates to less than all the other items.

- partition(): Takes a comparison function and divides the elements of the collection into those that match and those that don't, and then returns an array of arrays in the format [[trues], [falses]].

- pluck(): Takes a property name and grabs that property of each element in the array to create the results array. If you had a collection of items each with a name property, you could use pluck() to quickly gather all the names into a new array.

- reject(): Takes a comparison function and returns an array with only those elements that did not match the comparison.

- sortBy(): Allows you to pass in a function that lets you sort the items in a collection by a specific property.

- toArray(): Returns an array of the elements in a collection.

Element

Prototype introduces a new class, Element, that controls some basic styling properties of a DOM node. Element is a *static* class, in that you need not create an instance of it to access its functionality. Its various methods all take an element ID or an element itself as a parameter and perform some action on them.

We spend a lot of time hiding and showing nodes of a DOM tree. Error messages are invisible unless validation fails, for example, or trees contain collapsible nodes. Most of the dynamic nature of a web page is wrapped up in the mysterious appearance and disappearance of blocks of data. The standard JavaScript strategy for accomplishing that uses the .style.display property.

```html
<div id="hideOrShow">
    You can turn me on and off.
</div>
<input type="button" value="Toggle" onclick="toggle('hideOrShow');"/>

 <script type="text/javascript">
    function toggle(elemName) {
      var elem = document.getElementById(elemName);
      if(elem.style.display=='none') elem.style.display = '';
      else elem.style.display = 'none';
    }
 </script>
```

Element provides the .toggle command, which accomplishes the exact same thing but with the added benefit of being able to pass in as many element names (or elements) as you like to a single call. .toggle will iterate over all the arguments, toggling the state of each in turn. This provides a convenient way to swap the visibility of elements:

```html
<div id="up">
    <img src="images/up.gif"/>Up
</div>
<div id="down" style="display:none;">
    <img src="images/down.gif"/>Down
</div>
<input type="button" value="Toggle"
    onclick="Element.toggle('up', 'down');"/>
```

To be sure, we don't always want to toggle. Element also exposes show() and hide(), which each take a variable number of elements as arguments, and ensures that each has its display property set correctly. Sometimes, though, toggling isn't enough. Setting an element's display property to none renders the rest of the page layout as though the element did not exist in the DOM at all. However, the mere existence of the element might have other effects. If the hidden element contained form elements, for example, they would be submitted to the action as though they were visible. The same is true for scripts that traverse the DOM elements or manipulate page layout.

Instead of merely setting the div's display property to none, we can remove the <div> from the DOM tree entirely. Normally, this would mean navigating to the <div>'s parent node and removing the div from the parent's children. The DOM has a removeChild() method specifically

> ## Cross-browser Warning
>
> Not all browsers handle all DOM manipulations equally. For example, you cannot insert anything into a *<table>* in IE, or you will get an error. Once again, refer to www.quirksmode.org for full treatment of different behaviors in different browsers.

for this purpose. The node is removed from the tree, and the entire tree re-rendered to keep that block from influencing the flow. Furthermore, containing elements no longer have any knowledge of the node, and scripts will not be able to discover it. This is nonreversible, unless you have cached a copy of the node in another variable and add it back manually later. Prototype exposes the removeChild() feature as a function called Element.remove().

Inserting Data

Showing and hiding data is nice, but it implies that we have a nice container dedicated for displaying that piece of data. Showing an error message, for example, usually means that we have a hidden div or span standing by to take that data and then display it to the user. Quite often, though, what we want to do is add more data to an existing, visible element. Most commonly, we want to add items to an already-visible list of items. The standard DHTML way to do this is to re-create a new version of the list items that includes the addition and then replace the contents of the list with the new version. With Ajax, this would mean having a server-side method that you call that sends the list back with any new items appended. While effective, this might be extremely inefficient. The code that generates the content of the list might be long running and, if it involved a database, mandates at least a round trip to the datastore to refill the list.

Prototype introduces the Insertion class. Insertion allows us to add information to an existing container without replacing what currently exists in the list. Insertion.Top() enters the new data at the beginning of the container's body, while Insertion.Bottom() enters it at the end. This means you can easily append single lines to a list without re-rendering the whole list:

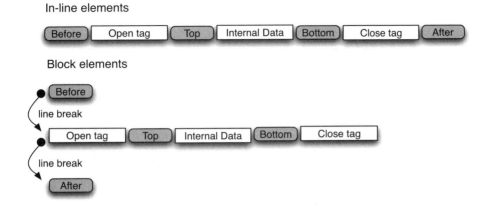

Figure 6.1: Insertion placement possibilities

```
<ul id="mylist">
  <li>one</li>
  <li>two</li>
  <li>three</li>
</ul>
<input type="text" id="newval"/>
<input type="button"
       value="Add Item"
       onclick="new Insertion.Bottom('mylist',
                          '<li>'+$F('newval')+'</li>');"/>
```

Keep in mind that you have to provide the full value you want rendered. In the previous example, we're appending the text value of the input field to the bottom of the list. We have to wrap it in the <li> tags in order to get it to render as a list item; without those tags, the new value is just pasted as text inside the list, which is rendered without the bullet and as inline text.

Prototype actually goes a little further and lets you append text around the container as well. In all, Insertion offers four placements for your new data: Before(), Top(), Bottom(), and After(). Figure 6.1 demonstrates where each lives.

This is fairly powerful, since you can modify a section of the page for which you do not have an ID (or there may be no ID at all).

Beware Before() and After()

Don't get too carried away with Before() and After(). While each will happily let you insert plain text or renderable markup into the document at the appropriate point, you cannot use them to create new containers around an existing item. To do so, you would have to execute two separate statements: an Insertion.Before() for the opening tag and an Insertion.After() for the closing tag. Modern DOM rendering engines will not allow you to add malformed XML to the document. Therefore, the first call, containing just the opening tag, will have a matching closing tag inserted at the end of the value you passed in. The second call will have the closing tag simply stripped from the input.

Imagine you have an element containing a new header tag that you want to surround with a new <div> tag. Your code would look like this:

```
<ul id="mylist">
   <li>one</li>
   <li>two</li>
   <li>three</li>
</ul>
<input type="text" id="newval"/>
<input type="button" value="Add Item"
   onclick="wrapList('mylist');"/>
<script type="text/javascript">
   function wrapList(listname) {
      new Insertion.Before(listname,
                  '<div><h2>New Title</h2>');
      new Insertion.After(listname, '</div>');
   }
</script>
```

When you execute this, the resulting rendered DOM tree, if you could see it using View Source, would look like this:

```
<div><h2>New Title</h2></div>
<ul id="mylist">
   <li>one</li>
   <li>two</li>
   <li>three</li>
</ul>
<input type="text" id="newval"/>
<input type="button" value="Add Item"
         onclick="wrapList('mylist');"/>
 . . .
```

Forms

Working with forms has historically been a bit of a drag. Forms are useful for only one purpose: collecting data from a user. The input fields that exist on a form, though varied in style, are essentially identical in nature. They represent an item that a user can use to tell us something. Before Ajax and the rethinking of the DOM that it brought with it, we had to treat forms and inputs just like any other HTML elements, navigating the DOM to find them and modifying their style properties to affect their behavior.

Prototype gives us tools to think about forms differently. Instead of representing a chunk of HTML that happens to have input boxes embedded in it, Prototype encourages us to think of forms as collections of data fields. Using the library, we can manipulate the properties of all the fields on a form simultaneously when that suits our needs and navigate them as an array of fields, not as scattered children in a subtree of the DOM.

The vehicles for this change are the new classes Field and Form. Field provides three major UI-related methods:

- select(): Selects the current value of the field

- focus(): Moves the focus to the field

- activate(): A combination of select() and focus()

For example, you could create a form with certain form fields visible at all times, a second set of more advanced options visible only when the user requests them. For convenience, you would want the user to begin typing into the topmost field immediately upon making it visible, which you could accomplish with activate:

```
<form action="postback.jsp" method="post">
  First Name: <input type="text" name="firstname"/><br/>
  Last Name: <input type="text" name="lastname"/><br/>

  <a href="#"
    onclick="Element.toggle('advanced_options');Field.activate('petsname');">
    Advanced Options
  </a>

  <div id="advanced_options" style="display:none;">
    Pet's name: <input type="text" name="petsname"/><br/>
    Favorite color: <input type="text" name="favoritecolor"/>
  </div>
</form>
```

Form offers three more UI-related methods:

- disable(): Disables every input field in the form (sets the background to gray and disallows changes)

- enable(): Enables every input field in the form

- focusFirstElement(): Sets the focus to the topmost field in the form

These methods allow you to work with the entire form as a single entity. For example, it is a common pattern to display information to the user that they may want to edit. Web developers have to decide between showing them the data as plain HTML then switching to a form view when the user chooses to edit, or just showing it to them in the form view from the get-go. With Form.enable and Form.disable, the decision is easier. You can display the data in a disabled form; when the user clicks the Edit button, simply enable the entire form.

Position

Prototype contains several methods for understanding the current position of elements on a rendered page. Specifically, they allow you to discover the relative position on an element on a scrollable page, including whether the element is on the currently visible portion of the page. If not, you can retrieve the scroll offsets (horizontal or vertical) to the element from the visible section. Most developers won't use these features directly but instead use frameworks that build on top of them to provide higher-level features (such as Script.aculo.us, for example).

Script.aculo.us

Thomas Fuchs has built on top of the base Prototype library to dramatically increase the number and kinds of effects that can be created with JavaScript. Script.aculo.us is the result of his efforts. Where Prototype is focused on extending the baseline capabilities of JavaScript and the DOM, Script.aculo.us allows web developers to make HTML look and act just like any other rich client platform. The kinds of effects range from simple hiding and showing tricks all the way up to drag-and-drop functionality and sortability.

Effects

The library is divided into the five core effects and a series of combination effects built on top of them. The core effects are Opacity, Highlight,

MoveBy, Scale, and Parallel. Every effect represents a transition between two states that occurs over time. The effects all have default values for start and end points, as well as duration. These defaults can be overridden for a fully customized effect. The various effects have different required parameters (for instance, MoveBy() requires x and y deltas), and each can accept any of the standard options as well. The general syntax for launching an effect is:

```
new Effect.EffectName( element, required-params, {options} );
```

The effects are all asynchronous, which means that if you launch several effects simultaneously, they will render simultaneously. This is true whether the effects target different elements or all target the same element. Quick-fingered users won't be surprised by browser lockups as your <div>s turn yellow and balloon to twice their size, and you can fade out as many deleted items from your list as you desire at the same time.

This section will examine all the possible ways to utilize the core effects from the library. In Chapter 7, *Ajax UI, Part II*, on page 125, we'll look at how to use them effectively to increase the usability of the user interface. For all their cool factor, these kinds of effects can be overused and become just another <blink> tag, so knowing why you would employ them is just as useful as knowing how.

The standard options you can pass to the effects are:

- duration: The number of seconds the transition will take, with a default of 1.0

- fps: Target frames per second rate (default is 25)

- transition: An algorithm for determining how to move from the starting point to the ending point. These are represented as a series of, essentially, enumerated constants. Can be one of the following:

  - sinoidal: Start slow, peak in the middle, and slow down on the way out
  - linear: Constant speed from start to end
  - reverse: Constant speed but from end to start
  - wobble: Reverse direction several times during transition
  - flicker: Jump to random values during transition
  - pulse: Progress from start to end, back to start, back to end, and repeat five times

- from: Starting point for transition,from 0.0 to 1.0 (default is 0.0). See the explanation that follows.

- to: Ending point for transition, from 0.0 to 1.0 (default is 1.0)

- sync: Whether new frames should be rendered automatically (the default is true)

Think of from and to as percentages. If you are using the MoveBy() effect to move an element 50px to the right and 50px down, then the starting point, (0.0), represents the original positions, and the ending point, (1.0), represents the original position +50px in both directions. However, if you launch the effect using the following options:

```
new Effect.MoveBy( 'movable_element', 50, 50, {from: 0.0, to: 0.5} );
```

then the actual endpoint would be the original position plus 25px in both directions, since your to: option requires the transition to end halfway through. The transition option just determines what algorithm to use to progress from the from: option value to the to: option value. Flicker, for example, uses the following algorithm:

```
return ((-Math.cos(pos*Math.PI)/4) + 0.75) + Math.random(0.25);
```

Effects also allow you to bind callbacks to various stages in the transition cycle. The callbacks are also asynchronous. The only caveat to this is that, in some browsers, popping up a dialog box through alert or confirm will allow the effect to progress, but its effects will be invisible until the user closes the dialog. This means that whatever state the transition is in when the dialog is closed will suddenly appear. If the transition's duration has already passed by the time the user closes the window, the effect will have finished and the user will never have been treated to your Ajaxy goodness.

Opacity

The Opacity() effect is straightforward. You can transition between an opacity of 100% to 0%. There are no specific parameters for the percentage opacity: you simply use the from and to options, using 1.0 as 100% opaque and 0.0 as 0%. If you get the element to 0% opaque (also known as 100% transparent), you have not hidden the element in the sense that we explained before with Element.hide()—it is simply invisible. Using the Prototype Element.show() method will not make the element reappear; to do that, you would need to readjust the opacity to something greater than 0%. Likewise, a 0% opaque element is still taking up space in the DOM layout.

To make an element fade quietly from sight over two seconds, you could use the following:

```
new Effect.Opacity('some_element',
                   { duration: 2.0, from: 1.0, to: 0.0 });
```

If you wanted the element to go out like a lightbulb (flickering on and off until finally going out), you would use the following:

```
new Effect.Opacity('some_element',
                   { duration: 2.0,
                     from: 1.0, to: 0.0,
                     transition: Effect.Transitions.flicker});
```

To simply flash the element a few times to draw attention to it, you can fade it in and out:

```
new Effect.Opacity('some_element',
                   { duration: 1.0,
                     from: 1.0, to: 0.0,
                     transition: Effect.Transitions.pulse});
```

Movement

Effect.MoveBy() provides easy control over repositioning elements. The beauty of Effect.MoveBy() is that it doesn't require the element to have any particular placement styles already associated with it. Regardless of whether it is an inline or block element or whether it is positioned absolutely or relatively, it can be moved around with the same call to Effect.MoveBy(). You can even run the element right off the right or bottom edge of the document, causing the page itself to sprout scrollbars to allow for the new position. Repositioning it off the top or left borders, of course, removes it from sight without affecting the overall position or size of the page.

Effect.MoveBy() has two mandatory parameters that must be specified in addition to the element name and options. They are the X and Y offsets to calculate the new position. The offsets follow a simple geometry: positive X means movement to the right, negative X means movement to the left. Positive Y means down, negative Y is up. Therefore, to raise an element 100px while moving it to the right by 20, you could use the following:

```
new Effect.MoveBy('some_element', -100, 20);
```

To shake the element in place to draw attention to it, but have it end up back at its starting point:

```
new Effect.MoveBy('some_element',
                  0, -100,
                { duration: 2.0,
                  transition: Effect.Transitions.pulse});
```

One thing to watch out for: in the documentation at Script.aculo.us' website, as of version 1.0, the API for the call is misrepresented. The function itself takes the offsets in the order Y, X, but the documentation lists them as X, Y.

Size and Scale

The Effect.Scale() method allows you to affect the overall size of an element. Sizing can be tricky; when the element is a container for other elements, you have to know whether you want the contents to scale as well as the container. If the object is going to grow, should the new size be anchored to the upper-left corner of the element or to its center? What if the element has parts that are visible only if you scroll to them? There are six scale-specific options you can use in the {options} part of the call, if necessary:

- scaleX: should the element scale horizontally (default is true)

- scaleY: should the element scale vertically (default is true)

- scaleContent: should the content of the element scale along with the container itself (default is true)

- scaleFromCenter: Keeps the center of the object stationary while expanding the four corners (default is false)

- scaleMode: a value of 'box' means scale only those parts of the element that are current visible on the page without scrolling, while content means scale everything (default box)

- scaleFrom: a starting percentage of actual size to scale from (default is 100%)

Scaling a container element is tricky if you also want everything contained inside to scale along with it. Graphical subelements scale automatically with the container except <img> tags. <img> tags must be scaled independently by applying a scale effect directly to the tag. For textual contents, the font size in the HTML page must be specified in *em*

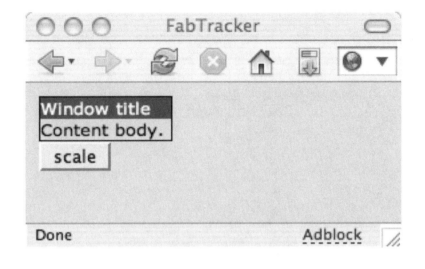

Figure 6.2: ELEMENTS BEFORE SCALING

units in order for scaling to work. Unfortunately, *em* isn't the default sizing unit for text in most browsers, so unless you explicitly apply a style to your text that sets it to *em* units, Effect.Scale() will ignore the text and scale the rest of the container around it.

Figure 6.2 shows a *<div>* with a contained *<div>* and some text in its original state:

```
<div id="window" style="border: solid 1px black;">
  <div id="windowbar" style="background-color: red; color: white;">
    Window title
  </div>
  Content body.
</div>
```

If you run a simple scale against this element, the container elements will scale but not the text. This call doubles the size of the elements, as shown in Figure 6.3, on the next page:

```
new Effect.Scale('window', 200);
```

In order to get the text to scale along with the graphics, we'd need to apply a style to the original elements to set the text to *em* units. Unfortunately, *em* units are not the standard in any browser. If you don't size your text specifically using styles based on *em* units, scaled

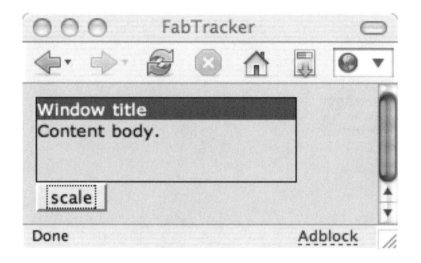

Figure 6.3: ELEMENTS AFTER SIMPLE SCALING

elements will look horrible by default:

```
<div id="window" style="border: solid 1px black; font-size: 1.0em;">
  <div id="windowbar" style="background-color: red; color: white;">
    Window title
  </div>
  Content body.
</div>
```

Applying the same scaling as before, we'd now get the result shown in Figure 6.4, on the facing page.

Highlight

Popularized by the venerable Yellow Fade Technique (or YFT, as it is more popularly known), this effect simply transitions the background color of an element from a start color to an end color by moving through the spectrum between them. The original YFT resets the background color to a buttery yellow and fades back to white. The effect brings the eye to an element where a change has occurred but then leaves the page in a pristine state after the transitions has completed. To enable this, Effect.Highlight() has three effect-specific options you can use:

Figure 6.4: SCALING TEXT

- startcolor: Instantly changes background color of element to this value at the start of the effect

- endcolor: Target end color to transition to

- restorecolor: Sets the background color to this after transition has completed

The animation transitions between startcolor: and endcolor:, and then the element is set to restorecolor:. The three color options accept only hexadecimal color values as strings. The hex values can optionally start with #. You can *not* use standardized color descriptors such as red and khaki nor shortform hex values such as f00. Here are two examples:

```
// simple Yellow Fade Technique
new Effect.Highlight('some_element');˚

// fade from red to blue, back to white
new Effect.Highlight('other_element',
                  { startcolor: '#ff0000',
                    endcolor:   '#0000ff',
                    restorecolor: '#ffffff' });
```

Parallel Effects

These four core effects are all very powerful by themselves. Since they are asynchronous, though, you can apply multiple effects simultaneously to get combined effects. Instead of having to wire up the combined effects yourself, Script.aculo.us supplies the Parallel() effect that takes care of it for you. Instead of supplying an element to Effect.Parallel(), you provide an array of other effects. They don't necessarily have to all target the same element. Effect.Parallel() will kick all the child effects off simultaneously. You could, for example, use Effect.Parallel(), to combine the Yellow Fade Technique and a pulsating Scale() effect to really draw attention to something:

```
new Effect.Parallel(
    [ new Effect.Highlight('window', { sync: true }),
      new Effect.Scale('window', 200,
                        {sync: true,
                         transition: Effect.Transitions.pulse}),
    ],
    { duration: 2.0});
```

Combination Effects

Luckily, Script.aculo.us already provides a wide variety of combination effects using Effect.Parallel() and the four core effects. Once again proving that you can build great complexity from a few simple building blocks, the range of available effects is impressive. Using the effects is no more complicated than using the core effects. The following is the list of combination affects available as of version 1.0:

- Effect.Appear(): Sets the opacity of the element to 0, fades it up to 100, and ensures that it is visible if it was hidden.

- Effect.Fade(): Sets the opacity of the element to 100, fades it to 0, then hides it at the end.

- Effect.Puff(): Combines Scale() and Opacity(), growing the element to 200% while fading it out and hiding it at the end.

- Effect.BlindUp(): Scales the image vertically to 0, without scaling the contents. Hides it at the end.

- Effect.BlindDown(): Scales the image vertically to full size, without scaling the contents. Ensures it is visible.

- Effect.SwitchOff(): Turns the element off like an old TV, shuddering slightly before collapsing. Uses Opacity() with Transitions.flicker to go from 100% to 0% while simultaneously scaling the image down to 0 with scaleFromCenter() set to true.

- Effect.DropOut(): Combines MoveBy() and Opacity(), moving the element down while fading it out.

- Effect.SlideDown(): Uses MoveBy() to animate sliding the contents of a *<div>* into view. Requires your *<div>* to be contained by an outer *<div>*.

- Effect.SlideUp(): Opposite of SlideDow()n. Hides the element after the transition.

- Effect.Squish(): Uses Scale() to go from full size to 0, ensures the element is hidden at the end.

- Effect.Grow(): Sets the size of the element to zero, uses Scale() to grow the element to full size with scaleFromCenter: set to true.

- Effect.Shrink(): Like Squish(), but with scaleFromContent: set to true.

- Effect.Pulsate(): Uses consecutive Fade()s and Appear()s to blink the item smoothly.

- Effect.Shake(): Uses consecutive MoveBy() effects to move the item left and right.

- Effect.Fold(): Combines BlindUp() and Shrink() to give the appearance that the item is folding up. First shrinks the element vertically, then horizontally, down to 0.

Advanced Techniques

Script.aculo.us also provides a series of more advanced techniques, such as drag-and-drop and sorting capabilities. We'll examine these in detail in the next chapter.

Dojo

Dojo is a different kind of animal than Prototype and Script.aculo.us. Whereas those libraries are smaller and more focused on UI goodness coupled with good XHR support, Dojo is essentially an entire platform for building client applications. In addition to its XHR and effects modules, Dojo includes a JavaScript collections library, widgets and widget-authoring utilities, a logging module, a math module, and lots more. As we demonstrated in the previous chapter, the beating heart of Dojo is the I/O libraries and the eventing system. We won't cover that ground again here. Instead, we'll introduce you to the idea of animations in Dojo, and take a look at how they are used to create effects like we saw in Script.aculo.us.

Animations

A Dojo animation is an object that defines the parameters of a transition between two states. The states can be anything: opacity levels, position, color, shape. The animation itself isn't concerned with the states, only the properties of the transition itself. When you create an animation, you supply four parameters:

- curve: A representation of an algorithm for returning values from 0 to 1. Like in Script.aculo.us, this value will be used as a multiplier against the current state of the element for creating steps, or *frames*, of the animation.

- duration: Number of milliseconds the animation will take.

- acceleration: Whether the animation is accelerating or decelerating (not implemented at time of writing).

- repeatCount: Number of times to repeat the animation (-1 means loop forever).

A curve is just an object that exposes a method, getValue(n), where n is a number from 0 to 1. The return value is an array of numbers that can be used to calculate current state. For example, you could create a linear curve to move from [0,0] to [100,100], thereby tracing a line through a Cartesian plane that creates a 45-degree angle in the upper-right quadrant. Or, you could create an arc curve to move from [255,0,0] to [0,0,255], thereby providing a transition from red to blue. The wiki for Dojo offers the following example of a curve implementation, representing a linear transition value set:

```
function Line(start, end) {
  this.start = start;
  this.end = end;
  this.dimensions = start.length;

  //simple function to find point on an n-dimensional, straight line
  this.getValue = function(n) {
    var retVal = new Array(this.dimensions);
    for(var i=0;i<this.dimensions;i++)
      retVal[i] = ((this.end[i] - this.start[i]) * n) + this.start[i];
```

```
    return retVal;
  }

  return this;
}
```

Dojo provides preimplemented curves in the dojo.math.curves module. They range from the simple Line curve, as shown previously, to Bezier curves, circles, arcs, and more. The API is simple enough to add your own implementations. Just make sure you remember your ninth-grade geometry. You simply provide an array of numbers, and the curve will be implemented upon each element in the array, with the return value being an array of the modified values.

To make the animation cause an element to transition, you have to wire up the events of the animation to the properties of the element you want to animate. Dojo's eventing library provides us with this ability. To create our own fade-out animation, we could use the following code:

```
function fadeOut(nodename) {
 var node = document.getElementById(nodename);

 var animation = new dojo.animation.Animation (
  new dojo.math.curves.Lin([100],[0]),   // linear progression from 100% to 0%
  2000,                                   // 2 seconds
  0                                       // not implemented, but must provide
 );

 dojo.event.connect(animation, "onAnimate", function(e) {
  node.style.opacity = e.x;
 });

 animation.play();
}
```

We must start the animation ourselves after it has been created. Then, as the animation progresses through the curve, retrieving values, those values are sent to the event listener. In this case, onAnimate is called for every frame in the animation, and it takes a special event argument that provides information about the status of the animation, including current values, percentage complete, designated end time, etc. Inside our anonymous listener for onAnimate, we retrieve the current value of our linear progression from 100 to 0 and use it as the value for the node's style.opacity property. This causes the element to fade out over two seconds, as per our duration parameter when we created the animation.

Effects

Dojo uses this animation system to build its library of effects. Creating an effect is an exercise in calling the appropriate method from the dojo.graphics.htmlEffects module. Each effect method returns a reference to the Animation object itself, so you can append your own listeners or modify the properties of the animation to suit your specific needs. To create a fade-out animation, for example, you could use this:

```
var node = document.getElementById('some_element');
var fader = dojo.graphics.htmlEffects.fadeOut(node, 2000);
fader.play();
```

If you wanted the element to be removed from the page after fading all the way out, you can utilize the optional third parameter to include a callback function for the onEnd event.

```
var fader = dojo.graphics.htmlEffects.fadeOut(
                node,
                2000,
                function(e) {node.style.display = 'none';})
```

The effects currently provided by Dojo are as follows:

- fadeOut(): Fades the opacity of the element from 100 to 0.

- fadeIn(): Fades the opacity of the element from 0 to 100.

- fadeHide(): FadeOut, but sets the .display property of the element to 'none' at the end.

- fadeShow(): FadeIn, but first guarantees that the item is being displayed.

- slideTo(): Moves an element to a given position on the screen.

- slideBy(): Moves an element a certain distance on the screen.

- colorFadeIn(): Uses a provided color as the starting point, fades to the original background color of the element. This effect is also called highlight (is officially aliased that way).

- colorFadeOut(): Fades from the original background color of the element to a provided color.

- wipeIn(): Sets the height of the element to 0, then grows it to its original size.

- wipeOut(): Sets the height of the element to its original size, then shrinks it to 0.

- explode(): Takes a from node and a to node, expands the size of the from node until it matches the to node.

- explodeFromBox(): Takes a set of four starting coordinates and an end node, grows the node from the starting coordinates to the end node position.

- implode(): takes a from node and a to node, shrinks the from node to fill the to node

- implodeToBox(): Takes a from node and a set of target coordinates, shrinks the from node to the shape specified by the coordinates.

6.2 Conclusion

In this chapter, we've exposed you to the basic UI elements of three different Ajax libraries. While Script.aculo.us and Dojo seem to provide a lot of overlapping effects, as you can see, the style of use is drastically different between the two libraries. Which you end up choosing for your own projects is a matter of both taste and need; Dojo provides a lot more in terms of functionality than Script.aculo.us, and if you require those features, then it makes sense to work with Dojo's effects as well. However, if you are less interested in those advanced features and just want the effects, Script.aculo.us is a much lighter-weight alternative. It has lower overhead from a bandwidth and a learning perspective.

In the next chapter, we'll use these libraries to reimplement our CRM application with whizzy UI features. We'll show server-side validation, notification techniques, progress indicators, and more. Additionally, we'll talk about what not to do with Ajax. There are some big anti-patterns waiting for you out there; we'll give you the heads up on how to keep your app clean.

Ajax UI, Part II

In the previous chapter, we started to look at using some of the available Ajax JavaScript libraries to drive the user interface in a browser. Understanding how these libraries help you more efficiently control the UI is Step 1. Step 2 is understanding what you should do with your newfound tools.

This chapter will present some of the standard techniques for utilizing Ajax on the UI. We'll talk about validation, notification, and data management strategies that have proven they increase the utility and usability of web applications. Later, we'll talk about some antipatterns, too, the things you should avoid and the tests you should apply when Ajaxifying your application. This chapter isn't an exhaustive treatise. Our intent is to give you a set of foundational tools for deciding how to (and when not to) proceed.

7.1 Some Standard Usages

Let's look at several common applications of Ajax using the libraries we talked about in the previous chapter: Prototype, Script.aculo.us, and Dojo.

Server-Side Validation

Web applications face a variety of standard problems. Validation is one that has spawned an infinite array of potential solutions. We have learned over time that there is one universal delineation to be taken into account: the server side versus the client side. Or so we thought. Client-side validation is handy for our users because they get "instant" feedback about the correctness of their data entry without having to wait for the whole page to refresh. Client-side validation is largely useless to the application developer, however, since it is trivial for a user to circumvent client-side JavaScript. Heck, users can ignore our rendered HTML entirely and craft requests to our system using Telnet. Therefore, server-side validation is always mandatory. Client-side validation is a usability enhancement for our users.

Ajax allows us to combine the two techniques for greater usability. The problem with client-side techniques is that the validation rule itself has to be portable to the browser. This means you can execute regular expression matches, required field checking, and even small-scale data comparisons (for example, is the state abbreviation one of the standard 50 two-letter abbreviations?). You can't, however, validate the inputs against your database or against any server-side resident data or rules. With Ajax, we get the benefits of client-side validation ("instant" feedback without a page refresh) but the power of server-side validation (comparison against server-resident data or rules).

This means we can create web applications with full validation the way we have historically been able to do only in *fat client* applications. We can use a full-fledged rules engine, for example, for validating individual data fields. But keep in mind that we are still required to re-validate the data on the final submission, because users can bypass an Ajaxified web application just as easily as a standard one, which means the final POST must be checked from top to bottom. So, this pattern gives us more powerful client-side usability but does not solve the underlying security problem at all.

We're going to modify the CRM application from the earlier chapters with our new Ajax patterns. For this validation example, we have to start by preparing the UI itself. Here is the original HTML for rendering the Customer Name and Address fields for input:

File 13
```
<tr>
  <th>Customer Name:</th>
  <td><input type="text" name="name"/></td>
</tr>
<tr>
  <th>Address:</th>
  <td><input type="text" name="address"/></td>
</tr>
```

It includes a label and an input field for each data value. It doesn't have any reasonable place to put an error message when validation fails. First, error messages should be conveniently colocated with the

---

Validation Error Messages

In addition to displaying error messages next to the fields they
are associated with, it is also common (and, dare we say,
appropriate) to include a general message area that provides
a summary of all error messages. Adding one is left as an exercise to the reader.

---

input fields they describe, so we'll add a new *<span>* element directly
beside the input fields. The *<span>* tags will be marked with a specific
CSS class so that we can control their look (in this case, we'll just style
the text red). Plus, we'll update the input fields to each have a unique
ID, which we can use to extract the values at runtime, and the new
<span> tags also have IDs so we can fill them in with a new innerHTML
after validation.

Second, we'll need to hook our validation code up to an event on the
input fields. The standard event to hook for this purpose is the onblur
event. This event fires whenever the user changes focus away from the
field, whether by clicking elsewhere or tabbing away from it. We'll call
a JavaScript method from the onblur event that will perform the validation. The method is called validateField(), and we'll examine it more in a
minute. For now, know that the function takes four parameters:

- field id: The ID of the input field being validated
- required: Whether this field is a required field
- validation: The validation rule to execute on the data
- update: The ID of the field used to display the error message

The new version of the UI elements looks like this:

File 8

```html
<tr>
  <th>Customer Name:</th>
  <td>
    <input type="text" id="name" name="name"
        onblur="validateField('name', 'required', 'name', 'nameError')"/>
  </td>
  <td colspan="2">
    <span style="border-bottom: solid 1px red;
              color: red;" id="nameError">
    </span>
  </td>
</tr>
```

```
<tr>
  <th>Address:</th>
  <td>
    <input type="text" id="address" name="address"
           onblur="validateField('address', 'required', 'address', 'addressError')
  </td>
  <td colspan="2">
    <span style="border-bottom: solid 1px red;
                 color: red;" id="addressError">
    </span>
  </td>
</tr>
```

Third, we need to write the method that calls the validation on the server. Its job is to launch an asynchronous request, passing in enough information to validate the field, and then update a named display element with the error message, if any. Our validateField() method first constructs a parameter list to append to the validation URL using the input parameters to the method. It then uses the Prototype library's Ajax.Updater to fire the request and fill in the display field with any error message generated.

File 8

```
function validateField(fieldname, required, validation, update) {
  var params = "type=" + validation    +
               "&required=" + required +
               "&value=" + $F(fieldname);

  new Ajax.Updater(update, validationUrl, {
    asynchronous: true,
    method: "get",
    parameters: params
  });
}
```

Finally, we need to create a server-based validation engine. You could call any standard platform validation engine you want: Struts validation, dyna-validation, Spring's Validator, the ASP.NET validation rules, a rules engine, whatever. Here, we've written a custom servlet that takes a field's value and the rules to invoke (required or not, plus specific rule) and returns either an empty string (meaning it succeeded) or an error message (for failure). Clearly, we'd add things such as i18n and SQL-injection protection if this were to be released to the public. The listing of that code, in its entirety, is on the next page.

```java
package ajaxian.book.crm.servlet;

import javax.servlet.http.HttpServlet;
import javax.servlet.http.HttpServletRequest;
import javax.servlet.http.HttpServletResponse;
import javax.servlet.ServletConfig;
import java.io.PrintWriter;
import java.io.IOException;

public class ValidationServlet extends HttpServlet {
    public void doGet(HttpServletRequest request,
                      HttpServletResponse response)
        throws IOException {

        response.setContentType("text/html");
        PrintWriter out = response.getWriter();
        System.out.println(request);
        String required = request.getParameter("required");
        String type = request.getParameter("type");
        String value = request.getParameter("value");
        String message = "";
        if(required.equals("required")) message += validateRequired(value);
        out.println(message);
    }

    private String validateRequired(String input) {
        if (null==input || 0==input.length()) return "Field required";
        return "";
    }
}
```

When the user first sees the page, as shown in Figure 7.1, on the next page, it looks like any standard HTML form, waiting for input.

As the user tabs through the fields, leaving data that breaks the rules, the page updates without a refresh, giving the user instant feedback, as shown in Figure 7.2, on the following page.

Request Notification

The asynchronous server-side validation we just created works well. The user gets a pretty big benefit without too much of a cost. We do have one problem, though. The user is firing server-side events via a nonstandard mechanism. Rarely does a web application user expect the TAB key to establish a connection back to the server. Without that expectation, they might be surprised to find that bandwidth is consumed at this point and even more surprised when, a half second later, the UI suddenly pops up a block of red text next to the field they

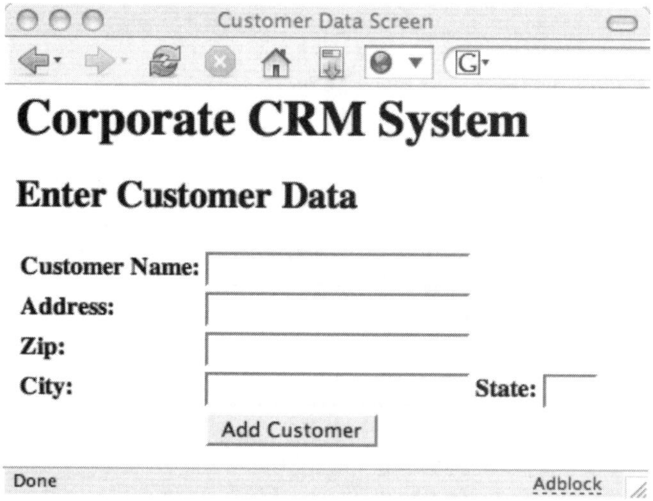

Figure 7.1: FORM WAITING FOR INPUT

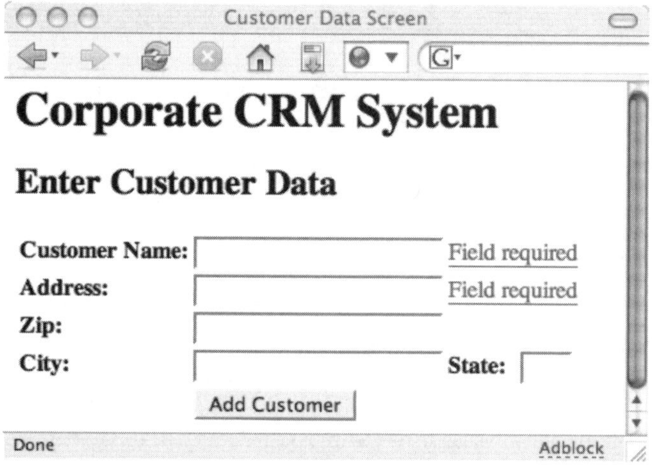

Figure 7.2: FORM DISPLAYING VALIDATION ERRORS

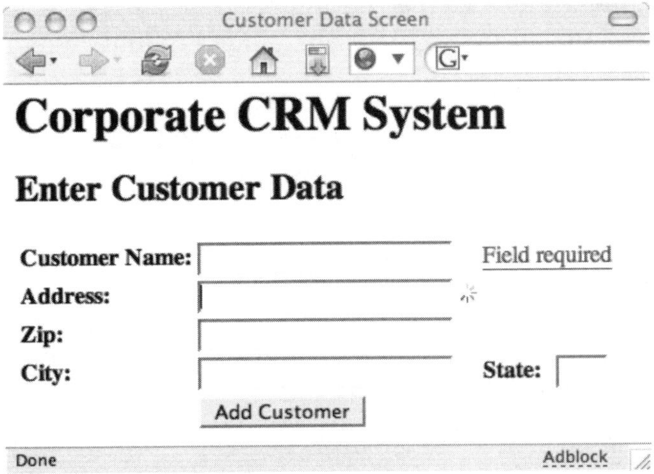

Figure 7.3: FORM PROCESSING VALIDATION REQUEST

just left. If you take into account the expected occurrence of network latency, suddenly you have the scenario of a user getting all the way to the bottom of a form before error messages start filling in at the top. How bad would it be if the error messages popped up in an area of the screen the user has already scrolled past? Fairly inconvenient, at the least.

The answer is to include a feedback mechanism that alerts the user that a request is in progress. Browsers typically accomplish this through a spinning/jumping/waving graphic in upper-right corner that animates only while a request is being processed. Ajax techniques can't take advantage of this UI convention, though, for two reasons: it is difficult to impossible to control the browser's request icon, and it can alert you to the status of only a single request at a time. With Ajax, and a technique like the validation described above, there can be multiple concurrent requests being processed.

The standard solution is to show an animated graphic that indicates a request in process. This is displayed inline, wherever the results of the request will be displayed, as shown in Figure 7.3. If the graphic pops up immediately, the user knows right away that something is happening and where to look for the results. Multiple graphics can be shown simultaneously by embedding them in multiple containers in the DOM.

The current standard is to use an animated GIF image, which is quick to load and implies activity without having to actually poll the current status of the request.

First, we'll add some <span>s to the page to hold our progress indicators. In this case, the image is an animated GIF called progress.gif, which is just a spinning wheel. We'll add them between the input fields and the associated error message containers; this will place the notification GIF approximately where the error message will appear, so the eye is drawn to the appropriate place. We'll go ahead and make a hard link to the image, rather than loading it dynamically with JavaScript, though either would be acceptable. The browser will natively attempt to cache the image for the first container, and all subsequent containers will use the cached GIF, preventing needless round-trips to the server for the same file. We'll simply place the image in a <span> whose display: style is set to none. When we want to notify the user, we toggle the <span>. When the request is complete, we toggle it again. Here's the code:

File 7

```html
<tr>
  <th>Customer Name:</th>
  <td>
    <input type="text" id="name" name="name"
        onblur="validateField('name', 'required', 'name', 'nameError')"/>
    <span id="nameProgress"
        style="display:none;"><img src="../progress.gif"/></span>
  </td>
  <td colspan="2">
    <span style="border-bottom: solid 1px red; color: red;"
        id="nameError">
    </span>
  </td>
</tr>
<tr>
  <th>Address:</th>
  <td>
    <input type="text" id="address" name="address"
        onblur="validateField('address', 'required',
                              'address', 'addressError')"/>
    <span id="addressProgress"
        style="display:none;"><img src="../progress.gif"/>
    </span>
  </td>
  <td colspan="2">
    <span style="border-bottom: solid 1px red; color: red;"
        id="addressError">
    </span>
  </td>
</tr>
```

Second, we have to update our request-generating code. In the previous example, we used the Prototype library's Ajax.Updater object to perform our round-trip. We'll extend that example here. The options collection contains four event hooks: onLoading, onLoaded, onInteractive, and onComplete, each corresponding to one of the four readystate values. Prototype simply implements the onreadystatechange hook and then publishes the specific events as those values arrive. We'll trap the onLoading and onComplete events, which allows us to show the image when the request begins and hide it once a response has been received. The values for the two events need to be function calls. Instead of simply calling Element.show() and Element.hide() directly, we'll wrap them in anonymous functions. If you don't do this, the onLoading call never completes, the validation result is never received, onComplete is never called, and the little spinning wheel becomes the only interesting thing about the page. Here's the code:

File 7

```
function validateField(fieldname, required, validation, update) {
    var params = "type=" + validation +
                 "&required=" + required +
                 "&value=" + $F(fieldname);

    new Ajax.Updater(update, validationUrl, {
        asynchronous: true,
        method: "get",
        parameters: params,
        onLoading:  function(request) {Element.show(fieldname + 'Progress');},
        onComplete: function(request) {Element.hide(fieldname + 'Progress');}
    });
}
```

Update Notification

Web surfers are largely trained to believe that something loaded on a page is static. They understand that in order to update the contents of a page, the page must be reloaded. The only cognitive exception to this rule is animations. The web-surfing population understands that certain graphics are not static but in fact loops of animation. These are expected to repeat the same set of information over time, though, and are not actually "dynamic" in any data-centric meaning of the term.

Ajax is all about breaking this particular expectation. That is, in fact, the core idea of Ajax: break free from the bonds of static information. But it goes against the foundation of most users' understanding of how the web works. This means we have to take special pains to ensure that when we do break this convention, users don't miss it.

The primogenitor of this pattern is the famous Yellow Fade Technique, or YFT. Apparently created (or at least named) by the good folks at 37signals, the YFT is a simple trick. Simply choose a color (canonically and eponymously yellow), reset the background color of an element to this new color and then slowly transition it back to the original. The effect is to highlight an area of the page as though with a highlighter so as to draw the user's attention but to have that intrusive effect disappear so as not to detract from the overall look and feel of the page.

To do this, you could write some code that manipulates the background-color style of an element. In order to return the element to its original state at the end of the effect, you'll need to capture its original background-color. You'd have to deal with the fact that most browsers internally store colors in the form rgb(nnn, nnn, nnn). If you would prefer to work in hex notation (#789abc), then you would have to convert them yourself. Likewise, you would have to come up with some strategy for moving from the original value to the target value for each color (red, green, and blue) simultaneously to get a smooth transition.

Luckily, somebody else has already done that work for you. Previously, we've used the Prototype library to do server-side validation and progress notification. We're now going to layer the Script.aculo.us library on top of that to get the highlight effect.[1] We'll modify the sample application to use the YFT to alert you when the content of the City and State fields has been updated.

First, we don't have to change the HTML at all. We already have a container element with a unique ID that we can use for the highlight effect. It's the <tr> that holds the City and State fields. Its ID is rewrite.

File 9

```
<tr id="rewrite">
    <th>City:</th>
    <td>
      <input id="city" type="text" name="city"/>
    </td>
    <th>State:</th>
    <td>
      <input id="state" type="text" name="state"
             size='3' maxlength='2' />
    </td>
</tr>
```

The second part is to update the getZipData() function to trigger the effect when the data has been loaded. Remember, XHR features the

---

[1]http://script.aculo.us/

onreadystatechange event to alert your code when the status of the request has changed. In this case, though, Prototype offers us another option. As we saw in Chapter 6, *Ajax UI, Part I*, on page 95, the Prototype library provides two new events, onSuccess and onFailure, so that we can write error-aware asynchronous methods. Our current version of getZipData() already uses onFailure to alert the user if the request fails:

File 13

```
function getZipData(zipCode) {
  new Ajax.Updater("rewrite", url, {
    asynchronous: true,
    method: "get",
    parameters: "zip=" + zipCode + "&type=html",
    onFailure: function(request) {
      assignError(request.responseText);
    }
  });
}
```

When the request fails, the assignError() function is called to display the message. We're now going to add a handler to the onSuccess method to perform the YFT. We use onSuccess instead of onComplete because onComplete will fire regardless of what's in the response. This would lead us to highlight City and State even if their data doesn't update. Instead, we use onSuccess, which fires only if the request returned data that ends up in the display fields:

File 23

```
function getZipData(zipCode) {
  new Ajax.Updater("rewrite", url, {
    asynchronous: true,
    method: "get",
    parameters: "zip=" + zipCode + "&type=html",
    onSuccess: function(request) {
      new Effect.Highlight('rewrite');
    },
    onFailure: function(request) {
      assignError(request.responseText);
    }
  });
}
```

The effect of this new handler is that the row containing City and State will go yellow whenever the request succeeds and then fade back to white over a one-second period. Bear in mind, as you learned in the previous chapter, you can affect the behavior of the transition by submitting options to the call. For example, you can change the transition to go from cornflower blue to white over three seconds with a linear transition by changing the call to the following:

```
new Effect.Highlight('rewrite',
                        { startcolor: '#92A4E2',
                          duration: 3.0,
                          transition: Effect.Transitions.linear } );
```

You can also choose the end transition color (endcolor) and the final color to use after the fade (restorecolor) if you need to.

Autocomplete

One of those things that often sets traditional thick clients apart from thin clients is the ability to quickly react to what the user is doing. For example, lots of locally installed applications can react to what a user is typing and make intelligent guesses about how to complete the word(s) for the user. Google (once again) showed that the same thing could be accomplished on the Web with Google Suggest. This feature has come to be known as *autocomplete*.

Script.aculo.us provides an amazingly simple-to-use version called the AutoCompleter. It watches an input field and sends a post parameter of the same name to a registered server endpoint. The results are rendered in another container node, allowing the user to choose from the results. The whole effect can be achieved with the addition of one container, one line of JavaScript, and a little simple CSS.

Let's add this feature to the sample CRM application. We'll prompt the user with potential Zip code matches based on what they are typing in the zip field. As they type into the zip field, we'll compare that against the list of available Zip codes and return those that are potential matches (the ones that start with the characters entered so far).

Let's start with a servlet that implements the autocompletion feature. Any reasonable production-quality version would use a database of Zip codes, and the SQL SELECT x WHERE zip LIKE 'y%' notation to retrieve values. To keep it simple for the book, the servlet will instead just keep an array of Zips as strings to compare against. Here's the servlet:

File 5
```
package ajaxian.book.crm.servlet;

import javax.servlet.http.HttpServlet;
import javax.servlet.http.HttpServletRequest;
import javax.servlet.http.HttpServletResponse;
import javax.servlet.ServletConfig;
import java.io.PrintWriter;
import java.io.IOException;
import java.util.Iterator;
import java.util.ArrayList;
```

```java
public class AutoCompleteServlet extends HttpServlet {
    public void doPost(HttpServletRequest request,
                       HttpServletResponse response)
        throws IOException {
            System.out.println(request);
        String[] zips = new String[] {
            "10010", "11035", "27707", "31000", "32230", "34434",
            "45555", "46666", "46785", "46699", "49999", "53711", "53703" };

        ArrayList results = new ArrayList();

        String val = request.getParameter("zip");
        for(int i=0;i<zips.length;i++) {
            if(zips[i].startsWith(val)) results.add(zips[i]);
        }

        String message = "<ul>";
        Iterator iter = results.iterator();
        while(iter.hasNext()) {
            message += "<li>" + (String)iter.next() + "</li>";
        }
        message += "</ul>";


        response.setContentType("text/html");
            PrintWriter out = response.getWriter();

        out.println(message);
    }
}
```

Next, we'll have to add the *Ajax.AutoCompleter* and a container *<div>* to hold the responses we get from the server. The entire update to the UI is as follows:

File 22

```html
<tr>
  <th>Zip:</th>
  <td>
    <input autocomplete="off" onblur="getZipData(this.value)"
           type="text" name="zip" id="zip"/>
    <div class="auto_complete" id="zip_values"></div>
  </td>
  <script type="text/javascript">
    new Ajax.Autocompleter('zip', 'zip_values',
                           '/ajaxian-book-crm/autoComplete', {})
  </script>
  <td id="zipError" style="color: red"></td>
</tr>
```

First, we had to make a minor change to the zip input field itself. We added the autocomplete="off" attribute, which prevents the browser from attempting to fill in the value itself. This would preempt our JavaScript version and nullify the whole exercise, so we'll disable it. Next, we have to add a container to hold the results; that's the *<div>* named zip_values. Finally, we add a *<script>* block to invoke the Ajax.AutoCompleter. The first parameter is the id of the input field to be autocompleted, the second is the ID of the container to display the results, the third is the server endpoint to send the request to, and the final parameter is a collection of options.

In our case, we're not using any of the optional parameters since the defaults work just fine for this purpose. However, the options you have to customize the behavior of the AutoCompleter are:

- paramName: A name to use for the value sent to the server. This defaults to the name of the target input field.

- frequency: How often to check for changes to the input field and send the request (defaults to 0.4 seconds)

- minChars: How many characters the user has to enter before the first request is sent (defaults to 1)

- afterUpdateElement: A hook invoked after the values are returned and set into the target container

Script.aculo.us also provides another object, AutoCompleter.Local, which uses a locally cached list of values instead of making round-trips to the server. This would increase speed at the expense of stale data.

To finish the example, we just have to make the results look pretty. Without any style help, the results will be displayed in a transparent *<div>* as a series of bulleted list items, without keyboard navigation. Clicking on one with the mouse would be the only way to select an entry from the list. We are using the styles provided by Script.aculo.us to make our list entries navigable and pretty, as shown here:

File 22

```
<style>
  div.auto_complete {
    width: 350px;
    background: #fff;
  }
  div.auto_complete ul {
    border:1px solid #888;
    margin:0;
    padding:0;
```

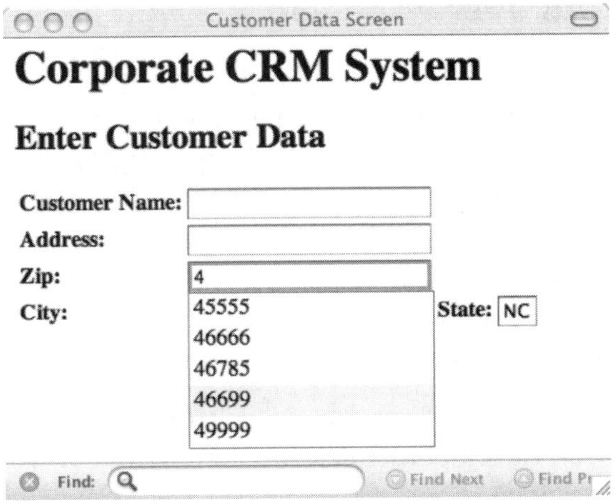

Figure 7.4: Autocomplete in Action

```
    width:100%;
    list-style-type:none;
  }
  div.auto_complete ul li {
    margin:0;
    padding:3px;
  }
  div.auto_complete ul li.selected {
    background-color: #ffb;
  }
  div.auto_complete ul strong.highlight {
    color: #800;
    margin:0;
    padding:0;
  }
</style>
```

Figure 7.4 shows the final result. Notice how the effect is like a drop-down box. The *<div>* has a narrow black border, the individual items are displayed without list bullets, and as you key up and down the list, the items highlight with (in this case) a pale yellow. Pressing enter while an item is highlighted, or clicking one with the mouse, causes that value to be set into the input field.

7.2 It Isn't All Just Wine and Roses...

Ajax is fantastic. It opens the Web to a whole new way of developing and delivering applications to your users. Largely, it changes the experience of using a web app from *reading* to *using*. As long-time instructors and trainers, we know firsthand the value of interaction in keeping students engaged and happy. The same phenomenon applies to applications. If your application is passive and makes your users passive consumers, then the application will not capture your users' attention. An interactive version, however, has the power to excite.

Even though Ajax has this power to change the Web so radically, it behooves us all as developers to remember why the Web enjoys such broad acceptance. It is based around certain standards (technical and visual) that have allowed users of all stripes to take advantage of services provided there. Those standards, some written and some simply understood, are vital to the success of all applications on the Web, whether or not they use Ajax.

The key to successful Ajaxification is to not ignore important conventions. Certain laws of the land made the Web so popular and accessible, in ways that other applications and technologies never were. As you add this new technology into your application, think both tactically and strategically. Ask yourself the following questions:

- "Is what I'm adding increasing the usability of my application, or the length of my resume?"

- "Does it break an ingrained habit of my users?"

- "Is the value worth the cognitive dissonance such a break will cause for my users?"

Tactically, the change might increase the usability of this single page but strategically reduce the usability of the application as a whole.

We'll walk through some of the biggest antipatterns to watch out for. This list is not exhaustive. When in doubt about something you are working on, check it against our previous smell-test questions. And keep in mind that the key is usability and fun: if it increases both, then do it!

Watch That Back Button!

Two features set the World Wide Web apart from everything that came before it: the back button and the bookmark. Applications historically were guided tours. Users were encouraged to follow certain paths through the information provided. At best, users might be able to search for a specific item or screen and navigate directly to it. If they moved on, the only way to return was to run the search again. And even this was a rare enough feature for an application. Consider Quicken circa 1998 or those multimedia encyclopedias we all bought back in '96. You had tables of contents and search capabilities but no notion of the history of your actions.

The back button isn't just a button; it's a symbol of freedom. It means that you are free from the shackles of the guided tour. You forge your own path through the information at your fingertips and can retrace your steps at your leisure. You become the master of the application, instead of the other way around. Don't believe me? Go into your browser, turn off the navigation bar, and see how long you go before having to turn it back on again.

Bearing this in mind, now picture how the back button actually works. The default behavior for a browser is to cache pages as they are downloaded. Clearly, this feature can be overridden at either the browser level or server level, but the default is to create a local cache. Only the original state of a page as downloaded from the server is cached. If the DOM is modified in any way by client-side JavaScript, those changes are not reflected in the cache at all. Conversely, if the page was *not* cached, then the back button merely sends a new request to the server to request the page, which will return the page in its original state anyway. The practical upshot of all this is that all your Ajax goodness is lost when the user navigates away from your page and back again.

It's even worse than it looks at first glance, as well. If the page has elements whose value is determined at parse time, then those values will be cached along with the rest of the page. Clicking the back button will normally result in a load from cache where possible; if the page was cached, the elements will contain possibly outdated values since the server-side parse never takes place a second time. At that point, only if the user manually refreshes the page will the new values appear.

It becomes incumbent on the designer of the application to distinguish between information retrieval and navigation. When a user wants to proceed to a new topic area, they generally want a history of where they were previously. The back button is the instant access to that history; navigating to a new subject area via an Ajaxian in-page replacement nullifies the ability of the back button to perform its appointed duties. Take, for example, the very common practice of online news-papers splitting its articles up over multiple pages. In standard HTML, the current page ends with a link to Next Page>>. Clicking that reloads the browser and shows page 2 of the article. At the bottom are now links to <<Previous Page and Next Page>>. Users can use either the link or the back button to navigate backwards. Since the pages are part of a unified whole, and the user is already trained to use the Next Page>> link for forward navigation, it wouldn't be too much of a stretch to do an Ajax version where the pages are loaded into a <div> on the fly. Users would use the built-in navigation as before; clicking the back button would take them away from the article entirely, back to the table of contents. This seems fairly natural.

Alternatively, imagine the same online newspaper site but with a table of contents whose links to articles operate in Ajax fashion. Clicking on the title of an article replaces the table of contents with the text of the article. Navigating forward and back in the article happens via Ajax as well. When the user clicks the provided Next and Previous buttons, new pages are loaded into the same <div>. What happens if the user clicks the back button now? They don't end up back at the table of contents; instead, they end up at whatever website they were at before coming to the newspaper site. This is because the table of contents was forced into the same page context as the articles it listed. By doing so, you have essentially eliminated the history of a topic transition for your user (TOC → article) that they would normally expect to be maintained for them.

It is hard to pin down the exact point at which Ajax breaks this rule. But it is really easy to spot it after you have done it. Just use your application a few times. Whenever you find yourself annoyed because you can't retrace your steps, you have probably found an instance of this antipattern.

Bookmarking Makes the Web

Bookmarking is the kissing cousin of the back button. It is a user-controlled metahistory of their browsing exploits. Bookmarking the index page (the welcome mat) is less useful now than it was in the past. With Google as our shared bookmarks, most people don't bother book-marking the index page anymore. It's just as easy to run to Google, type in the page name, and click the resulting link (or even the I'm Feeling Lucky button, which we almost never are). Instead, we use bookmarks for *deep linking*. This means capturing the state of the application or site at some point after you have begun interacting with it. Perhaps this is the result of a search at Amazon or the report of your current holdings at your financial institution, or some particular article at the *New York Times*.

Deep linking means that users have the complete ability to pause and return to your application. If state is maintained (cookies, long-term sessions, back-end storage, whatever) and users can specify where in the application flow to resume their work, then they are not chained to your timetable. We often find ourselves in the middle of something on an application but forced to take a call or run to a meeting. We want to know that we can pick up right where we left off at some later time. So we bookmark the page. If we come back, open the bookmark, and end up back at the index page instead, we're displeased.

When a user arrives at an Ajaxified page, the URL that appears in the address bar is whatever they typed in or clicked on to get there. When a bookmark is added to a browser, it makes a copy of the current address in the address bar. If the page has allowed the user to progress through tens or hundreds of interactions, the URL in the address bar is exactly the same as it was for the initial request. A user who navigates to the bookmark will always end up at the original state of the page; Ajax-based changes will be long forgotten.

Once again, we are faced with the distinction between a major topic area of the application versus a minor shift in focus. Users will accept certain limitations on their bookmarking ability; for example, most people don't expect to be able to bookmark a page halfway through the checkout wizard at an e-commerce site. Clearly, users have come to learn the difference between static pages and stateful processes that can't be captured in a snapshot. Developers now have to come to the same questions: what transitions can I encapsulate in a nonbookmarkable process, and what requires page transitions in order to allow pause-and-resume behavior?

GET Is for Getting, POST Is for Doing

In the world of HTTP, browsers communicate with servers using (typically) either GET or POST requests. A GET request is generated whenever you click a hyperlink; the idea is that it *gets* the next page. A POST request is sent when you hit the submit button on an HTML form. It *posts* the data from that form to the application for processing.

In May 2005, the team that created Basecamp (and Ruby on Rails) learned this really valuable lesson: GET is for getting things and POST is for doing things. The HTTP specification is pretty specific on this topic. GETs are for retrieving data. POSTs are for interacting with the server in a way that might change server state. When you avoid the recommendations of a specification, bad things can—and often do—happen. Basecamp's public tussle with this issue serves as a cautionary tale for the rest of us: if these kinds of issues can affect the best and brightest, we need to be extra careful in our own applications to avoid similar problems.

Basecamp's problem was that, at the time, the default method for creating links back to the server with Rails was a GET. It didn't matter what the link was doing: redirecting to a new page, reading a record, or deleting a record. Then, Google released Google Accelerator. Google Accelerator installs in your browser and redirects requests through Google's servers. If Google has already cached the page, you'll be rewarded with the previously cached version, thus speeding up your access time. If the page has not been cached, then the request is forwarded as normal. Google Accelerator then walks all the links off of the returned page, thus caching it and all of its subpages.

For an application whose controls are all provided as simple GET-method links, Google Accelerator becomes the most efficient destructive force imaginable. Think of it as the Terminator of web apps. It is single-minded: fire a request to every link on the page. It is efficient. And it absolutely will not stop until your app is dead.

37signals didn't realize there was a problem until data started disappearing from the Basecamp database. As users began reporting that their data was mysteriously missing, the team finally realized that the common thread was Google Accelerator. Normally, such a thing wouldn't be a terrible problem. After all, Google's indexing worms follow essentially the same path; find a page, navigate to all the link endpoints, cache, and continue. But with Google Accelerator, the worm finally has access to information it has never had before: your username and password. Navigate to your Basecamp account, for example, and log in. Google Accelerator can now follow all the links on your private page. It then clicks everything it can, as fast as possible. And some of those links are labeled *Delete This Item*.

The solution was to change their framework, Rails, to create POST-method links for update methods. They did this by creating a second view helper in addition to link_to() that creates a *<form>* element to surround a button. The parameters are embedded as hidden *<input>*s. The *<form>* is set to POST as its method. Now, your update-related links don't fall prey to Google Accelerator.

When you Ajaxify an application, the temptation to write pages this way is strong. You present your user with a list of items. You want them to be able to add new ones or delete existing ones from the page without a refresh. So you add a link to the bottom, New Record. Embedded in each item on the list is a link called Delete. You use a simple GET with a URL such as http://www.mydomain.com/my/app/delete?recId=545. What could be easier? Of course, Google Accelerator will knock on your door. "Sarah Connor?" it will ask. And that will be the end of that.

Tell People When Updates are Happening

When browsing a Web 1.0 application, pay careful attention to the feedback you get from the application, the browser, and your OS. For example, when you click a link to another page and the data has started to render (but slowly), what feedback are you getting? The refresh icon in the upper-right corner of your browser begins to spin or jump or change colors. On the Mac, the cursor turns into the Rainbow Wheel of Doom and you can't click anything in the browser window (though the browser's menus are usually still accessible). That's because the navigation operation is synchronous: you are forced to wait until it has completed before you can use the contents of the window, or until you choose File→Print from the menu. The dialog box often takes a second or two to appear as it scans your network for configured printers. While this is happening, your cursor might turn into an hourglass, and you won't be able to click anything in the browser window or on the menus.

Synchronous operations come with their own feedback. If it is related to requesting new information, the browser tells you via the refresh icon. You get feedback in the form of not being able to click resources. Even your cursor changes to tell you "Quit clicking that." You know that the browser is attempting to do work on your behalf. Now, enter Ajax. The *asynchronous* part makes everything different. When you fire an asynchronous request back to the server, there is nothing that the browser will do for you automatically that provides feedback to the user that something is going on. It will quietly and invisibly wait for the response to return and then put it wherever your JavaScript tells it to go. Suddenly, as if by magic, the rendered HTML is updated. Voila!

Some previously hidden *<div>* pops into view, filled with useful but surprising information! Unfortunately, your user has already scrolled past that part of the page and misses all the fun.

It is up to you to provide adequate warning to your user that some activity is being performed on their behalf. Because they are able to continue to work with the page and the browser after firing an asynchronous call, you have to provide visual cues to them to let them know that something is on the way. Earlier in this chapter, we showed you a technique for popping up a notification animation. Often, this technique is enough. But sometimes, you'll have to do more. Perhaps you have to change the cursor or perhaps show a full progress bar. Regardless of the specific technique, you should always provide a mechanism to warn your users that clicking that link, pressing that button, or doing whatever it is, has now fired a request and the browser is waiting for a response.

Don't Reinvent the Wheel

We've grown accustomed to certain UI conventions. Modern operating systems and their windowing toolkits all offer us certain abstractions that have settled in our consciousness. We know what a *window* is, for example. Even our parents know that when they see a box on the screen with an outset border, a header at the top, and some buttons in upper-left or upper-right corners, that that thing can be dragged around on the screen and it can be closed. We know what a button looks like and that the appropriate thing to do is click it, once, to press it. We've been trained that the words along the top edge of a window are probably menus and that if we hover the mouse over them or click them, they are likely to spawn little submenus. We've actually run this experiment with our family. They are Microsoft Windows users. If we put them in front of a Mac, they know how those conventions work even though the actual graphical look is entirely different. They have no idea what the Dock is for, but the common abstractions are plain and clear. Likewise, when they sit at a Gnome or KDE desktop on a Linux box, everything is fairly straightforward.

The Web has taught us some additional standards. Now, we agree that text along the top or left edges may be a menu and that hovering the mouse over a menu is preferable to having to click it to get the submenu to appear. We know that words underlined and often blue are *hyperlinks* that will navigate us to a new page. Square gray boxes next to words are check boxes, which can be checked and unchecked individually, while groups of gray circles are *radio buttons*, and clicking one affects the others. And when the cursor turns into a little pointing hand, that means whatever we're hovering over is clickable.

These conventions enable a common computing experience. They are the very thing that allows users not to have to RTFM every time they encounter a new application. They allow us to surf the Web, which is really just the accumulation of a billion applications designed by a billion monkeys. Without those conventions, every new web page would be a new cognitive experience; we'd have to take a day to read the help before being able to check the Eagles' score. The Web would be useless.

So don't be tempted to think you are smarter than the collective. As programmers and designers, we often suffer from a certain hubris that says "I can be better than the lowest common denominator." The problem isn't believing that. The problem is mistaking "common" for "lowest common." Just because everybody is doing it doesn't make it bad. That kind of logic is just counterintuitive enough to appeal to our old high-school self, whose fascination with The Cure and Metallica was fed by the belief that Phil Collins couldn't possibly be any good because so darn many people listened to his music.

For example, Ajax enables us to create portal sites the right way. Basically, a portal is a website that displays multiple disparate content areas on a single page. There could be local weather, last five e-mail messages, who is currently logged into the site, RSS feeds, etc. Each content area is self-contained, and they can be added and removed individually, often minimized, closed entirely, and dragged around and repositioned. That reminds us of something we were just thinking about...hmmm, what was it...oh, right, a *window*! That's it! A content area in a portal is just like a window! And we currently have a convention for drawing a window so that the user knows what to do with it. This means a really good portal site should look something like Figure 7.5, on the following page.

The individual portlets clearly are closeable and minimizable, and it shouldn't surprise us at all to find out that they are draggable. The temptation can be strong to reinvent all of this—rounded windows without obvious title bars, little dots in the lower-left corner to click to close the window, etc. While we're fans of avant-garde design, we don't like struggling with an interface to figure out how it works. We like being surprised by an interface even less. Stick with what works.

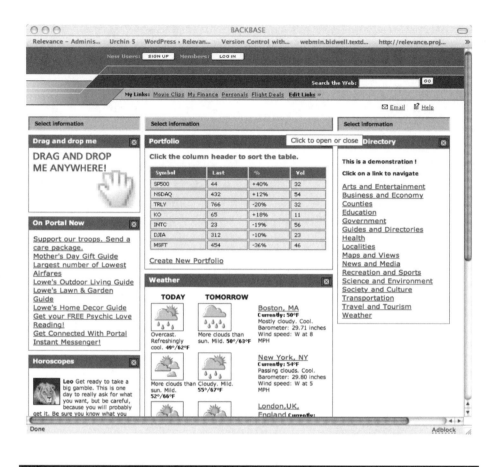

Figure 7.5: A Well-Designed Portal

Likewise, launching asynchronous calls to the server based on non-standard interactions with a page will be disconcerting to your users. Running your mouse over an obvious menu at the top of the screen and causing a menu to pop up is fine, even if it involves (quick) round-trips. Having menus pop up as you mouse over random words in a paragraph would be alarming. Causing data to refresh when users click buttons is expected. Causing data to refresh when users click links might be surprising. And for crying out loud, think very, very carefully before you start shaking, puffing, and squishing elements on the screen. Ask yourself whether the effect is something the users will understand in context or whether they will just be surprised by it.

7.3 Conclusion

In this chapter, we've talked about some common patterns for making effective use of Ajax in the UI. For the most part, what we've shown is how to use Ajax to make web pages respond more like the rest of the user interfaces that our customers have grown accustomed to using. Alerting our user to changes in data, that background processing is ongoing, or that they have committed errors in their data entry are all just ways of increasing the responsiveness of the application while keeping with standard conventions. Techniques like autocompleting text boxes allow customers to use our applications more efficiently. Sorting data and drag-and-drop capabilities make the UI more like the standard "thick" UI components of our desktop systems.

As with anything, though, the trick is knowing when *not* to do it. The second half of our chapter was all about keeping ourselves focused on the most important point: usability. When these techniques make it easier for our users to accomplish a task, then the technique is successful. When they get in the way, when they cause our users to have to think about what they are doing, then we should reevaluate our decision. And above all, never surprise the user.

Chapter 8

Debugging Ajax Applications

One of the simple pleasures of software development is the gratification that comes from writing code and seeing it work right away (or, if you're a Java programmer, seeing it work several minutes after you've written it). Of course, this concept can be symmetrically applied to the grief felt when the code *doesn't* work right away.

This chapter discusses the various tools and techniques that you can use to discover why your code doesn't work on those (rare?) occasions when things just aren't going your way.

8.1 View Source

The time-honored mechanism for debugging web applications is the View Source mechanism, which is as ubiquitous in modern browsers as back and forward buttons. In the Ajax world, however, the View Source function becomes of limited utility.

Consider the following example:

File 24
```
Line 1    <html>
    -       <head>
    -         <script type="text/javascript">
    -           function init() {
    5             document.getElementById("foo").innerHTML = "Goodbye, world!";
    -           }
    -         </script>
    -       </head>
    -       <body onload="init()">
    10        <p id="foo">
    -           Hello, world!
    -         </p>
    -       </body>
    -     </html>
```

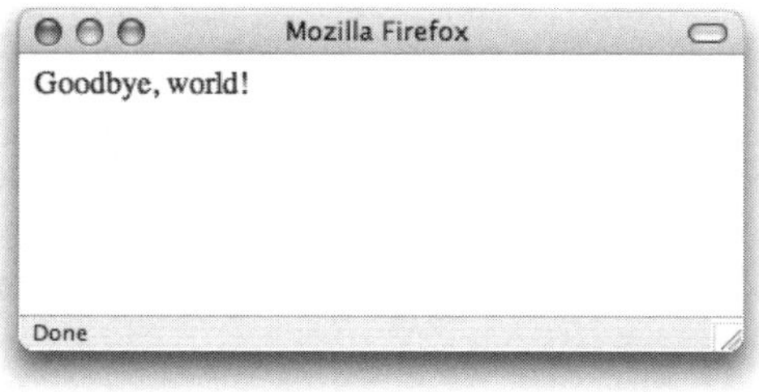

Figure 8.1: THE SOURCE CAN BE MISLEADING...

Open this page in your browser and you'll see something like Figure 8.1.

If you use the your browser's View Source option, you'll see the code as listed in this book. That's great. The problem is that source is not in sync with what you actually see in the browser. In the source code, line 11 says "Hello, world," but as you can see in Figure 8.1, the page displays "Goodbye, world"—obviously because of the JavaScript we have in the source code that modifies the web page.

For this trivial example, that may not seem like a big deal, but for more complex Ajaxian applications, this is a major problem. You will often want to see exactly what the current state of the web page source is.

8.2 DOM Inspectors

DOM inspector

Enter the *DOM inspector*. As we explained earlier, browsers maintain an XML version of the web pages they display in memory, and this XML document is available as a DOM tree via the document variable. While View Source will display only the source code that was originally sent to the browser, by inspecting the web page's DOM tree, you can see the exact current state of the web page.

Firefox and Safari both include built-in DOM inspectors, and Microsoft makes one available for Internet Explorer as a separate download. Of these three browsers, Firefox's is the most powerful, so we'll take a look at that one and then discuss the limitations of the DOM inspectors available in the other browsers.

Firefox DOM Inspector

The Firefox DOM inspector is available in the Tools pull-down menu.

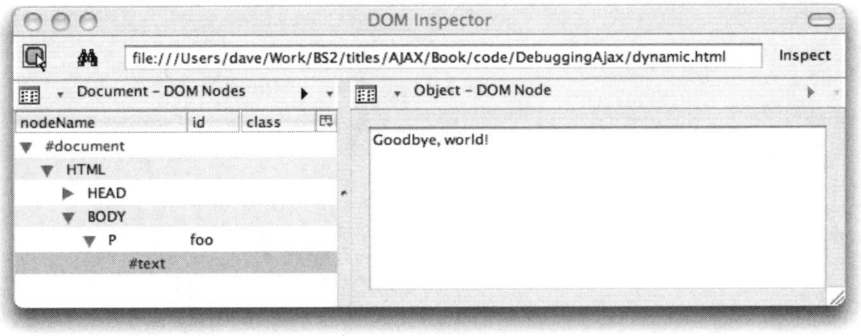

Figure 8.2: THE FIREFOX DOM INSPECTOR

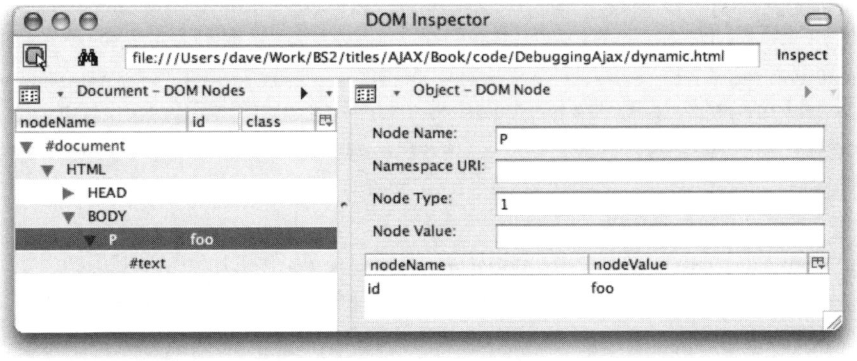

Figure 8.3: A SELECTED ELEMENT IN THE DOM TREE

Figure 8.2 shows it revealing the secrets of our dynamic page. On the left side is a depiction of the DOM tree, starting with the top-level document. Beneath this are all the elements that compromise the DOM tree—our web page, in other words. In this case, the highlighted line represents the text within the <p> element that our JavaScript created.

On the right side are the properties of the element selected in the tree on the left side; in this case the contents of the text node that we've highlighted. And here we actually see what the contents of the table cell are—the phrase "Goodbye, world!"

Figure 8.3, shows the properties available if we select a different type of element; in this case, it shows the <p> element itself.

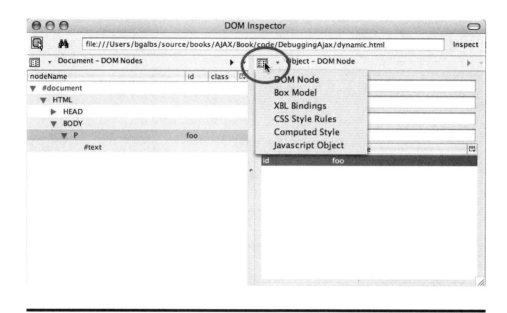

Figure 8.4: THE DOM INSPECTOR PROPERTY SHEET ICON

The pop-up window on the right side is the context menu that appears if you right-click the properties table. Most interesting is the ability to edit any of the properties on the table element or even insert new properties. In fact, Firefox's DOM Inspector will also let you cut, copy, paste, and delete all of the various elements in the DOM on the left side of the inspector as well.

The properties on the right side of the DOM Inspector are the properties of the XHTML elements in the DOM tree (actually, the properties of the DOM API's representation of the XHTML element, but that's not a terribly important distinction). There are, in fact, other properties you can view for each of the elements in the DOM tree. You can switch to these other property sheets by clicking the property sheet icon as shown in Figure 8.4.

The DOM Node sheet is the one we've been looking at up to now; it displays those properties that are defined by the DOM specification as belonging to the particular element type. The other property sheets are explained by the following list:

- *Box Model*: Displays the position, dimensions, margin, border, and padding information for the box that represents the selected

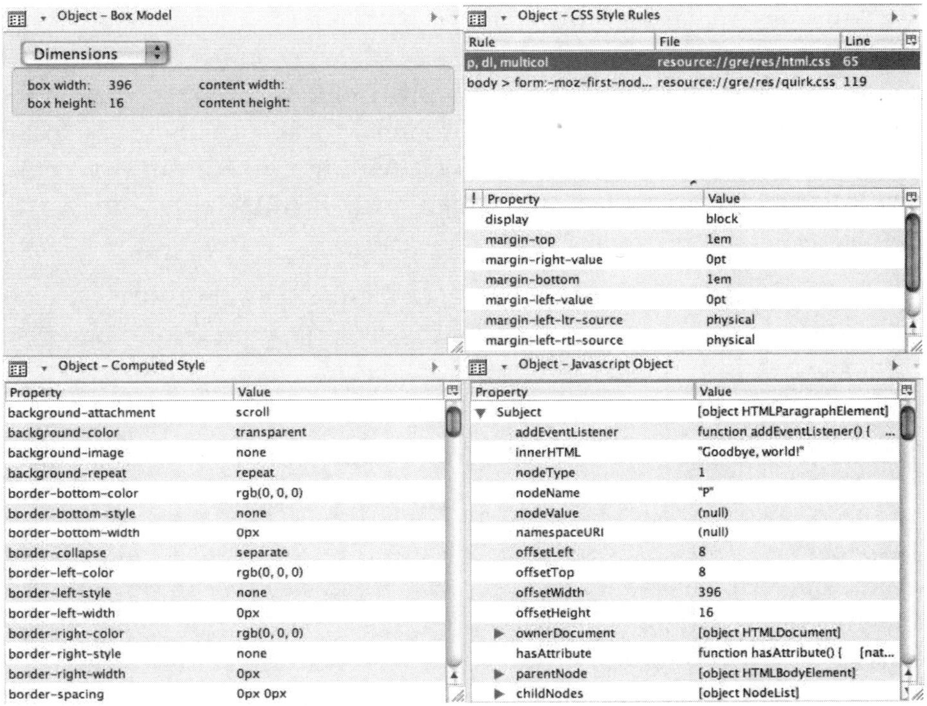

Figure 8.5: VARIOUS DOM INSPECTOR PROPERTY SHEETS

element (or, if the element does not have a box, the information for the elements containing box).

- *XBL Bindings*: Relates to Firefox's proprietary XUL API; we won't discuss this here.

- *CSS Style Rules*: Displays the CSS rules that are being explicitly applied to the selected element.

- *Computed Style*: Lists all of the CSS styles that are being applied to the selected element. This is different from CSS Style Rules as all of the styles that this element inherits are displayed, rather than just those that are explicitly applied to it.

- *JavasSript Object*: Lists all of the properties on the JavaScript object that represents the selected element.

Figure 8.5, shows a view of each of these sheets (except the boring XBL Bindings) for the table element we saw earlier.

We'll discuss one more feature of the DOM Inspector before moving on. Often times, you can get lost in the tree of nodes on the left side of the inspector. Actually, to be fair, it's really much more the opposite; it's pretty difficult *not* to get lost. Fortunately, there's a handy way to get your bearings. By right-clicking an element in the DOM tree, you can *blink* it, which causes it to be momentarily highlighted on the actual web page.

There's more we could say about the DOM Inspector, but we've got lots of other debugging tools to show you yet, so let's move on—but first, we'll say a few words about the DOM inspectors in other browsers.

Safari Debug Menu and DOM Inspector

Here's a surprise for some readers: Safari actually does have a DOM inspector, contrary to popular belief, but it is hidden away in a Debug menu that isn't visible by default. In fact, as we'll see throughout the chapter, Safari's debugging tools are quite capable. But before we get carried away singing its virtues, let's first figure out how to get that invisible Debug menu to show up.

Revealing the Debug Pull-Down Menu

Finding the Safari debug menu requires the use of the OS X Terminal application. Once open, you need to execute the following command:

```
$ defaults write com.apple.Safari IncludeDebugMenu 1
```

After executing that command, the next time you launch Safari, you'll see the magical Debug menu, as shown in Figure 8.6, on the next page.

You'll find that Safari's debugging capabilities are quite competitive with Firefox, sporting such niceties as such as a built-in profiler and some neat helper functions that automatically launch a web page in all of the browsers installed on your system. Safari's DOM Inspector is best-of-breed, giving you the functionality of Firefox's in a much more aesthetic package.

While Figure 8.7, on page 158, doesn't show it, Safari's DOM Inspector is partially transparent and is launched by right-clicking on an element in the web page. It then floats over the page, highlighting the element currently being inspected. Leave it to Apple to make a gorgeous DOM Inspector.

Figure 8.6: Safari's Debug Menu

Internet Explorer Developer Toolbar and DOM Inspector

IE does not have a built-in DOM inspector, but Microsoft does provide a free Developer Toolbar for IE 6+ that comes with a DOM inspector.[1] Note that the toolbar is not yet officially released, so the final URL is likely to change. Actually, with a URL like that, it's probably guaranteed to change; just use Google to find it ("Internet Explorer developer toolbar").

Once you've installed it (and you've restarted IE), you can add the Developer Toolbar to your IE toolbars using the View -> Toolbars -> Developer Toolbar pull-down menu, as shown in Figure 8.8, on the next page. Note that, depending on your system's configuration, you may need to reposition the Developer Toolbar to see all of its options (which may require you to unlock the toolbars before you can move them).

---

[1] http://www.microsoft.com/downloads/details.aspx?FamilyID=e59c3964-672d-4511-bb3e-2d5e1db91038

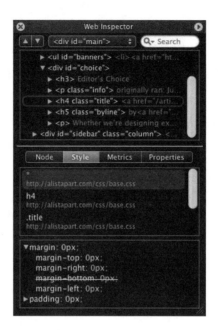

Figure 8.7: Safari's DOM Inspector

Figure 8.8: Internet Explorer's Developer Toolbar

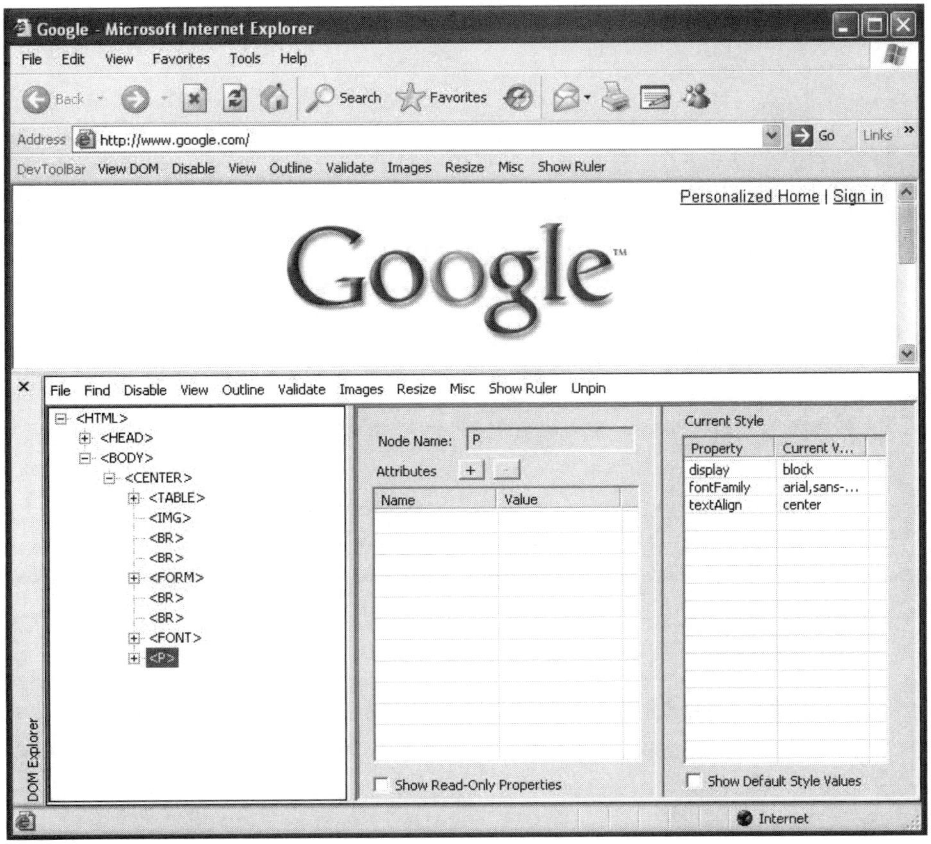

Figure 8.9: INTERNET EXPLORER'S DOM INSPECTOR

The View DOM button on the Developer Toolbar will produce a DOM inspector for the current page, as shown in Figure 8.9.

While the layout is different from Firefox, most of the functionality is still present. (The only notable absence is an equivalent for the JavaScript Object property sheet.) You can see the XHTML properties set on the elements in the middle area, and on the right side you can see the explicit styles on the element and, by checking the Show Default Style Values, all of the inherited CSS properties, too.

Live View Source

DOM inspectors remain the definitive mechanism for exploring the contents of a web page at runtime, allowing you to inspect every detail and

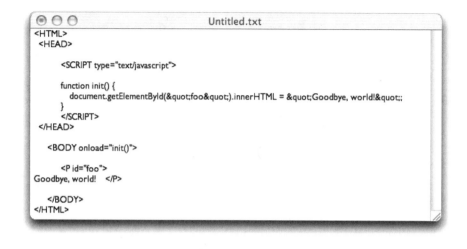

Figure 8.10: FIREFOX-GENERATED LIVE SOURCE CODE

make tweaks to explore alternative options at runtime. Still, none of the three DOM inspectors we looked at scores any points for revealing the big picture or giving you a quick view of the runtime document contents. Oftentimes, what you really want is just a View Source facility that shows you the *live* copy of document.

Firefox and Safari both provide this capability out of the box through their DOM inspectors. In Firefox, to view a live copy of the document, you can right-click any element in the DOM tree and select Copy XML. Then, in your favorite text editor, select Paste, and you'll have a nicely formatted copy of the source tree, as shown in Figure 8.10.

Firefox has another neat feature. If you select some portion of the web page in the browser window and right-click, you can select the View Selection Source option and see the subset of the DOM tree that is responsible for rendering your selection. You can therefore use the Control-A key combination to select the entire page and use View Selection Source to see something very close to a Live View Source option. As a bonus, Firefox provides syntax highlighting with this view.

In Safari, the DOM Inspector always shows a copy of the live web page documentation when you select a node in the DOM tree.

Internet Explorer does not provide a mechanism for viewing the live source of a web page. At least one third-party commercial plug-in pro-

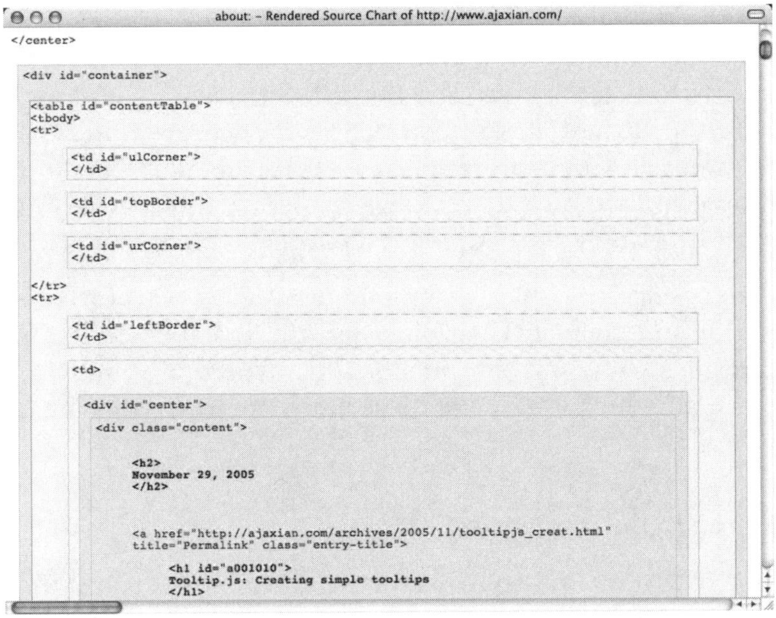

Figure 8.11: THE VIEW RENDERED SOURCE CHART PLUG-IN

vides this functionality; we recommend Instant Source,[2] which displays a window beneath the current web page that displays the live DOM source for the page and provides a number of other convenient functions, such as limiting the display to only the select or hovered-over item and allowing you the edit the source in place.

Firefox Plug-ins

The Firefox community has developed at least two plug-ins that provide useful functionality related to viewing the live source. The View Rendered Source Chart,[3] displays the DOM tree for any web page as a colorful chart depicting the box model of the web page, as shown in Figure 8.11.

View Rendered Source Chart is open-source (though a $1 commercial version is available that adds a few features).

---

[2]http://www.blazingtools.com/is.html
[3]http://jennifermadden.com/scripts/ViewRenderedSource.html

Another plug-in, View formatted source, displays a syntax-highlighted view of the live source. As a bonus, this live source view allows individual elements to be collapsed, like the DOM Inspectors, and when you mouse-over an element in this source view, a pop-up window displays the CSS properties that are applied to the element. View formatted source can also decorate the web page rendering and provide links that allow you to view only the source for a particular element.

To our knowledge, no third-party plug-ins for Safari provide similar functionality to either of these plug-ins; the Instance Source plug-in for IE provides some of this functionality. There are probably other commercial plug-ins for IE along these lines, but we aren't familiar with them.

Mouseover DOM Inspector

The final tool that we find quite useful is compatible with all of the major browsers: the Mouseover DOM Inspector, or MODI for short. MODI is a *bookmarklet* that you can use with any web page; you bookmark a link from the MODI website[4] and then click the bookmark to use it to examine any site in the future.

bookmarklet

When you click the bookmark, you'll see the MODI pop-up box appear in the web page, as shown in Figure 8.12, on the next page.

You can click and move the MODI window wherever you like. As you move the mouse around, the MODI window displays useful DOM information about the area of the page the mouse is over, such as the children of the element, its ancestry, and various attributes about the element.

Were this all MODI did, it would be pretty interesting. But, there's more. MODI lets you modify the DOM as well, through a series of keystroke listeners it installs. These listeners also provide some additional DOM inspection functionality that's pretty neat.

Our favorite feature is the V key—press this while hovering over an element, and a pop-up window appears that contains the element's source code. You can edit the source directly within this pop-up window and apply it live to the document. MODI also has a sort of clipboard: press A whilst hovered over an element, and the element is copied into

---

[4]http://slayeroffice.com/tools/modi/v2.0/modi_help.html

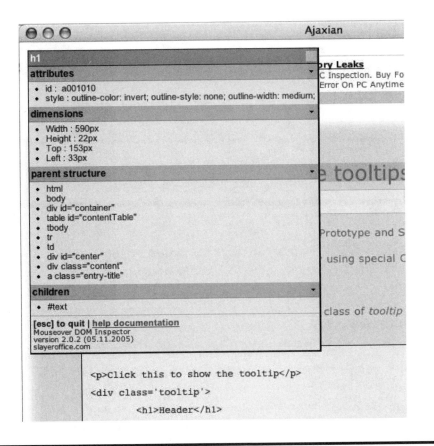

Figure 8.12: MODI IN ACTION ON AJAXIAN

the clipboard. Press S over another element, and the copied element will be appended as a child to that element.

MODI does much more than this; we highly recommend that you check it out.

8.3 JavaScript Debugging

The live DOM-viewing features we just discussed are absolutely vital for understanding the current state of a web page, but they're only half the story, of course. Any Ajax application will also make extensive use of JavaScript. Let's talk about what to do when your JavaScript doesn't do what you expect.

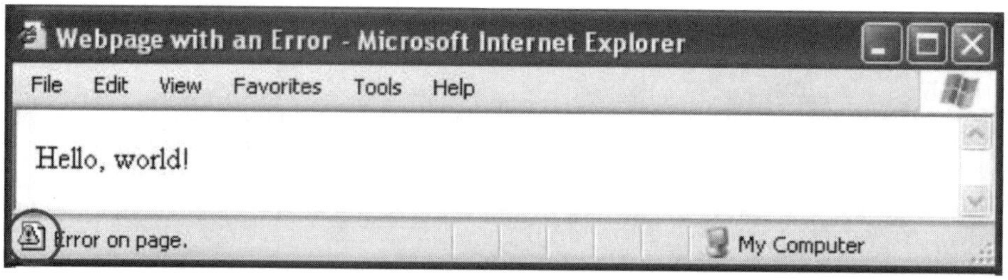

Figure 8.13: INTERNET EXPLORER ERROR ICON

Two basic types of errors can occur in your scripts: syntactical and behavioral. Let's discuss how to handle both types of errors in your scripts.

Syntactical Errors

If you are accustomed to using a compiled language, such as Java or C++, then you're probably not used to dealing with syntactical errors at runtime. If you mistype a function names or abuse operators, compiled languages spit out syntax-related error messages when the compiler converts source code into a lower-level form. In the case of JavaScript, however, these errors are detected at runtime. The browsers differ in how they handle displaying these error messages.

Internet Explorer

In the case of Internet Explorer, the presence of a JavaScript-issued error message is indicated by a changed icon in the lower-left corner of the browser window, as shown in Figure 8.13.

By double-clicking the icon, you'll see a pop-up dialog that displays information about the error, as shown in Figure 8.14, on the next page.

IE will record every script error that occurs on the current web page and save them for your review in this dialog; by clicking the next and previous buttons, you can cycle through these messages. Once you leave the web page, these errors will be cleared.

It can be easy to overlook IE's subtle icon-change error indication, but fortunately, you can configure IE to display a dialog each time an error occurs, saving you the bother and extra step of dealing with the icon.

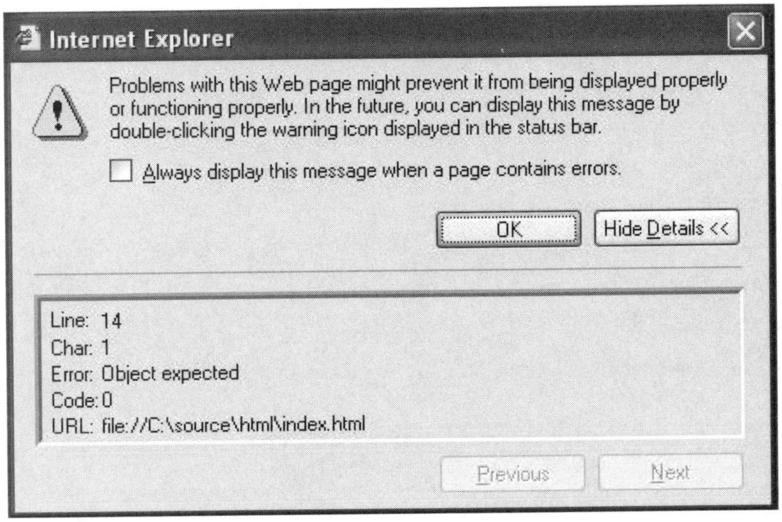

Figure 8.14: INTERNET EXPLORER ERROR DIALOG

The Browsing section of the Advanced tab in IE's Internet Option's dialog window contains a preference item named "Display a notification about every script error"; check this, and the dialog will automatically appear.

Before we move on to the other browsers, we should mention a quirk in Internet Explorer's error display mechanism. If you fail to turn on the "Display a notification about every script error" option, Internet Explorer will fail to display a notification about errors that occur in the JavaScript before the page is completely loaded. For example, consider the following simple web page:

```
Line 1    <html>
   -          <head>
   -             <script type="text/javascript">
   -                 alerrrrrrrrt("Too many R's");
   5             </script>
   -          </head>
   -          <body></body>
   -      </html>
```

You would expect IE to complain about line 4, but alas, no complaint is made. It turns out that when IE finishes displaying a page, it clears all script errors currently tracked, including those caused while the page was rendered. Bummer.

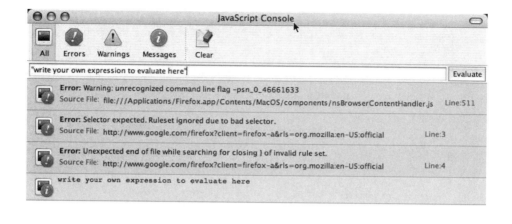

Figure 8.15: FIREFOX JAVASCRIPT CONSOLE

Firefox

If you find IE's mechanism for displaying error messages lacking or annoying, you're not alone, and fortunately, the other browsers provide a superior mechanism: the JavaScript console.

Available from Firefox's Tools menu, the JavaScript console (shown in Figure 8.15) records every error that occurs during the entire browser session. Unlike IE's modal pop-up dialog, the console window may be kept open during a browsing session.

In addition, you can evaluate JavaScript expressions—a handy way to test JavaScript expressions without creating an entire web page as a container for them. The console has access to the various implicit objects that the browser makes available to the JavaScript environment, such as the document object, but it does not have access to the variables that are created by the page. When you evaluate an expression in the console, the result of the evaluation will be displayed as a message in the console itself.

Safari

Like Firefox, Safari includes a JavaScript console, available from the Debug menu. It also comes with a helpful bonus feature—the ability to log your own messages to the console by executing this expression, passing in the string to log: window.console.log("string to log").

Actually, Firefox also includes the ability for scripts to log messages to the console, but unlike Safari, this ability is far more difficult to use, requiring you to delve into native Firefox functionality, which includes the requirement to request advance script permissions, and so forth. For more information on using this ability, please go online.[5]

Safari also allows for interactive script evaluation using the Snippet Editor, also available from the Debug menu.

MochiKit Interpreter

We should also mention that a popular third-party JavaScript framework, MochiKit, allows you to interactively evaluate JavaScript expressions in any browser.[6] If you run Internet Explorer, this provides a nice alternative to Firefox's own JavaScript console for evaluating JavaScript expressions, as shown in Figure 8.16, on the next page.

Behavioral Errors

As we all know too well from personal experience, even when a script does not contain syntactical errors, it may still fail to do what we want it to do. The process of discovering and removing these types of errors from your scripts is often more art than science, but contrary to common belief, a number of tools enable script debugging.

Alert Stinks

The most common way to debug scripts is by inserting alert() statements through your code, as in the following:

```
function foo() {
  var result = someFunction();
  alert(result);
}
```

This technique is cross-browser and can potentially be used in production code with the use of a debugging flag:

---

[5]http://kb.mozillazine.org/JavaScript_Console
[6]http://www.mochikit.com/examples/interpreter/index.html

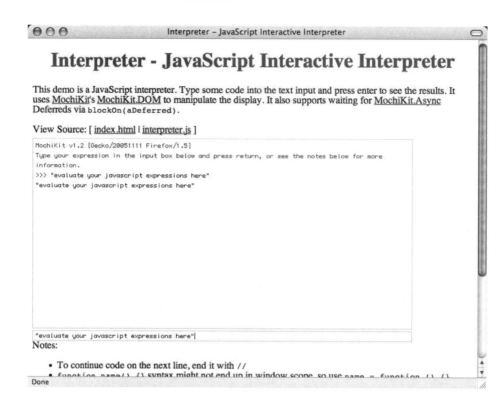

Figure 8.16: MOCHIKIT'S INTERACTIVE INTERPRETER

```
var debugging = false;

function foo() {
  var result = someFunction();
  if (debugging) alert(result);
}
```

However, using alert() this way grows tedious (quickly), because the resulting JavaScript pop-up dialog forces you to modally process each and every value you pass to alert() and furthermore gives you no way to leave a record of each displayed value—even copy-and-paste techniques don't work since the dialog doesn't use a text control to display the message. There has to be a better way.

MochiKit Logging

While the JavaScript console in Firefox and Safari could provide an ideal platform for logging arbitrary output from your own scripts, the omission of such a console from Internet Explorer limits the utility of such an idea. A number of third-party JavaScript libraries have emerged to fill the gap by providing logging functionality without the use of a browser-provided console.

MochiKit contains a useful cross-browser logging feature. It also adds the concept of multiple logging levels as is so popular in frameworks such as Java's log4j and Python's logging module. The following code shows an example of using MochiKit's logging framework:

File 26

```
Line 1   <html>
    -        <head>
    -            <title>MochiKit Logging</title>
    -            <script type="text/javascript" src="js/MochiKit.js"></script>
    5            <script type="text/javascript">
    -                logDebug("This is a DEBUG level message");
    -                log("This is an INFO level message");
    -                logWarning("This is a WARNING level message");
    -                logError("This is an ERROR level message");
    10               logFatal("This is a FATAL level message");
    -
    -                function showLog() {
    -                    createLoggingPane(true);
    -                }
    15           </script>
    -        </head>
    -        <body onload="showLog()">
    -            MochiKit Logging is cool.
    -        </body>
    20   </html>
```

The code on line 13 causes the logging statements to be displayed in a div element appended to the bottom of the page, as shown in Figure 8.17, on the following page.

If you prefer, you can display the logging statements in a separate pop-up window by passing true to createLoggingPane().

MochiKit's logging functionality is well documented online.[7,8]

---

[7]http://www.mochikit.com/doc/html/MochiKit/Logging.html
[8]http://www.mochikit.com/doc/html/MochiKit/LoggingPane.html

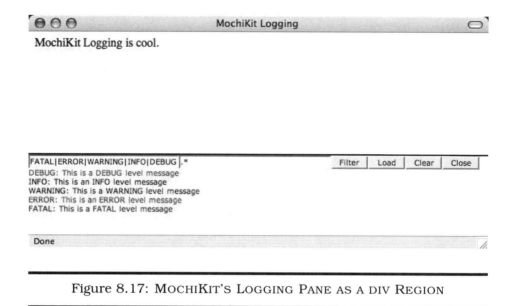

Figure 8.17: MochiKit's Logging Pane as a div Region

Step Debugging

The last debugging technique we'll discuss is *step-through debugging*: the ability to step through each line of your scripts whilst examining the state of the JavaScript environment. Often, this is a much more efficient than inserting individual logging statements throughout your code.

Step Debugging in Firefox

The Mozilla foundation created the Venkman JavaScript debugger,[9] which integrates very nicely with Firefox. After installing Venkman, you can launch it from the Tools menu by selecting JavaScript Debugger.

Venkman is very sophisticated; we'll cover only the basics here. In the upper-left corner of the Venkman window, all of the currently loading scripts from all browser sessions are displayed. By clicking one of the script items, the source code will be displayed in the upper-right corner. You may set breakpoints on any of the dashed lines.

After a breakpoint is set, the Venkman debugger will pause the execution of your script when the breakpoint is reached, allowing you to

---

[9]http://www.mozilla.org/projects/venkman/

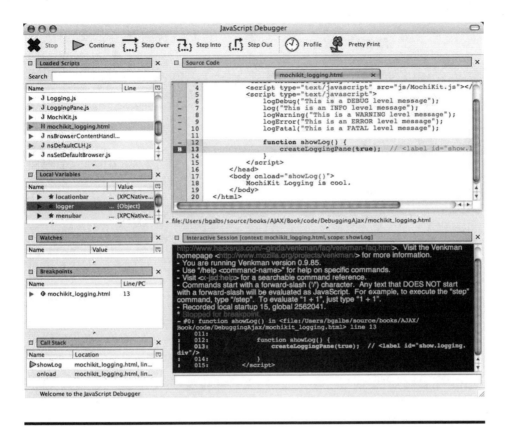

Figure 8.18: The Venkman Debugger for Mozilla-based Browsers

examine local variables and interact with the current script. This is the state displayed in Figure 8.18.

For more information on Venkman, see the Venkman FAQ.[10]

Step Debugging in Internet Explorer

Microsoft has also created a script debugger for Internet Explorer, imaginatively named Script Debugger[11] (or, just Google for "microsoft script debugger"). Once installed, you must enable script debugging in Internet Explorer by unchecking the Disable Script Debugging option.

---

[10]http://www.hacksrus.com/~ginda/venkman/faq/venkman-faq.html

[11]http://www.microsoft.com/downloads/details.aspx?FamilyID=2f465be0-94fd-4569-b3c4-dffdf19ccd99

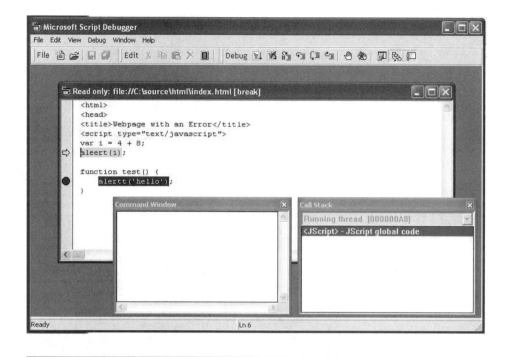

Figure 8.19: 1999 CALLED; IT WANTS ITS INTERNET EXPLORER SCRIPT DEBUGGER BACK

If you perform these two steps and Internet Explorer encounters a script error, you will have the option to enter the Script Debugger environment, as shown in Figure 8.19. You can also enter the Script Debugger at any time through the View -> Script Debugger pull-down menu.

As with Venkman, the Script Debugger is most useful for setting breakpoints that allow you to examine the state of your script at runtime. While IE's Script Debugger does not provide a view of all currently defined objects as Venkman does, you can enter arbitrary expressions in the Command window to discover object properties yourself.

If you buy Microsoft FrontPage 2003 or Visual Studio .NET, you get powerful script debuggers than we've shown here.[12]

To learn about the Visual Studio .NET Script Debugger, check out the Microsoft Word document available online.[13]

---

[12]http://msdn.microsoft.com/library/en-us/dnfp2k2/html/odc_fpDebugScripts.asp

[13]http://www.gotdotnet.com/team/csharp/learn/whitepapers/How%20to%20debug%20script%20in%20Visual%20Studio%20.Net.doc

Step Debugging in Safari

Unfortunately, no script debugger is available for Safari.

8.4 Conclusion

A number of effective quality tools and techniques exist for debugging your Ajax code. DOM-viewing tools and techniques help you view the current state of your page; the JavaScript consoles (and pop-up dialog in IE) can show you what went wrong with your script's syntax, MochiKit's logging framework can you help investigate behavioral problems in your scripts, and when you need a more powerful tool, Venkman and Microsoft's Script Debugger can take you further by enabling step-through debugging.

Degradable Ajax

One of the first questions that gets asked with respect to Ajax is "Can I create a cool Ajax application that still works for non-Ajax-enabled browsers?". This seemingly simple question is actually quite complex; what makes a browser "Ajax-enabled?" Is it JavaScript support? CSS and DHTML capabilities? Secure access to server-side callbacks? And what do we mean when we say the "application works"? Your definition of *degradable Ajax* could be very different from ours. Over the course of this chapter, we'll explore various ways of providing *graceful failback* in your applications.

9.1 What Is Degradable Ajax?

As we said, defining *degradable Ajax* is not a simple thing. Different people might have different ideas about what it means, and a single person might define it differently in different contexts. At a high level, most people think that degradable Ajax means your Ajax-based application will run with browsers that don't support Ajax. The problem is this: what does "run" mean?

Degrading, But Working

We have seen many of techniques that allow your Ajax application to still work as advertised without sacrificing much, if any, of the benefits of Ajax. This is where the power of the toolkits that we talked about (e.g. Dojo Toolkit, Prototype) come into play.

For instance, Dojo will automatically detect whether a given browser supports XMLHttpRequest or the Microsoft equivalents and replace their use with hidden <*iframe*> tags if not. This is the best form of degradation, because the user sees the same results as a user with a browser that supports XHR. Of course, the browser has to support <*iframe*> tags, which means IE 4+, Netscape 6+, or newer browsers such as Firefox and Opera.

Refusing to Play at All

Ideally, all of our users would run the latest and greatest browsers, and this entire chapter would be moot. Unfortunately, this isn't the case. We sometimes dream about a world in which autoupdate was embedded into our PCs many years ago. In that world, the computer was upgrading the browsers for our user. We wouldn't see IE 4 or Mac IE 5. Some applications may choose simply to not support those older browsers at all. Instead, the application simply renders a warning screen to those users, in effect telling them to upgrade to more modern software. When you are creating free Web 2.0 applications to be used by the masses, this might be acceptable. When you are creating business applications for a closed environment with strict software control policies, this is probably a bad choice to make.

Drawing a Line

This brings us to choice. As developers, we need to make the call on what kind of degradation we will allow. Our company/team/project will have to support a subset of the browsers out there, and we need to be explicit about who makes the cut. If you want to support lynx, Mac IE 5, and that weird browser your uncle whipped together, you will have to narrow down the features that you can use for your web-based application. That's life.

Making the choice isn't always easy, and it is best done with data. Do you know what browsers will be coming to your new shiny app? Are you building an intranet site with a known world, or are you developing a public-facing application? Are you writing for a government application that needs to be accessible? If you can possibly narrow down the acceptable or expected browsers that will utilize your application, you can tailor the feature set to the available capabilities of that universe of browsers. This means having a thorough understanding of what is possible in what browsers and having the wherewithal to tell your customers or team what *isn't* going to be in the app.

Degrade == Perfect || Not Crash

The final choice for degrading your application is deciding how much you want to degrade. You could take the tack that degrading means the application needs to work just as well as the full-on Ajax version. Or you could acknowledge that the app won't work that well, but it won't crash the browser.

Part of this decision is helped by what you want to do with your Ajax application. If you are building a rich application to replace the Win-Forms app that your brokers use, it may be asking a lot for a fully featured experience using lynx. But there are all kinds of interactions with an application that Ajax makes *better* that might be *acceptable* using older Web 1.0 standard techniques. For example, we've explored the idea of asynchronous validations with dynamic rendering of error messages; this is a great use of Ajax in an application, making it more usable to the average user. In the absence of XMLHttpRequest or advanced DHTML support, it is silly to not just go ahead and use good ol' server-side validation on post. This is the kind of degradation that is most pragmatic but also hardest to provide, because it involves making decisions and writing code for lots of special cases all over your application.

9.2 Ensuring Degradable Ajax Applications

Let's face it, you have lots of ways to get a degradable Ajax app. However, the truth is that we are human, and the best way to ensure that your application truly works without the Ajax magic is to...wait for it...write it first without Ajax!

That can sound like a lot of work, and it also isn't as sexy as going right for the Ajax coolness, but if you get the application working as a traditional web application first, you will know that any browser can run it. Once the app or a piece of the app is running, you can go in and Ajaxify it. Let's see how to do that.

Ajaxifying a Traditional Web Application

Let's take a simple form that we want to Ajaxify. Imagine a typical to-do list that gives you a set of inputs, allowing for you to add them all to a to-do list, show in Figure 9.1, on the next page.

Nothing earth-shattering here; let's take a look at the simple HTML:

Figure 9.1: TRADITIONAL TO-DO LIST

File 29

```html
<html>
  <head>
    <title>Traditional Todo List</title>
  </head>
  <body>

    <h2>Traditional Todo List</h2>

    <form method="post" action="/addtotodo">
      <table border="0" cellspacing="0" cellpadding="5">
        <tr>
          <td>Add Item</td>
          <td><input type="text" name="add1" value="" /></td>
        </tr>
        <tr>
          <td>Add Item</td>
          <td><input type="text" name="add2" value="" /></td>
        </tr>
        <tr>
          <td>Add Item</td>
          <td><input type="text" name="add3" value="" /></td>
        </tr>
        <tr>
          <td>Add Item</td>
          <td><input type="text" name="add4" value="" /></td>
        </tr>
```

```
      <tr>
        <td>Add Item</td>
        <td><input type="text" name="add5" value="" /></td>
      </tr>
    </table>

    <input type="submit" name="submit" value="Add Todo Items" />
  </form>
 </body>
</html>
```

This works, but using it might be painful. Forcing users to enter all of their items and clicking a button can be slow going. When http://tadalist.com came up with its Ajax version, everyone cried "Yes!". This was not necessarily because everyone wants to make lists but because everyone understands that this is how most people use applications: provide a little data, the app responds, provide a little more data, etc. So let's take this clunky interface and put on an Ajax touch.

Instead of requiring a clunky Web 1.0 submit button, let's add the list item when the user tabs out of the text box. JavaScript, and its access to the DOM, is our ally in this. We can begin to associate new behaviors with our existing elements without necessarily interfering with how the original application works.

Cleaning Out the Submit Button

We don't need no stinking submit button! We'll want to suppress it when we are in Ajax mode. To do that, we need to mark up our HTML view with a CSS ID attribute which will allow us to affect the element directly in our JavaScript code. Our submit button gets tagged with the todolist ID:

```
<input type="submit" id="todosubmit"
       name="submit" value="Add Todo Items" />
```

Now we have an ID attached, we can make our Ajax-aware folk not even know it exists via some simple JavaScript/DOM. We will be good JavaScript citizens and attach the button-suppressing code by putting it in an onload handler of the DOM window object:

```
window.onload = function() {
  document.getElementById("todosubmit").style.display = "none";
}
```

Chances are that in real applications, there will be a whole set of buttons that we can get rid of in our Ajax applications, and rather than manually putting in each id, we can use one class to tell us that this shouldn't be viewable. Unfortunately, the DOM folk didn't give us getElementsByClassName(), so we need to use our own. Luckily, libraries such as Dojo and Prototype add these convenience methods for us. This is how we could implement nuking all items where the class is deleteforajax, using Prototype:

```
getElementsByClassName("deleteforajax").each(function(element) {
  element.style.display = "none";
});
```

This approach requires us to be smart about how we structure our data, because cleaning out any such element will also suppress that element's children.

Stop Submitting My Form!

Our traditional application relies on a standard HTML form. We set this up to submit to the server (using the action= attribute). But since we have suppressed the submit button, we feel a false sense of security; if the user can't see the submit button, how could they submit the form? The answer is that the user can hit Enter or Return—in most browsers the form will still be sent back to the server, which we don't want. This means that we need to change the action on the form to do nothing if the user somehow manages to submit it. First we add id="todoform" to the form, and then we change the action:

```
document.getElementById("todoform").action = "javascript:;";
```

We can do the same trick as with deleteforajax by having a standard CSS class that defines forms that we will not submit anymore.

Now, How Do I Submit To-Do Items?

All of a sudden we have no way to submit anything to the server, which means we can't add to-do list items! To fix this, we need to add events that will kick off Ajax requests back to the server. We can do this by adding an onblur event such as the following:

```
<input type="text" name="add1" onblur="addTodoItem(this);"/>
```

The addTodoItem() JavaScript function is then responsible for making an Ajax request, getting back a message from the server (such as "ok, added it" or the HTML element itself), and then inserting the response back into the page.

We already discussed dealing with the returned data in earlier chapters. We can get HTML, JSON, your own custom format, or whatever you want. Later in the chapter we will see that using HTML may well be the best choice.

Putting It All Together

After going through these steps, you will end up with a file that looks like this:

File 28

```html
<html>
  <head>
    <title>Degradable Todo List</title>
    <script type="text/javascript">

      window.onload = function() {
        document.getElementById("todosubmit").style.display = "none";
        document.getElementById("todoform").action = "javascript:;";
      }

      function addTodoItem(el) {
        // make the ajax call
      }
    </script>
  </head>
  <body>
    <h2>Degradable Todo List</h2>

    <form method="post" action="/addtotodo" id="todoform">
      <table border="0" cellspacing="0" cellpadding="5" id="todolist">
        <tr id="row1">
          <td>Add Item</td>
          <td>
            <input type="text" name="add1" value=""
                   onblur="addTodoItem(this);"/>
          </td>
        </tr>
        <tr id="row2">
          <td>Add Item</td>
          <td>
            <input type="text" name="add2" value=""
                   onblur="addTodoItem(this);"/>
          </td>
        </tr>
        <tr id="row3">
          <td>Add Item</td>
          <td>
            <input type="text" name="add3" value=""
                   onblur="addTodoItem(this);"/>
          </td>
```

Figure 9.2: DEGRADABLE TODO LIST

```
        </tr>
        <tr id="row4">
          <td>Add Item</td>
          <td>
            <input type="text" name="add4" value=""
                   onblur="addTodoItem(this);"/>
          </td>
        </tr>
        <tr id="row5">
          <td>Add Item</td>
          <td>
            <input type="text" name="add5" value=""
                   onblur="addTodoItem(this);"/>
          </td>
        </tr>
      </table>

    <input type="submit" id="todosubmit"
           name="submit" value="Add Todo Items" />
    </form>
  </body>
</html>
```

And if you open the file in a browser that likes JavaScript, you will see
the submit button has disappeared, as shown in Figure 9.2.

getElementsBySelector

Take a peak in behaviour.js, and you'll see the wonderful methoddocument.getElementsBySelector(selector).

You will also see another helpful function,getAllChildren(), which returns all of the children of a given element, including a workaround for IE5/Windows:

```
function getAllChildren(e) {
  // Returns all children of element.
  // Workaround required for IE5/Windows. Ugh.
  return e.all ? e.all : e.getElementsByTagName(' *');
}
```

Using JavaScript Behaviour to Keep Us Clean

One valid concern with the previous approach is that our HTML starts to get very ugly, very quickly. Your nose probably turns up like ours does when we see a lot of JavaScript appearing in our HTML pages. We don't mind sprinkling CSS around, though, which is the core piece that we need for this technique. If only we could make do with just having CSS information and having our JavaScript out of the way, out of the view.

It turns out that we are not the first people to think about this issue. Building on the work of Simon Willison, Ben Nolan created a small library called Behaviour (http://bennolan.com/behaviour/), which allows you to attach JavaScript behavior to CSS selectors.

To see this in action, let's use Behaviour to get rid of the onblur event handlers from our To-Do list example.

Add Behaviour

We first need to clean out the onblur handlers, and instead we tag the input elements with a CSS class addtodo:

```
<input class="addtodo" type="text" name="add1" value=""/>
```

At this point we can attach our behavior by loading the Behaviour JavaScript library and then setting up simple rules that attach the JavaScript method to the onblur event on the given input types:

File 27

```
<script type="text/javascript" src="scripts/behaviour.js"></script>
<script type="text/javascript">
  var myrules = {
      '.addtodo': function(element) {
      element.onblur = addTodoItem(element);
    }
  };

  Behaviour.register(myrules);
</script>
```

The myrules variable declares an associative array of CSS selectors map-ping to elements to which we can attach logic. In the previous code, we look for all addtodo CSS classes via .addtodo, and then we attach the logic via code such as this:

```
element.onblur = addTodoItem(element);
```

We register these rules by calling Behaviour.register(myrules), which parses out the selector, grabs all elements in the DOM that match the selector, and applies our callbacks to the appropriate events.

If we change the DOM, we need to let Behaviour know, so it can apply its rules again. For example, if we append any new children to the document or replace the innerHTML of any element, we have probably modified the DOM. To attach the behaviors to the new elements, make sure you call Behaviour.apply().

We can take this a lot further. Ideally we wouldn't have multiple text boxes as we do now. It makes sense in a world where you can't make dynamic Ajax calls, but since we can, we should get rid of all but one of the text inputs and make it look more like TadaLists (Figure 9.3, on the next page).

We would replace the multiple inputs with one that allows you to type a to-do item, hit Enter/Return, and have your to-do added to the page. At that time the input box would move down and clear off to allow you to type in the next one. Now your data entry becomes as simple as the following:

- Type in entry.
- Hit Enter/Return.
- Repeat.

Validation would be added here, as shown in the early CRM examples.

Figure 9.3: DEGRADABLE TODO LIST

Using HTML to Enable Degradability

We have discussed the Ajax approach of always returning HTML to the browser and using innerHTML to apply it to the DOM. Some frameworks, such as Ruby on Rails, favor this tactic. It has the nice side benefit of making degradable applications easier to build.

Decorating for non-Ajax

discusses the way that the Ruby framework allows you to call *partials*, which are small snippets of HTML. You can think of a page that goes through a loop of some kind, and calls a partial, which produces the HTML for each loop. Partials give you a nice way of gaining reuse and keeping DRY.

The beauty of this reuse is when you make remote Ajax calls that can access these partials. Your non-Ajax application view can access a full page load, and Rails will kindly render everything for you, calling into the partial when needed. An Ajax-enabled view will not need to access a Rails full controller but can instead offer a remote Ajax call that hits the partial, gets the same HTML, but just a snippet, and then applies it dynamically to the DOM via innerHTML.

Suddenly you find that you can apply the previous rules, starting with a normal web application, and then apply the Rails magic to have an application that runs with or without Ajax support in the browser.

This isn't just for Rails users, though. You can see that this is a common pattern that we can follow. Your framework can have actions on the server that are able to render full pages, and for pieces, they chain calls to subactions that know how to render small pieces. If you then have Ajax calls, they can directly access the subactions, and now you get to reuse all of your work!

Filtering Out for Ajax

We can take this approach further too. Most server technologies have a notion of filters (such as servlet filters in Java). You can set up a filter that understands and looks for a particular URL token such as ajaxCall=true. (In Rails, for example, the request object has an xhr?() method.) When a request comes in, the filter can see this variable and do one of the following:

- Add site content: If this is an Ajax call, just return the simple HTML from the action. If this isn't an Ajax call, then decorate the HTML that comes back with the full application skeleton.

- Filter out content: If this is an Ajax call, use XQuery to grab just a small piece of the HTML that the call needs. If this isn't an Ajax call, do nothing, and allow the entire page to be sent back.

You will use the technique that fits best for your application.

We can see that if we choose to do most of our Ajax by returning HTML, it becomes fairly easy for us to reuse our server code and degrade our application cleanly. However, what if we are returning JSON or some other kind of data structure?

Degrading with JSON

There is a lot of debate over techniques for building Ajax applications. A common discussion revolves around what data format to use. Should we use XML? HTML? JSON? JavaScript? We discussed how HTML fits in with respect to degrading your application. What about the others? Let's take an extreme way of building your Ajax applications.

Web Services-Driven Ajax

Tools such as TIBCO General Interface, Backbase, and others allow you to build web services-driven Ajax applications. This means that you can treat your Ajax apps as you would other rich client applications. In this model you separate your client and server side:

- Client side: The client side is a rich JavaScript application that talks to the server tier to gather content and displays it dynamically using JavaScript, HTML, and CSS.

- Server side: On the server side, we develop Web services, which can be RESTful or WS-* based. This tier responds to requests from the client side, taking in arguments and returning data. Often we will return only XML or JSON representations that thus can be used by any type of client representation. Not every application has an HTML-based front end, you know.

With this strong separation, the client side and server side teams can define interface contracts, create mock versions, and get to the races. With a mocked-out interface the client side could be totally written without the server-side piece being in place. This approach also allows you to reuse a lot of your work across projects.

Google has an Ajax widget that offers user feedback on the strength of passwords (https://www.google.com/accounts/NewAccount). With this approach, you have a web service that is responsible for taking a password and returning the strength. This can obviously be reused across applications.

So, how do you degrade in this world? One way is to bite the bullet and acknowledge that your Ajax application is so rich that it is not like a web client, and you have to fork the client side and create a second version. One client is the Ajax one, and another is the traditional web one. In this case the web server framework becomes the client itself. This doesn't mean you cannot get reuse, though, because you can tie into the web services just as easily as your Ajax client. This means that the more you put in the web services tier, the easier your life is.

Remember, though, that for many, many situations, you can take the hit on not allowing non-Ajax-aware browsers and environments. Time will be on your side too as people get new computers; they will get new environments.

Dynamic Web Sites vs. Web Applications

We often talk about the difference between dynamic websites and web applications. Dynamic websites focus on sending back HTML content and often have small pieces of Ajax such as form validation. Web applications are more than this. They are rich applications that happen to use the Web platform. An example of this is Yahoo! Mail. It looks like a web page, but it smells like a rich app.

If you are looking to build web applications, then widget libraries such as Zimbra AjaxTK, Backbase, TIBCO General Interface, and others in that family make sense. You have IDEs to drag and drop components, and you end up building something that looks like VB on the Web. These applications do not degrade easily because they rely heavily on dynamic DOM manipulation on the client side to achieve rich UI effects.

9.3 Wrapping Up

Degradable Ajax is not a simple topic. You need to define how much you are willing to degrade and what you will be willing to support.

The answer to these questions can change the technology and toolset that you choose for your application and the approach that you take on items such as return data formats.

Keeping your HTML clean will help out in many ways. Using techniques such as using Behaviour will help make this happen and will make life easier when you degrade your Ajax application.

But, if you are building a rich application that makes Yahoo! Mail look like Squirrel mail, maybe you just tell certain environments "Sorry!" Spend time working on functionality for the 90%, rather than accessibility for the rest. The key is understanding who your user base is and providing the maximum value for the maximum number of potential users.

Chapter 10

JSON and JSON-RPC

In the next few chapters, we'll introduce you to four server-side web application development frameworks and the different strategies they employ for integrating Ajax techniques into their workflow. Before we get there, we need to stop and look at the integration that's sweeping the nation, JavaScript Object Notation (JSON).

JSON is an open format describing how to represent JavaScript objects in a simple text representation that can be easily created and parsed. In other words, you can send data to the browser encoding as JSON objects instead of XML, and the JSON objects can be converted easily into JavaScript objects.

JSON has two advantages over XML when it comes to receiving data in JavaScript. First, with JSON, there's no manual parsing necessary. JSON objects are typed: values are either strings, numbers, arrays, booleans, objects, or null. Compare this to XML, which is typeless; all element values are strings. This loss of types means added complexity when trying to interpret the values within the XML; you have to adopt some sort of layer on top of XML (such as the W3C XML Schema typing system) to impose types on XML. And, chances are, unless you invent your own typing system to use with XML, you'll have yet another layer of complexity because the type system is likely to be an imperfect fit with JavaScript's own type system.

Second, JSON frees you from having to parse data. If you've spent too many days writing mind-numbing DOM code, you'll appreciate this advantage. Your application data is readily accessible as objects, so retrieving values is as easy as reading from an object property or invoking a function.

It is better to look at an example. In a CRM application like Hector's, maybe you'd like to return a list of addresses for use in printing labels. On the server, you generate the addresses as an ordered collection of objects, sorted alphabetically by addressee. You need to transfer this data to the client tier, where it will be consumed by JavaScript for rendering into an Ajax UI.

Conceptually, the data looks like this:

```
ADRESSES
      DOE, JANE
                111 Appian Way
                Atlanta
                GA
                11111
      DOE, JOHN
                222 Something Street
                San Diego
                CA
                22222
      MCKENZIE, DOUG
                333 Maple Leaf Avenue
                Toronto
                ON
                L4Z 1X2
```

This simple structured data could be rendered in XML fairly easily from most server-side frameworks. Depending on how you are collecting the data in the first place, it is even possible that your database will render it directly to XML for you. But consuming it as XML from JavaScript is tedious at best. At a bare minimum, you have to be very cognizant of which browser you are using the XML in, because that drives how you create the document object that will load the XML (one strategy for IE, another for everyone else). Then, you have to use standard DOM manipulation code, which we've talked about before, to navigate and consume it. Yuck.

JSON offers a lighter, faster alternative. Rather than rendering the data as XML, your server could render it as serialized JSON data, which is to say a string. That string might look like this:

```
{"addresses" :
  [
    { "name": "DOE, JANE", "street": "111 Appian Way",
      "city": "Atlanta", "state": "GA", "zip": "11111"},
    { "name": "DOE, JOHN", "street": "222 Something Street",
      "city": "San Diego", "state": "CA", "zip": "22222"},
    { "name": "MCKENZIE, DOUG", "street": "333 Maple Leaf Avenue",
```

```
           "city": "Toronto", "state": "ON", "zip": "L4Z 1X2"}
   ]
}
```

To use this on the client, you would receive this packet as the responseText from an XHR call. It's just a string at this point, and needs to be converted into data. Instead of launching some kind of external parser (a la XML), you can simply evaluate this string, because it is just idiomatic JavaScript. It conforms to the EcmaScript specification and when evaluated, becomes an object whose properties you can query to access the data.

```
var data = eval(xhr.responseText);

for(i=0; i < data.addresses.length; i++)
{
  new Insertion.Bottom('names', "<li>" + data.addresses[i].name + "</li>");
}
```

Immediately after evaluating the string, we have an object with a series of properties containing the data from the JSON serialized data. To access any single address, we just use an ordered array called addresses, accessing them by numerical index. To access the properties of each address, we just refer to them by name: name, street, city, state, and zip.

JSON is also very flexible. Because that third address is in Canada, we might want to refer to state as province and zip as postalcode. Just replace those names in the serialized version:

```
{"addresses" :
  [
    { "name": "DOE, JANE", "street": "111 Appian Way",
      "city": "Atlanta", "state": "GA", "zip": "11111"},
    { "name": "DOE, JOHN", "street": "222 Something Street",
      "city": "San Diego", "state": "CA", "zip": "22222"},
    { "name": "MCKENZIE, DOUG", "street": "333 Maple Leaf Avenue",
      "city": "Toronto", "province": "ON", "postalcode": "L4Z 1X2"}
  ]
}
```

Now, as you navigate the data, if you ask for the state property of addresses[2], you'll get undefined. Ask for province, and you'll be told ON. Because JavaScript allows you to construct objects on the fly and because requesting a nonexistent property is not an exception, this behavior is built into the language. Addresses could even have different numbers of properties (some might have street2, for example) and it would be perfectly acceptable.

JSON is interesting because it is easier to work with than XML and because it is already ubiquitously available across many server-side frameworks, from Java to C# to PHP to ActionScript and many more (see http://www.crockford.com/JSON/ for a list). Most modern browsers support it in their current version of JavaScript. And deserializing the data is extremely fast (faster than parsing an XML document) because it simply involves invoking the JavaScript interpreter.

Another interesting benefit of JSON is that it gets around the JavaScript sandbox for fetching data from multiple servers. Normally, you cannot make JavaScript calls to remote servers that aren't the originating server unless you have distributed your JavaScripts in signed JARs. This means you can retrieve data only from your own server. However, the HTML specification allows you to embed <script> tags that import JavaScript from any server you'd like through the src attribute. As long as you point that src at a URL that emits JSON data, it will be automatically evaluated for you. The Yahoo! APIs all provide JSON output that is used this way.

The biggest problem is one of security: just using eval on any inbound text might be too trusting (can anyone say "cross-site scripting?"). To get around that, you can also use a JSON parser, which essentially is a wrapper around eval that validates the string as JSON (and *not* arbitrary executable JavaScript) before evaluating it. This seems reasonable, but it means including a nonstandard library (the parser) in your client-side code, even though it is just a JavaScript file, but it also eliminates the cross-site import ability that JSON provides, since <script> tags are automatically evaluated without the chance to run them through a custom parser first.

10.1 JSON-RPC

JSON provides another notable benefit: it is the core of a widely available proxy-based Ajax framework known as JSON-RPC.

JSON-RPC (http://json-rpc.org/) is an emerging standard that builds on the JSON foundation to standardize how JavaScript applications can retrieve JSON objects from a server.

While in theory this means you can create a JavaScript client that can talk to multiple back ends in different programming languages that implement a JSON-RPC interface, the reality is that this is of specious benefit. Chances are, a back end implemented in different languages is going to look rather different from an API perspective. It's probably unrealistic to assume that you can code your JavaScript layer once and simply plug in other back ends.

Having said that, you can of course abstract the code that does the object remoting and have more general code that works on JavaScript objects (converted by JSON-RPC), but this is at a higher level than any particular JavaScript proxy implementation.

James Britt has created an implementation of JSON-RPC for Ruby on Rails based around the Orbjson library (http://rubyforge.org/projects/orbjson/). To see what JSON means from a coding perspective, let's use James's library as an example and implement a JSON bridge for a Rails application. A JSON-RPC package is available for almost any language/framework (Perl, Python, PHP, .NET, Smalltalk, etc.). The details will be different, but the concepts will be nearly identical.

JSON on Rails

Orbjson is the Ruby version of JSON-RPC. Like any JSON-RPC implementation, its job is to expose methods on server-side objects to client-side JavaScript through one or more proxies. In this case, the proxy is a JavaScript object that can marshal JavaScript objects to JSON and JSON back to JavaScript. In addition, it knows how to wrap the XML-HttpRequest object for use as the communication pipeline for the JSON data.

In the Ruby world, you use a program called gems to install libraries. To get Orbjson, then, you simply have to execute the following:

```
> gem install orbjson
```

This installs two important pieces: a Ruby object called Orbjson that is in charge of receiving JSON from the client and turning it into a call to a server-side Ruby object, and then serializing the result back to JSON, and a couple of JavaScript files.

These two script files provide the same facilities (sending data to the server via JSON and XMLHttpRequest) and differ only in style. json-rpc.js provides the synchronous implementation, while jsonrpc_async.js is asynchronous. In general, the only difference from the programmer's perspective is that, when using jsonrpc_async.js, the first parameter to any JSON-RPC call is the callback function which deals with the results, while the synchronous version just takes the outbound data parameters.

The Server Side

Let's talk about the server side first. We'll gloss over some of the underlying Rails principles (for more information, see Chapter 13, *Ajax with Rails*, on page 217) and focus on what you have to do to get Orbjson working with your Rails app.

First, you have to pull Orbjson into the project. Following the author's style (James Britt), you first create an object in your app that includes the base JSON-RPC functionality. In the /lib directory, add a file called hyper-active-orbjson.rb, which pulls in the Orbjson gem and defines a single class:

File 62

```
require_gem 'Orbjson'

class HyperActiveOrbjson
  include Orbjson::Common
end
```

Next, you'll define one or more objects that you want to expose to the client through the JSON-RPC bridge. Technically, you can put them anywhere your Rails app can load objects from, but by convention, they also go in the /lib directory. In our case, we're going to create an object that exposes a single method, get_city_state(), which takes a Zip code and returns an array containing the city and state that maps to it.

File 63

```
class Zipdata
  def get_city_state(zip)
    if(zip == '90210')
      return ["Beverly Hills", "CA"]
    else
      return ["Durham", "NC"]
    end
  end
end
```

Notice that this class has no base classes and seems to have no specific features that tell you that it is for use as a remote target. That's the point of JSON-RPC; the server objects are just plain old whatever-your-platform-is.

Finally, you have to tell Rails about Orbjson and your new service. Rails lets you make global configuration decisions in the environment.rb file. Here, we have to tell Orbjson which objects we want to wrap up as remote targets and then pull in the core functionality of the Orbjson library:

File 61

```
cfg =
'lib/zipdata:
    - Zipdata'

Orbjson::System.init( cfg )
require 'hyper-active-orbjson'
ORBJSON = HyperActiveOrbjson.new
```

The first statement creates the configuration data that tells Orbjson which objects to wrap. The string itself is just YAML (Yet Another Markup Language). The second statement consumes the YAML. You could pass in a string, as seen here, or the path to a stand-alone YAML file. The third and fourth statements simply instantiate the core Orb functionality and store it in a global variable.

The final step is to create a Rails controller that can receive the remote calls and call Orbjson to do the work based on the request payload:

File 52

```
class ServicesController < ApplicationController
  def jsonrpc
      post = @request.raw_post
      render(:text => ORBJSON.process(post))
  end
end
```

This controller has a single action method, jsonrpc(), whose sole purpose in life is to grab the raw post payload of the request, send it into the JSON library, and send the results back as the payload of the outbound response.

The Client Side

The bulk of the complexity came on the server side. For the client, you have to pick your RPC strategy (synchronous or asynchronous) and include the correct JavaScript file. This example will use the synchronous version, which means we put a copy of jsonrpc.js in the public/javascripts folder of our Rails application. To include it into our page, we use the Rails javascript_include_tag() method (again, for more details, see Chapter 13, *Ajax with Rails*, on page 217).

File 55

```
<%= javascript_include_tag 'controls', 'dragdrop', 'effects',
                            'prototype', 'jsonrpc' %>
```

This line, in addition to pulling down the JSON-RPC library, also pulls in Prototype and Script.aculo.us.

Next, we include some custom JavaScript to enable our JSON calls:

File 55

```
<script type="text/javascript">
  var jsonurl = "http://localhost:3000/services/jsonrpc";
  var jsonrpc = null;

  function init() {
    jsonrpc = new JSONRpcClient(jsonurl);
  }

  function get_city_state(val) {
    var zips = jsonrpc.zipdata.get_city_state(val);
    $('address_city').value = zips[0];
    $('address_state').value = zips[1];
  }
</script>
```

The first two lines simply set up a couple of convenience variables; one holds the URL to the services controller that we just established, and the second holds the proxy we'll use to invoke the services.

The init() method establishes the JSON-RPC proxy to point to the service. Underneath, this object uses XMLHttpRequest or its Microsoft equivalent to pass the calls to the server and retrieve the results. In addition, it has methods for serializing JavaScript objects, strings, arrays, and dates to JSON notation.

Lastly, we create a function to invoke the proxy and use the results to modify our page. The get_city_state() method takes a Zip code and invokes the remote method by calling jsonrpc.zipdata.get_city_state(). The proxy takes care of taking the JSON results and marshaling them back to a JavaScript array for us; we can simply peel the data out of the array and assign it to fields using standard Prototype access.

JSON-RPC is about the seamless interconnection of JavaScript and your server. In addition to simple arrays, Orbjson will marshal arbitrary JavaScript or Ruby objects, arrays, strings, and dates both directions. However as a general solution, JSON-RPC might be too different than your current environment. Many platforms have a more tightly integrated solution for using JSON as a marshalling layer between the framework and the client (see Chapter 15, *ASP.NET and Atlas*, on page 253 and Chapter 14, *Proxy-Based Ajax with DWR*, on page 237 for the .NET and Java versions). We view JSON-RPC as it currently stands as a solid remoting technology for languages that don't currently have something better, such as DWR. So while there is a port of JSON-RPC for Java[1] we strongly recommend you pass it by and use DWR instead.

---

[1]JSON-RPC–Java, http://oss.metaparadigm.com/jsonrpc/

Chapter 11

Server-side Framework
Integration

In this chapter and the next four, we'll introduce four web application development frameworks and examine the server-side integration techniques they use for incorporating Ajax. This kind of integration can be valuable for a development team, allowing the members of the team to focus their efforts on one logical tier (the server) while simultaneously generating artifacts for two physical tiers (server and client).

To explore these frameworks, we'll walk Hector's team through porting their CRM application to each framework. Along the way, we'll talk about the reasons why Hector might consider each port and the relative strengths and challenges each choice presents. The four frameworks we'll examine are as follows:

- *PHP*: Sajax is the first Ajax integration toolkit for PHP, and we'll examine it plus the newer Najax library.

- *Ruby on Rails*: Rails integrates closely with Script.aculo.us and Prototype. In fact, the authors of those two frameworks are also Rails committers.

- *Spring (Java)*: We'll look at the integration of the DWR framework with Spring for Java web applications.

- *ASP.NET*: We'll look at both Ajax.NET, an open-source Ajax library, and the upcoming Atlas toolkit from Microsoft.

As we look at these four frameworks and port Hector's application to each, bear in mind that we can't compare and contrast every aspect of the frameworks. This isn't a book about comparative web development; it's a book about Ajax and how to use it to make applications today. We hope that these server-side chapters give you the introduction you need to evaluate how your current platforms are approaching Ajax and how other frameworks you might not be familiar with are tackling the same problems with different strategies.

11.1 Different Strategies for Integration

Development teams can choose from several strategies for integrating Ajax with their framework. The choice largely depends on the philosophy of the framework team: should developers be using visual tools for assembling the application? Are web applications really about HTML? Should my server-side code be the primary metaphor for the entire application? In general, the strategies fall into three major categories: visual tool support, custom tag libraries (and helpers), and ORB-like remoting.

Tooling

Some server frameworks are built around the idea of using visual development tools for creating the view artifacts. Examples are the ASP.NET framework with its support in Visual Studio .NET and the JSF toolkit for Java with support in several Java IDEs. The aim of such frameworks are to provide developers with drag-and-drop development. To be brief, the programmer uses components that are in charge of their own client-side rendering (such as data tables and date pickers). These are assembled into a unified page. The components themselves are manipulated through a series of declarative properties that affect everything from their visual style to the component's life cycle.

These frameworks now integrate Ajax support through these declarative properties. In fact, ASP.NET has had such support for some time now. The programmer merely selects one of the properties (such as autoupdating for the data table), which enables in-page callbacks to the server to refresh data. The programmer might not even be aware that the result is, in fact, Ajax, just that the component now exhibits the desired behavior.

Later, in Chapter 15, *ASP.NET and Atlas*, on page 253, we'll take a look at Ajax support in ASP.NET.

Helper Tags

A second approach to Ajax integration is custom tag libraries. Toolkits like AjaxAnywhere[1] and Ruby on Rails use custom tag libraries (or similar constructs) as HTML-embedded stand in for server-side functionality. These tag libraries, sometimes referred to as *helper tags*, are parsed by the template engine of the given framework, which in turn generates client-side artifacts based on the attributes of the custom tag.

helper tags

The result is a page that looks like HTML, but whose actual content is determined at parse time. The tags provide a layer of abstraction for integrating server-side code into client-side templates. This can be quite a powerful ability, because it allows the developer to focus on a single artifact (the template) instead of jumping around between template and alternate code files.

We'll look at Ruby on Rails' Ajax integration in Chapter 13, *Ajax with Rails*, on page 217.

ORB-like Remoting

Our last category of Ajax integration with a server framework is to use ORB-like remoting to connect client-side JavaScript to existing server-side functionality. Using tools such as JSON-RPC, DWR (for Java), Ajax.NET, or several PHP frameworks, a developer can write JavaScript code for the browser that can seemingly access the server-side domain model directly. The effect of these frameworks is that your existing domain code is now reusable across to the client tier, providing a seamless object model for the code on both tiers.

We'll examine ORB-like remoting in Chapter 12, *Ajax with PHP*, on page 201, as we discuss PHP and its Ajax integration. First, we'll look at the granddaddy of all the PHP/Ajax integration projects, Sajax. Next, we'll compare to a newer player, Najax.

---

[1]http://www.ajaxian.com/archives/2005/09/ajaxanywhere_aj.html

Ajax with PHP

PHP is the framework of choice for many web developers. It is free and open source, which means it is widely adopted. For those who use it, they find it is a pragmatic choice, one with a bustling community of users and developers. The community is so strong, in fact, that the library of available additions to the framework is quite large. If you find yourself wanting a piece of functionality that isn't in the PHP core, make sure you have Googled around a bit before running off and implementing it yourself. Chances are, someone in the PHP community has done that work already.

This is true with the marriage of Ajax and PHP. Several PHP-based frameworks are available, of various quality and richness of features. In fact, the first PHP frameworks were announced within days of the coinage of the term Ajax. In this chapter, we will look at the most popular of these frameworks and will again rewrite Hector's CRM application. We'll finally focus on the server side of the application. Server-side framework integration means that we can utilize the same abstractions we have available on the server to implement a decidedly client-side set of features. The JavaScript frameworks we've talked about already (Dojo, Script.aculo.us, etc.), will be put on the back burner for now as we see what the server side can provide us.

12.1 The PHP Frameworks

Back in Chapter 5, *Ajax Frameworks*, on page 79, we discussed that Ajax support has been announced in JavaScript frameworks left, right, and center. Those frameworks were all written to run on the client, which in this case means within a browser. Server-side development frameworks face the same pressures for innovation that client-side frameworks do.

We've long had support for client-side technologies in our server-side frameworks. From template-based view-rendering technologies such as JSP, ASP and RHTML, to server-side objects with self-rendering capabilities such as ASP.NET and JSF components, these frameworks use a wide variety of methods to influence the client view. Now, they are adding the ability to generate JavaScript for the client to create Ajax effects and sometimes to hook up that JavaScript to server entities for data transfer. There are three major categories of Ajax integration support: visual tool support, tag libraries, and ORB-like remoting.

12.2 Working with Sajax

Let's return now to Hector and his CRM application. He has decided to move his team to an open-source platform, namely PHP. He's convinced that his team will be able to get more leverage by using an integrated Ajax framework. This means the team can add these new effects and callbacks without leaving the confines of PHP. We'll first port the application to Sajax.[1]

What Is Sajax?

Sajax is one of the earliest Ajaxian web frameworks available, originally written for PHP. It is an open-source project and allows you to bind your web UI to server-side functions. It accomplishes this by exporting client-side JavaScript functions that invoke a Sajax bridge back to the server-side code that is actually executed, wrapping it all in an XHR request.

Sajax is an ORB-like remoting layer, which means we will be able to first write the server-side functions we need (consisting of talking to the database and returning the correct data) and then bind our HTML UI directly to these functions. There will be no XMLHttpRequest object to be found, and you may even be surprised with some of the JavaScript method calls that we can run, since we will not see them in the PHP code itself.

There is some tension in the development community surrounding this kind of object remoting strategy. Some developers are keen on using

---

[1] http://www.modernmethod.com/sajax/

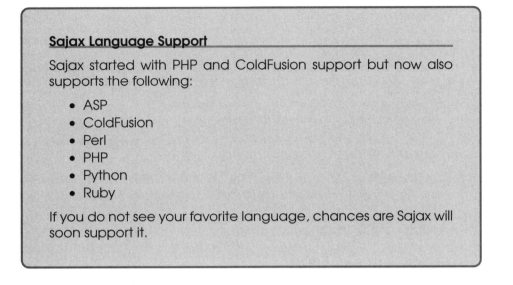

Sajax Language Support

Sajax started with PHP and ColdFusion support but now also supports the following:

- ASP
- ColdFusion
- Perl
- PHP
- Python
- Ruby

If you do not see your favorite language, chances are Sajax will soon support it.

web (XML) services as the primary channel for communicating between different application tiers. Depending on who you talk to, this can mean anything from a RESTful, loosely coupled, XML-over-HTTP architecture all the way to a WSDL, SOAP, and WS-* implementation. What they have in common is a move away from object (and method) orientation and to a message transport and service-oriented architecture.

Object brokers, on the other hand, are entirely about enabling remote communications without disrupting the mental model of the object oriented developer. You can tie client-side methods to server-side objects as though they were physically colocated, thus giving the illusion that there are no network calls and round-trips separating the different entities. While this is a powerful abstraction, it is still just an abstraction. There are, in fact, network round-trips involved, and if you look at the messages that are sent, they look surprisingly just like the messages sent through service-oriented frameworks.

Sajax chooses to expose its functionality through an object broker, thus placing a higher value on a standard experience for the developer across the physical application tiers. This might provide more efficiency at development time but may come at the expense of efficiency at run-time. This is because any abstraction that hides the underlying remote nature of an architecture runs the risk of causing developers to forget about the costs of having such a remote system. It is the responsibility of developers using such a framework to remember the costs associated with making remote calls and to program accordingly.

> **mysqli and PEARDB Interfaces**
>
> The service code uses the original mysql PHP library. If you are running later versions of PHP, you can use libraries such as mysqli and PEARDB:
>
> - mysqli offers increased functionality such as support for prepared statements and other performance-related improvements.
>
> - PEARDB is a DBI/JDBC-like database abstraction layer. This allows you to easily move between various databases.

Porting CRM to Sajax PHP

In order to port the CRM application to Sajax, we will be changing the way we think about the application. Back in the chapters on JavaScript toolkits and frameworks such as Dojo and Prototype, we were very focused on the front-end HTML and JavaScript code, and little was mentioned about the back end. Now we will focus behind the scenes and will use Sajax to generate the front end as much as possible. This means that instead of writing all of the JavaScript ourselves, we will have helper functions that do some magic for us.

Building Back-End Functions

Let's create PHP back-end functions for the Zip to city/state service. We will build the get_city_state() function that will use a MySQL database to return the city and state for the given Zip code. We will place this functionality in its own PHP file, zipService.sajax.php, and will include it from our web-facing PHP code.

We'll start with the small things. We define some constants to hold information on the database itself:

File 19

```
define('DB_HOST', 'localhost');
define('DB_USER', 'crmuser');
define('DB_PASS', 'crmpasswd');
define('DB_NAME', 'crm');
```

Then we create the get_city_state() method:

File 19

```php
function get_city_state($zip) {

  if (!mysql_connect(DB_HOST, DB_USER, DB_PASS)) {
    bail("Could not connect to MySQL");
  }

  if (!mysql_select_db(DB_NAME)) {
    bail("Could not use the " . DB_NAME . "      database in MySQL");
  }

  $q = sprintf("SELECT city,state FROM zips WHERE zip = '%s'",
               mysql_real_escape_string($zip));

  $r = mysql_query($q);
  $row = mysql_fetch_assoc($r);

  if ($row['city'] && $row['state']) {
    $return_string = $row['city'] . "," . $row['state'];
  } else {
    $return_string = "Could not find a city or state for this zip code";
  }

  mysql_free_result($r);

  return $return_string;
}
```

You'll see quite a few lines of code here, but it should be familiar to most PHP developers. We start by connecting to MySQL and selecting the CRM database with mysql_connect() and mysql_select_db(). We then build the query, making sure to escape the input via the method mysql_real_escape_string(). We escape the input string to give our application some protection against cross-site scripting and SQL injection attacks.[2] Finally, we fetch a row from the database using the methods mysql_query() and mysql_fetch_assoc().

After all of this, either we have a matching city and state to return, or we pass back an error message. Since we are good developers, we don't forget to free up our resources with mysql_free_result() before returning our results. This ensures that any memory being hogged by our results is eagerly released. We don't necessarily need to call this for the script you see here, because the results are automatically released upon termination of the script, but for the sake of explicitness, we include the call.

---

[2]For more information about these kinds of attacks, see http://en.wikipedia.org/wiki/Cross-site_scripting and http://en.wikipedia.org/wiki/SQL_injection_attack.

You may have noticed the helper function, bail(), that reports errors
to the browser if there are serious system issues (e.g. the database is
down). This is one benefit of integrating Ajax directly into the server-
side implementation framework. When bad things happen during the
server's execution of an asynchronous callback, it helps to have a built-
in channel for expressing the error information back to the browser:

File 19

```php
function bail($message) {
  header('Content-Type: text/html; charset=utf-8');
  echo "<html><head><title>Zip Error</title></head>" .
      "<body><h2>$message</h2>" .
      mysql_error() . "</body></html>";
  die();
}
```

Migrating to Sajax

Our back-end code is written, so now we move to the client browser
view. We'll create a PHP file that creates the HTML for display, as well
as exports our server functions to the browser as JavaScript methods. In figure_ed_screen_sajax.php, we include the main Sajax PHP module (Sajax.php), as well as the Zip service code that we created earlier
(zipService.sajax.php). In addition, we have to initialize Sajax and choose
the function that we want to be able to call from the client. We export
the method via sajax_export("get_city_state").

File 15

```php
require_once("sajax/php/Sajax.php");
require_once("zipService.sajax.php");

sajax_init();
//$sajax_debug_mode = 1;
sajax_export("get_city_state");
sajax_handle_client_request();
```

What about the sajax_handle_client_request()? That is where the magic
happens. If we take a step back and think about what actually happens
at runtime, we realize that for this to work, three things have to be true:

- Something has to generate the client-side Ajax call.

- Something has to be listening on the server for callback from the
  generated method.

- The listener must be able to invoke the original server-side method
  (with parameters) based on the callback from the client, and then
  return the results.

This is the job of sajax_handle_client_request(). Though this is standard boilerplate code that doesn't change and that you don't have to write, it is still important to understand what is happening here. This is true both for debugging purposes, and for making appropriate use of the framework. First, the method harvests the server-side function name and arguments from specific parameters of the request. Next, it uses those to dynamically invoke the server-side function. Notice also that for GET requests, the method makes sure (as much as is possible) to prevent client-side caching of the results, whereas for POST requests, it doesn't bother. This is because the HTTP specification notes that POST responses are not, by default, cachable, so there is no need to specify the various no-cache headers as in the GET version.[3]

File 18

```
function sajax_handle_client_request() {
  global $sajax_export_list;

  $mode = "";

  if (! empty($_GET["rs"]))
    $mode = "get";

  if (!empty($_POST["rs"]))
    $mode = "post";

  if (empty($mode))
    return;

  if ($mode == "get") {
    // Bust cache in the head
    header ("Expires: Mon, 26 Jul 1997 05:00:00 GMT");      // Date in the past
    header ("Last-Modified: " . gmdate("D, d M Y H:i:s") . " GMT");
    // always modified
    header ("Cache-Control: no-cache, must-revalidate");  // HTTP/1.1
    header ("Pragma: no-cache");                          // HTTP/1.0
    $func_name = $_GET["rs"];
    if (! empty($_GET["rsargs"]))
      $args = $_GET["rsargs"];
    else
      $args = array();
  }
  else {
    $func_name = $_POST["rs"];
    if (! empty($_POST["rsargs"]))
      $args = $_POST["rsargs"];
    else
```

---

[3]http://www.intertwingly.net/blog/2005/03/16/AJAX-Considered-Harmful

> ### Sajax Debug Mode
>
> By setting $sajax_debug_mode = 1;, Sajax will provide you with helpful tracing information during the execution of code within the page. The framework delivers the information via alert() calls which pop up modal dialog boxes to display the information. The type of information you'll see includes the following:
>
> - Notification of the begin and end of server callback functions
>
> - The name and parameters of the server function to be called
>
> - The raw result of the callback
>
> Other responses are also possible. Be forewarned that turning on debug mode will severely hamper a user's ability to actually use the application, so use it only for designated testing purposes.

```php
    $args = array();
  }

  if (! in_array($func_name, $sajax_export_list))
    echo "-:$func_name not callable";
  else {
    echo "+:";
    $result = call_user_func_array($func_name, $args);
    echo $result;
  }
  exit;
}
```

With this code in place, the work of the developer is largely complete. Since so much of the Sajax framework is handled in the bridge code, your job is largely one of configuration (denoting which methods are to be exported). However, about 80 or so lines of JavaScript are required in the browser to wire all this up; one line of PHP code is all that is required to generate and embed the scripts:

File 15

```php
<?php sajax_show_javascript(); ?>
```

You can examine the generated JavaScript code by doing a View Source on the page. In addition to a bunch of standard code for instantiating the XHR object and wiring up its state callbacks, you will also see methods generated specifically by your sajax_export() calls from before.

Each method that was exported gets a client-side helper method whose name is x_(name of original function)(). In our case, the function is called x_get_city_state(), shown here:

```
function x_get_city_state() {
  sajax_do_call("get_city_state",
                x_get_city_state.arguments);
}
```

What is the x_get_city_state.arguments() all about? To allow for a variable length parameter list, we are packaging up all the inputs to the method into a single collection of values. These values mimic the server-side function definition exactly, with one addition. To enable the full Ajax life cycle of a Sajax method, we have to provide an extra parameter, which is a function to use as a callback when the request returns without an error. This method harvests the results of the server call and performs the client-side work to display and/or utilize the data. The function we have been using to this point is assignCityAndState(), which we will just reuse in this context:

File 15

```
function assignCityAndState(data) {
  if (data.indexOf(',') > 0) {
    var cityState = data.substring(1).split(',');
    document.getElementById("city").value = cityState[0];
    document.getElementById("state").value = cityState[1];
    document.getElementById("zipError").innerHTML = "";
  } else {
    document.getElementById("zipError").innerHTML = "Error: " + data;
  }
}
```

Since we are leaving the main part of our HTML the same as the early Ajax examples, we can wrap these calls with our faithful getZipData():

File 15

```
function getZipData(zipCode) {
  x_get_city_state(zipCode, assignCityAndState);
}
```

Gaining and Losing

So there you have it. We have shown how you can use the Sajax framework to export server-side functions. Sajax really is simple to use, but it has some drawbacks. The main drawback is that you have the ability to return only simple types from your exported functions. You can't return a rich object and have it jump into a JavaScript object (via JSON or anything else). This means you may often create wrapper functions around existing server-side code to wrap their return types with simple string-based information that can be parsed manually on the client.

Similarly, other frameworks (such as Dojo) offer transparent failover support for older browsers. For example, Dojo can switch to use iframes for remoting when the XHR object is not available. Sajax provides no such support; it is a no-frills framework designed to make it easy to take advantage of Ajax features in modern browsers. What you gain is simplicity: a standard programming model with little to no JavaScript code to be written.

12.3 XOAD

Sajax isn't the only PHP Ajaxian framework in town. A newer kid on the block is XOAD. We will port our CRM application from the Sajax version and get a good view of the similarities and differences between the two popular frameworks.

From Procedural to OO

XOAD is similar to Sajax in that it also uses an ORB-based remoting model where you bind your JavaScript layer to your server-side code. You would think that we would be able to use the same Zip service that we already created for the Sajax version. This isn't going to be the case, because XOAD cares about classes and OO. We will not export just methods, but will give XOAD objects and classes. This means we need to change the Zip service to be a class.

Changing the Back End

We can do this in a slightly cheeky manner. We are going to take the get_city_state() and bail() functions and make them static methods in a Zip service class. We wrap the code in class ZipService {...}, and we make the functions static by adding the static keyword before their definitions (so we have static function get_city_state($zip) {...}).

The one change we need to make to the back end for XOAD is the addition of metadata to the class that describes what should be exported. This metadata gets added via a simple instance method on the Zip service:

| File 20 |
```php
function xoadGetMeta() {
        XOAD_Client::mapMethods($this, array('get_city_state'));
        XOAD_Client::publicMethods($this, array('get_city_state'));
}
```

> ### Sajax Could Work This Way
>
> At this point in time, Sajax could work with this code too. A simple way to get it to work is to create a wrapper function that we utilize like this:
>
> ```
> function get_city_state($zip) {
>   return ZipService::get_city_state($zip);
> }
> ```
>
> Soon we will change the class more though for XOAD, and it will no longer work with Sajax.

You have some options on what you want to export. In our example, we give the map of methods that we want to export, and we assign the access to public methods. You can access private methods via XOAD_Client::privateMethods(), and you can access variables using the methods XOAD_Client::privateVariables() and XOAD_Client::publicVariables(). Any OO purist will tell you that doing so violates the principles of encapsulation: namely, private members and data fields should be accessible only by the defining class or specifically trusted entities. Therefore, be careful when utilizing these methods and ensure that you are getting the functionality you actually need.

Back to Front

We start on the client side as we did with Sajax. We load everything we need and define the base directory for all things XOAD. In this case, we are using a subdirectory called xoad:

File 16

```
define('XOAD_BASE', 'xoad');

require_once('xoad/xoad.php');
require_once('zipService.xoad.php');

XOAD_Server::allowClasses('ZipService');

if (XOAD_Server::runServer()) {
        exit;
}
```

We will also register the classes we want to be remotable. It is not technically necessary to do this, but it is considered the polite thing

---

XOAD Serializer

At this point, XOAD uses a serializer object to be able to convert between the two worlds. We found an issue when running on PHP 5.1 and had to change the Serializer.class.php file so that the function function serialize(&$var) became function serialize($var) (i.e., we removed the ampersand). PHP 5 has different rules for handling pass-by-reference semantics. The error we were receiving was as follows:

```
PHP Fatal error: Only variables can be passed by reference
in /path/to/xoad/classes/Serializer.class.php on line 294
```

---

to do. XOAD keeps two hashes full of classes, one for allowed classes and one for denied classes. Calling methods on denied classes results in an error; calls to methods on allowed, or *unassigned*, methods will proceed. However, in keeping with suggested usage, we'll register the ZipServer class with XOAD_Server::allowClasses().

XOAD sets up XHR requests to come back to the same PHP server page. This means our PHP page is accessed in two modes. One is to display the main page, and the other is to access the callback function. The check in XOAD_Server::runServer() is there to handle the XHR request; it returns false immediately if the request is not an XHR callback. Otherwise, this method fires off the bound server methods according to the request parameters and returns the results.

Once again we are quickly done with the PHP header code, and we are into the HTML itself. We need to include all of the XOAD helper JavaScript code, which is done at the top of the HTML head element:

File 16
```
<?= XOAD_Utilities::header('xoad') ?>
```

We mentioned that XOAD is all about classes and objects, not just functions. To register a class and have access to it via JavaScript, you just need another helper function:

File 16
```
var obj = <?= XOAD_Client::register(new ZipService()) ?>;
```

We are registering a named object from the server, but you can also register anonymous items such as inline lists. To do that, you would just do something like the following:

```
var arr = <?= XOAD_Client::register(array(1, "bob", array("nested"))) ?>;
```

To handle errors that may occur, you follow a naming convention that allows you to have handlers for every method you call. The format of the handler in question is obj.on(Name of method)Error(), where the first character of the method name gets uppercased. We handle errors in our application with the following:

File 16

```
obj.onGet_city_stateError = function(error) {
  document.getElementById("zipError").innerHTML = "Error: " + error.message;
  return true;
}
```

The final piece of the pie is to wrap getZipData() once again to tie into our object:

File 16

```
function getZipData(zipCode) {
  obj.get_city_state(zipCode, assignCityAndState);
}
```

Returning Rich Types

We mentioned that XOAD is able to deal with richer return types than Sajax. Let's change our code to try that out for size. To do this, we will change get_city_state() to return an object of type ZipCityState. This is a structure that has all of the data needed, instead of having a strange string representation that you then need to parse on the client side.

The ZipCityState structure is a simple type. We just give it some public variables that can store and retrieve our data. Why even bother with accessors and mutators when it is this simple? (We can sense the OO purists out there squirming).

File 21

```
class ZipCityState {
  var $zip;
  var $city;
  var $state;

  function ZipCityState($theZip, $theCity, $theState) {
    $this->zip = $theZip;
    $this->city = $theCity;
    $this->state = $theState;
  }
}
```

Now we have a rich type to pass around between layers. We can create an object of this type in get_city_state() using the constructor provided previously in the ZipCityState class:

File 21

```php
if ($row['city'] && $row['state']) {
  $return_object = new ZipCityState($zip, $row['city'], $row['state']);
} else {
  $return_object = NULL;
}
```

Our back-end code has now been updated to return the rich object, so we need to change our browser code to be able to understand this object when it comes back. Remember, the original version expects a custom string representation of the data that it has to parse manually. The best thing about this example is that we are hardly having to change anything, and in fact we get to delete the string-parsing code. XOAD is handling the marshaling of the return type for us. It is creating a ZipCityState JavaScript object that has the same methods as the PHP version.

This means that the only change we make is to the assignCityAndState() JavaScript function. XOAD passes the return object from the PHP get_city_state() to assignCityAndState(). It just so happens that it now gets the rich ZipCityState, and we can use this object to get the city and state data by simply using zip.city and zip.state. It looks like this:

File 17

```javascript
function assignCityAndState(zcs) {
  if (zcs.city) {
    document.getElementById("city").value = zcs.city;
    document.getElementById("state").value = zcs.state;
    document.getElementById("zipError").innerHTML = "";
  } else {
    document.getElementById("zipError").innerHTML = "Error: " + zcs.zip;
  }
}
```

So there we have it. XOAD successfully managed to take a rich return type and generate a JSON representation to pass down to the client. This allowed us to map object return types versus simple strings and the like. You probably don't want to get too carried away, though. While it is theoretically possible to create insanely complex return types, with nested complex structures for data, this can lead down a long road of debugging, testing, and possibly even modifying the marshaling code buried inside XOAD. Besides, even if the marshaling code handled the data structures without a problem, large types still take up a lot of bandwidth. Keep it simple, and everyone is happy.

There is More to XOAD

This concludes the port to XOAD, and we have seen how it is an OO-based system versus the function-based structure of Sajax. The XOAD serializer allows you to return rich objects that will get converted to JSON objects that the browser JavaScript engine can consume.

There are other interesting features of the XOAD library that we haven't seen in this use case. One of these is *XOAD Events* which allow you to fire events from one computer and catch and process them on another. This is all done by using an observer pattern and having one piece of code firing events and another listening for them. This is useful for Ajax applications that need to be very responsive to data being passed between tiers (such as a chat client, for example).

12.4 Wrapping Up

We have shown you two of the most popular PHP-based Ajax frameworks. These frameworks amply demonstrate the power of integrated Ajax code; the simplicity of the model is evident. You never have to leave the cozy confines of PHP to achieve dramatic Ajax results. In fact, you don't even have to look at the JavaScript if you don't want to do so. However, just because these frameworks *can* hide the details of JavaScript on the client, that doesn't mean you have to ignore it yourself. There can be quite a lot of benefit to leveraging a high-level abstraction layer like Sajax or XOAD but manipulating the DOM directly with JavaScript to achieve more complex client-side behavior as well.

Chapter 13

Ajax with Rails

It is easy to talk about the degree of integration between some of the existing Ajax JavaScript frameworks and the Ruby on Rails platform. Thomas Fuchs (of Script.aculo.us) and Sam Stephenson (author of Prototype) were both announced as Rails committers in the summer of 2005, which means that integration with their frameworks is a given. As those Ajax frameworks continue to evolve, you can be guaranteed that the Rails support for the new features will be the first on the street.

The integration itself takes the form of a series of helper methods that can be embedded in the RHTML files that make up the view portion of the application. These helper methods allow you to attach behavior and logic to DOM elements through the same syntax with which you interact with server-side objects. The result is a clean, consistent RHTML file without a lot of visible JavaScript to muddy the water.

13.1 Ruby on Rails

Let's first take a brisk walk through the architecture of Rails itself. Rails, through its convention-over-configuration strategy, relies on a lot of naming conventions and simple generators to create the plumbing for your applications. Understanding how these things interact will allow us to better understand what the Ajax helpers are doing at runtime and thus how to better employ them to the benefit of our application.

Controllers and Actions

The logic of a Rails application is centralized in one or more controllers. These are classes that extend the ApplicationController class provided by

Rails and that adhere to a specific naming convention. For the example of Hector's CRM application, we would create a controller for the address functionality called AddressController. The filename for the class would be address_controller.rb, and it would be found in the app/controllers folder of the Rails project.

Controllers contain one or more public methods that are referred to as *actions*. Any public method of a controller is addressable via a URL. We'll add a public method called edit to the AddressController for rendering the address page of an application. The URL to reach this page would then be /address/edit, or the controller name followed by a path separator and then the action name.

Action methods can access a number of state management resources, notably the session, request, response, and params objects. Each is relatively self-explanatory; params might be the only exception. Rails takes any inbound query-string (GET) or form body (POST) parameters and creates a hash out of them.

Additionally, actions can create values that they can pass to the view (which we'll examine in the next section). Specifically, any instance variables are accessible in the view templates. In Ruby, instance-scoped variables are just variables prefixed with @. Here is the controller code for our edit page that passes the page title to the view via an instance variable:

```
class AddressController < ApplicationController
  def edit
    @page_title = 'Edit Address'
  end
end
```

Finally, actions have default views that are rendered if the action makes no alternate specification. The view that gets rendered for the previous controller and action would be /app/views/address/edit.rthml, again based on simple naming conventions. However, actions can specify lots of other options for what to output through the render method. Using render, the action might directly supply text to display, specify an alternate action to invoke, redirect to an external URL, etc. We'll see more about that in a minute.

RHTML

Rails uses a template-parsing engine called ERB as the underlying view technology. You create templates as .rhtml files, which use standard web template notation to layer server-side code with static HTML. In this case, the server-side code is Ruby, but it is still separated from the static HTML through the <% %> constructs. When an action is performed and the render logic causes an RHTML template to be parsed, the Ruby blocks are evaluated, and any output values are inserted amongst the static output before rendering.

Though it is possible to interleave real business logic into the view templates through these code segments, such behavior is considered (in Rails as in every other web development framework) gauche. Any Ruby code found in a template should be entirely devoted to making data presentable in that view, not controlling the application's core behavior.

Rather, the most common usage of Ruby blocks in an RHTML page is to render a piece of data using the <%= %> construct. The equals sign specifies that the result of whatever code is in the Ruby block should be rendered inline as text for purposes of outputting the view to the user. Here is the top part of the edit.rhtml template that uses this construct to place the page title in the header of the HTML page:

File 53

```
<html>
  <head>
    <title><%= @page_title %></title>
    <style type="text/css">
      th { text-align: left; }
    </style>
    <!-- etc. -->
```

Helpers

Helpers are special modules that provide methods for injecting HTML into a view. Helpers can be application-wide or localized to a specific controller. They are essentially just public methods of a specially named class whose output is text that can be utilized in a view.

Rails provides a series of helper classes and methods that make creating complex HTML, especially forms, quite simple. Take, for example, the FormHelper class provided by Rails. It contains a series of methods for outputting the various kinds of form elements: text boxes, check boxes, selection lists, etc. Here's the whole form for editing an address in the CRM application:

File 53

```
Line 1    <%= start_form_tag :action => 'update' %>
     -      <table>
     -        <tr>
     -          <th>Customer Name:</th>
```

```
 5      <td><%= text_field 'address', 'name', {:size => 30} %></td>
 -    </tr>
 -    <tr>
 -      <th>Address:</th>
 -      <td><%= text_field 'address', 'address', {:size => 30} %></td>
10    </tr>
 -    <tr>
 -      <th>City:</th>
 -      <td>
 -        <div id="city">
15          <%= text_field 'address', 'city', {:size => 20} %>
 -        </div>
 -      </td>
 -    </tr>
 -    <tr>
20      <th>State:</th>
 -      <td>
 -        <div id="state">
 -          <%= text_field 'address', 'state',
 -                          {:size => 3, :maxlength => 2} %>
25        </div>
 -      </td>
 -    </tr>
 -    <tr>
 -      <th>Zip:</th>
30      <td>
 -        <%= text_field 'address', 'zip',
 -                        {:size => 10, :maxlength => 10} %>
 -      </td>
 -    </tr>
35    <tr>
 -      <th></th>
 -      <td><%= submit_tag %></td>
 -    </tr>
 -  </table>
40  <%= end_form_tag %>
```

On line 1, you see the first helper we employ: start_form_tag. We've
provided only a single parameter, :action, which specifies the action to
invoke on the target controller. We could specifically name the controller as well; in the absence of one, the helper uses the current controller, which in this case is AddressController. When the template is
parsed and the helper is executed, the result is the following line of
HTML:

```
<form action="/address/update" method="POST">
```

In the rest of the code, you can see many uses of the text_field helper
to render text boxes within the form. The first two parameters to this
function are the name of the object whose property this field repre-

sents and the name of the property itself. For this example, there is a model object in @address and the form allows us to edit its properties. Rails uses the parameters to construct an input field for the data that matches a specific naming scheme: the id attribute takes the form object_property, while the name attribute is object[property].

After the two mandatory properties, you can also pass in an optional hash of values. Each key/value pair in the hash is turned into an HTML attribute on the form field using the key as the name of the attribute, and the value as the attribute's value. Thus, the following helper call:

```
<%= text_field 'address', 'city', {:size => 20} %>
```

becomes the following HTML after parsing:

```
<input type="text" id="address_city" name="address[city]" size="20"/>
```

13.2   Ajax Integration

Ajax integration in Rails generally takes the form of helper methods. The Ajax helpers are provided in the ActionView::Helpers::JavaScriptHelper class. These helpers, when parsed, render JavaScript code that utilizes the Prototype and Script.aculo.us libraries.

The Basics

The following sections highlight the Rails 1.0 way of doing Ajax. In further sections, we'll examine some parts of edge Rails as well.

javascript_include_tag

Of course, for any page to use a JavaScript library, it must import that script library. Rails provides a helper, javascript_include_tag(), that creates the script import statement for you. The only parameter is one or more script library names, minus the path or suffix. Rails assumes that the script files end with .js and are found in the public/javascripts folder.

Rails ships with Prototype and the core Script.aculo.us scripts already installed in public/javascripts. To import them all, you could use:

```
<%= javascript_include_tag 'prototype', 'effects', 'controls' %>
```

Or, you can do it more succinctly:

```
<%= javascript_include_tag :defaults %>
```

link_to_remote

The link_to_remote() helper method creates an href element that invokes a JavaScript function when clicked. The JavaScript function uses the XMLHttpRequest object to create a request back to the server. The helper creates both the HTML and the JavaScript to make it all happen.

You have to pass several mandatory parameters to the helper to get it to work: the text of the link, the URL to post to, and either an element to update with the results or a JavaScript function to invoke upon completion. If you specify a DOM element to update, the helper will generate inline JavaScript code on the href's onclick handler that uses Prototype's Ajax.Updater to make an outbound request and set the innerHTML of the target element to the results. For example, the following:

```
<%= link_to_remote 'Update A Field',
    :url => {:controller => 'my_controller', :action => 'my_action'},
            :update => 'an_element'
%>
```

is rendered as this:

```
<a href="#" onclick="new Ajax.Updater('an_element',
                                    '/my_controller/my_action',
                                    { asynchronous:true,
                                      evalScripts:true}); return false;">
  Update A Field
</a>
```

This construct is useful for situations where the results from the call are just HTML that can be placed into a single DOM element for rendering. However, this is often not the case, because the results might need to be spread out among several DOM elements or there might be more complex post-processing of the results necessary. In such cases, you would specify a JavaScript function to be called upon completion of the XHR request. The function should be defined to take the XHR object itself as its only parameter. The following code:

```
<%= link_to_remote 'Remote Call',
    :url => {:controller => 'my_controller', :action => 'my_action'},
    :complete => 'use_results(request)'
%>
<%= javascript_tag <<-END
                    function use_results(request) {
                    // harvest the results, parse them,
                    // distribute them, etc.
                    }
                    END
                    %>
```

becomes the following:

```
<a href="#"
   onclick="new Ajax.Request('/my_controller/my_action',
               { asynchronous:true,
                 evalScripts:true,
                 onComplete:function(request){
                 use_results(request)}}); return false;">
  Remote Call
</a>
<script type="text/javascript">
  //
  function use_results(request) {
      // harvest the results, parse them,
      // distribute them, etc.
  }
  //
</script>
```

The helper also allows a series of optional parameters for creating everything from confirmation alerts to readystate callbacks. For example, we could add a confirmation dialog to the previous request and also update the user when the response has been fully loaded, by writing the following:

```
<%= link_to_remote 'Remote Call',
    :url => {:controller => 'my_controller',
            :action => 'my_action'},
            :complete => 'use_results(request)',
            :confirm => 'Are you sure?',
            :loaded => 'show_loaded'
%>
```

which becomes this:

```
<a href="#"
   onclick="if (confirm('Are you sure?')) {
            new Ajax.Request('/my_controller/my_action', {
                    asynchronous:true,
                    evalScripts:true,
                    onComplete:function(request){
                      use_results(request)
                    },
                    onLoaded:function(request){
                      show_loaded
                    }
                });
            }; return false;">
 Remote Call
</a>
```

form_remote_tag

Quite often, we use Ajax techniques to take the results of a user's interaction with a form, post them to the server, and render the results on the page. Think of comments on a blog, where you enter your e-mail and the comment, you then submit it, and it magically appears appended to the bottom of the comments list. To accomplish this, you have to employ some JavaScript wizardry to serialize the elements on the form into a parameter you can pass via XMLHttpRequest.

With Ajax-enabled forms, you have to be wary of browsers without Ajax capabilities. A user trying to add a comment to a blog shouldn't be required to have a modern browser to accomplish such a simple task; if XHR is available, your page should take advantage, but you should provide reasonable failover behavior for older browsers. In the case of forms, this means allowing the form to be posted the normal HTML way.

Use the form_remote_tag() helper to create an Ajax-enabled Rails form. It creates a form tag with an onsubmit event to invoke a custom JavaScript function that uses Prototype's Ajax.Request (or Ajax.Updater) to send the form fields to the server. It takes the same parameters as link_to_remote apart from the initial text parameter (because the form has no visible artifact that requires it). The following:

```
<%= form_remote_tag :url => {:controller => 'my_controller',
                             :action => 'my_action'},
                    :update => 'my_element' %>
```

becomes this:

```
<form action="/my_controller/my_action"
      method="post"
      onsubmit="new Ajax.Updater('my_elem', '/address/my_action',
                { asynchronous:true,
                  evalScripts:true,
                  parameters:Form.serialize(this)}
              ); return false;">
```

The helper automatically creates failover support to post the form to the same destination as the Ajax version of the request. If JavaScript is not enabled, the onsubmit event is never bound, and the Ajax.Updater is never created. The default action and method are then used to send the form fields to the server.

Notice also that the helper automatically uses the Prototype method Form.serialize, which gathers all the input elements on a form into a single textual representation of a hash, which is then passed as the parameters value of the request.

You can specify an alternate destination for the non-Ajax version of the form by providing an optional hash of values to create the HTML version of the target URL:

```
<%= form_remote_tag :url => {
                      :controller => 'my_controller',
                      :action => 'my_action'
                    },
                    :update => 'my_element',
                    :html => {
                      :action => {
                        :controller => 'other_controller',
                        :action => 'non_ajax'
                      },
                      :method => 'post'
                    }
%>
```

Also, just like with link_to_remote, you can specify a JavaScript function to execute upon completion of the request instead of a DOM element to update with the results if the request requires more complex post-processing.

Observers and Updaters

The first two helpers we looked at require the user to click on something to generate the Ajax behavior, either a link or a form submit button. As we have already seen, this is not always how we want to trigger these callbacks. Instead, we want to observe elements of the page and either periodically send their current value to the server or watch for a change in the value and send the request upon that change.

If you want to watch a single field on a page for changes, you can use the observe_field helper. It allows you to monitor a field for changes (either periodically or using event-based semantics) and send those changes to the server. Periodical polling uses a timer to grab the value of the target field every n seconds and send it to the server (regardless of whether the value changed in the intervening interval). Event-based polling uses the onblur event, which means changes are sent only when the user shifts focus away from the target field. As such, periodical polling is useful for things such as autocomplete fields that display a list of choices based on the current contents of the field (like Google Suggest). Event-based polling is more useful when you want to wait until the user has entered a complete value in the field before causing a round-trip (like Hector's Zip lookup function).

By default, both versions of the observer send the value of the field as the raw post data to the server. However, you'll often want to label that value as a specifically named parameter. Rails provides the option with parameter for the observer which allows you to construct the parameter list for the request using a piece of JavaScript.

Here is an example of using a half-second interval periodic observer to send the value of a text field to the server, using with to construct the parameter list:

```
<%= text_field 'my_object', 'my_property' %>
<%= observe_field 'my_object_my_property',
    :url => {:controller => 'my_controller',
             :action => 'my_action'},
:update => 'display_target',
:frequency => 0.5,
:with => "'my_param = ' + value"
%>
```

The results look like:

```
<input id="my_object_my_property"
       name="my_object[my_property]"
       size="30"
       type="text" />
<script type="text/javascript">
  //
  new Form.Element.Observer(
          'my_object_my_property',
          0.5,
          function(element, value) {
            new Ajax.Updater('display_target',
                             '/my_controller/my_action',
                             { asynchronous:true,
                               evalScripts:true,
                               parameters:'my_param = ' + value
                             })
          })
  //
</script>
```

Conversely, to create an event-based observer, just leave out the frequency parameter.

If your page requires you to watch an entire form, rather than just a single field, Rails also provides the observe_form helper. Simply provide the form's ID rather than a specific field ID to the helper, and it will watch all the inputs on the form. The form observer can be periodic or event-based, just like the field observer. It uses Prototype's Form.serialize method to harvest all the form values, and you can use the optional with parameter to construct the request parameters as before.

Other Assorted Helpers

Rails provides a slew of other minor helpers to make accessing and utilizing Prototype and Script.aculo.us easier and more consistent with the rest of your RHTML code. For example, we already saw the javascript_tag helper, which simply creates a <*script*> block with the contents we passed into it. Additionally, there are helpers for the Script.aculo.us visual effects libraries, for creating remote JavaScript functions that aren't bound to change events, and for doing even more.

For example, the visual_effect helper takes the name of a DOM element, a symbol representing the desired effect, and a hash of parameters for controlling the effect and generates the appropriate JavaScript to launch it. To cause an element to fade, we could write the following:

```
<%= visual_effect :fade, 'target_element' %>
```

This helper is often used in conjunction with other helpers, specifically to generate the onComplete action for the request:

```
<%= observe_field 'my_object_my_property',
    :url => {:controller => 'my_controller', :action => 'my_action'},
    :update => 'display_target',
    :frequency => 0.5,
    :with => "'my_param = ' + value",
    :onComplete => visual_effect(:highlight, 'display_target')
%>
```

If you need to create an XHR round-trip but attach it to a nonstandard event on the page (anything other than a field's onblur event), you can utilize the Rails remote_function helper. It takes all the same parameters as link_to_remote but is useful for generating the JavaScript in arbitrary locations on the page.

```
<input type="text" id="my_text_field"
        onfocus="<%= remote_function :url => {:action => 'my_action'},
                                      :update => 'target' %>"/>
```

becomes the following:

```
<input type="text" id="my_text_field"
        onfocus="new Ajax.Updater('target', '/address/my_action',
                {asynchronous:true, evalScripts:true})"/>
```

CRM, Again

So, back to Hector's address entry form again. Let's see how to utilize these Ajax helpers to create the functionality we've already implemented. Then, we'll go a step further and see how easy the integration helpers make some seriously advanced Ajax functionality, such as sortable lists and autocomplete fields.

Observing the Zip Field

Our first thought as we begin adding the Ajax feature to our address form is that we should utilize the observe_field helper to watch the Zip field and update the values of the city and state elements when it changes. We can use the update parameter to specify where to write the prerendered output, or we can create custom JavaScript to handle it for us.

Let's start by using update. First, we need to figure out what DOM element to update. It can't be the city and state fields individually, because update let's us specify only a single DOM element to overwrite. The next option is to pick a container element that contains both address and city. Given the table structure of our form, we could create a *<div>* that wraps just the table rows containing the city and state. This is a bad idea, since injecting new table rows into an existing table has radically different effects on different browsers. Internet Explorer will just ignore the new rows entirely, while Safari will inject them but at the top of the table (and leave the existing values that you thought you were overwriting in their original locations).

So, to use update, we would have to overwrite the entire form whenever we post back the current Zip code value to the server. Here is the form that accomplishes the goal:

File 57

```
<html>
  <head>
    <title>Customer Data Screen</title>
    <style type="text/css">
      th { text-align: left; }
    </style>
    <%= javascript_include_tag 'controls', 'dragdrop', 'effects', 'prototype' %>
  </head>
<body>
  <h1>Corporate CRM System</h1>
  <h2>Enter Customer Data</h2>
  <div id="whole_form">
    <table>
```

```
<tr>
  <th>Customer Name:</th>
  <td><%= text_field 'address', 'name', {:size => 30} %></td>
</tr>
<tr>
  <th>Address:</th>
  <td><%= text_field 'address', 'address', {:size => 30} %></td>
</tr>

<tr>
  <th>City:</th>
  <td><%= text_field 'address', 'city', {:size => 20} %></td>
</tr>
<tr>
  <th>State:</th>
  <td>
    <%= text_field 'address', 'state', {:size => 3, :maxlength => 2} %>
  </td>
</tr>
<tr>
  <th>Zip:</th>
  <td>
    <%= text_field 'address', 'zip', {:size => 10, :maxlength => 10} %>
  </td>
  <%= observe_field :address_zip,
                    :url => {
                        :action => 'get_city_state_whole_form'
                    },
                    :with => "'zip=' + value",
                    :update => 'whole_form' %>
</tr>
<tr>
  <th></th>
  <td><%= submit_tag %></td>
</tr>
        </table>
      </div>
    </body>
</html>
```

Notice that observe_field helper right beneath the Zip field. You have to place the helper after the definition of the field it watches, or the generated JavaScript won't be able to find the target element at run-time. Here, we're specifying an event-based observer (no frequency specified) to watch the Zip field. Upon any change in the value, we call the get_city_state_whole_form of the current controller, passing in the Zip field's value as a parameter called zip.

The controller contains a method called get_city_state_whole_form that utilizes the Zip code data to create the output:

```
def get_city_state_whole_form
  @zip = @params[:zip]
  if(@zip=='90210')
    @city = "Beverly Hills"
    @state = "CA"
  else
    @city = "Durham"
    @state = "NC"
  end
end
```

Finally, there is a view called get_city_state_whole_form.rhtml in the file app/views/address that renders the new form:

```
<table>
    <tr>
        <th>Customer Name:</th>
        <td><%= text_field 'address', 'name', {:size => 30} %></td>
    </tr>
    <tr>
        <th>Address:</th>
        <td><%= text_field 'address', 'address', {:size => 30} %></td>
    </tr>

    <tr>
        <th>City:</th>
        <td>
          <%= text_field 'address', 'city', {:size => 20, :value => @city} %>
        </td>
    </tr>
    <tr>
        <th>State:</th>
        <td>
          <%= text_field 'address',
                         'state',
                         { :size => 3,
                           :maxlength => 2,
                           :value => @state} %>
        </td>
    </tr>
    <tr>
        <th>Zip:</th>
        <td>
          <%= text_field 'address',
                         'zip',
                         { :size => 10,
                           :maxlength => 10,
                           :value => @zip} %>
        </td>
        <%= observe_field :address_zip,
                          :url => { :action => 'get_city_state_whole_form'},
```

```
                                  :with => "'zip=' + value",
                                  :update => 'whole_form' %>
    </tr>
    <tr>
        <th></th>
        <td><%= submit_tag %></td>
    </tr>
</table>
```

Whenever the Zip field changes, the page posts the current Zip value back to the server, which in turn renders the HTML found in the template get_city_state_whole_form.rthml. This HTML is used to overwrite the entire form table on the page. This technique is remarkably unwieldy because it duplicates code in the views (edit_whole_form.rhtml duplicates much of get_city_state_whole_form.rthml).

Observing the Zip Field, Part II

To make this form less unwieldy, we'll eschew the update parameter of the observer and instead use custom JavaScript to parse the result data and assign the returned values to the city and state fields specifically. We'll make two simple changes to the original form. First, we'll modify the observer to call a custom JavaScript function upon completion of the request:

File 56

```
<tr>
    <th>Zip:</th>
    <td>
      <%= text_field 'address',
                     'zip',
                     { :size => 10, :maxlength => 10} %>
    </td>
    <%= observe_field :address_zip,
                      :url => {
                         :action => 'get_city_state_parse_data'
                      },
                      :with => "'zip=' + value",
                      :complete => 'update_fields(request);'%>
</tr>
```

In this version, we specify a new action method on our controller, get_city_state_parse_data. On completion of the remote call, we'll pass the XHR object to a function called update_fields. Bear in mind that this construct means that the update_fields function will be called regardless of the success of the remote call; if we need to create a different function for when the call fails, we would use :success and :failure instead of :complete.

The second change to the page is the addition of the JavaScript for dealing with the results. We use the javascript_tag helper to output the function:

File 56

```
<%= javascript_tag <<-END
    function update_fields(xhr) {
        result = xhr.responseText.split(',');
        $('address_city').value = result[0];
        $('address_state').value = result[1];
    }
END
%>
```

This function expects a string composed of a city and state separated by a comma. We split the result on the comma and assign each value to its appropriate field.

The action method is largely identical to the previous example; the biggest difference is the rendered view for returning the data:

File 58

```
<%= @city -%>,<%= @state -%>
```

Even this is overkill, though. Since the view is so compact, we can render it directly from the action method itself. Doing that would eliminate the view file entirely (get_city_state_parse_data.rthml), and the action method would become as follows:

```
def get_city_state_parse_data
  zip = @params[:zip]
  if zip == '90210'
    render(:text => 'Beverly Hills,CA')
  else
    render(:text => 'Durham,NC')
  end
end
```

We've used the Rails helper methods to add the Ajax functionality to the address form as we have in our previous examples. Let's look at doing something a bit more difficult.

Autocomplete Fields

Let's use Rails' Ajax helpers to add an autocomplete feature to the form. As users type their Zip code into the Zip field, the form will provide possible results in a drop-down beneath the field. The list of available results will be based on what has been typed already.

First, we'll add a <div> tag to hold the autocomplete results. We'll give it a particular class name (auto_complete) and place it directly after the

Zip field for which we'll be providing the functionality. Second, we'll add the auto_complete_field helper to create the JavaScript.

`File 54`

```
<tr>
  <td>Zip:</td>
  <td>
    <%= text_field 'address',
                   'zip',
                   {:autocomplete => 'off'} %>
    <div class="auto_complete" id="address_zip_auto_complete">
    </div></td>
    <%= auto_complete_field 'address_zip',
                            :url => {:action => 'get_zips'} %>
     <%= observe_field :address_zip,
                       :url => {:action => 'get_city_state_parse_data'},
                       :with => "'zip=' + value",
                       :complete => 'update_fields(request);'%>
</tr>
```

We also have to add a set of styles to the page to allow the autocomplete block to look and act like a drop-down list. We've lifted this style directly from Script.aculo.us:

`File 54`

```
<style type="text/css">
  th { text-align: left; }

  div.auto_complete {
    width: 350px;
    background: #fff;
  }
  div.auto_complete ul {
    border:1px solid #888;
    margin:0;
    padding:0;
    width:100%;
    list-style-type:none;
  }
  div.auto_complete ul li {
    margin:0;
    padding:3px;
  }
  div.auto_complete ul li.selected {
    background-color: #ffb;
  }
  div.auto_complete ul strong.highlight {
    color: #800;
    margin:0;
    padding:0;
  }
</style>
```

Last, we'll add the get_zips method to AddressController to take the current value of the Zip field and return a list of possible matches:

File 51

```
def get_zips
  @orig = ['11111', '11222', '13444', '13555', '13556',
           '13557', '22222', '23333', '23444']
  zip = @params[:address][:zip]

  @zips = @orig.select {|z| z.starts_with?(zip)}
end
```

And finally here is the RHTML file for rendering the matches:

File 60

```
<ul>
<% @zips.each do |zip| %>
    <li><%= zip %></li>
<% end %>
</ul>
```

13.3 The Future of Ajax in Rails

Rails moves fast; version 1.0 was just released while we were writing this chapter. Features are added all the time. The team has just introduced a new feature called *RJS templates* that is making Ajax even easier with Rails.

RJS templates

So far, we've see the use of helper methods to help automate the generation and inclusion of JavaScript into the rendered page. With methods such as javascript_include_tag, we can inject application-global scripts into our pages. With helpers such as link_to_remote and javascript_tag, we can add page-specific JavaScript. The missing piece has been reusable Ajax methods for pages that share behavior and elements but that isn't general to every page in the application.

Imagine that your site is based on the idea of group membership; you may belong to multiple groups, and what you see on some pages is based on which group is currently "active." Those pages all have a drop-down box that lists your current groups. Switching between groups changes the header of the page (to show the new group name and logo) and a box that shows how many messages you have waiting from other members of the group.

Creating the drop-down box and its Ajax callback event is simple. We simply use the observer, as we saw earlier in this chapter:

```
<select id="group_select" name="group_select">
  <%= options_from_collection_for_select @user.groups,
                                         'id',
                                         'name',
                                         @user.current_group %>
```

```
</select>
<%= observe_field 'group_select',
    :url => {:action => 'change_group'},
    :with => "'group_id = ' + value"
%>
```

When this call is made, the change_group action will be invoked back on the server. This action will retrieve the new group from the selected ID and make it available to view:

```
def change_group
  @group = Group.find(@params['value'])
end
```

The key is the view that gets rendered as a result. Instead of a standard .rthm template, we'll use the new .rjs template extension. The template's full name would be change_group.rjs, and it looks like this:

```
page.replace_html 'header', :partial => 'shared/header'
page.replace_html 'status', :partial => 'shared/status'
page.visual_effect :highlight, 'status', :duration => 1
```

Rails uses this template to create a JavaScript block that is rendered back to the current page, evaluated, and executed within that page's context. It will replace an element called header with the results of parsing the shared _header.rhtml template. It will likewise replace the contents of status with the results of another partial rendering and finally trigger the highlight effect on status to let the user know that a change has been made.

The page object is just an instance of the JavaScriptGenerator class, part of the Prototype integration code. Its purpose is to provide a single provider of the various standard JavaScript blocks that your Ajax pages will need. Through the RJS templates, it becomes a conduit for interacting with the DOM elements of the current page. Now, when the drop-down box for selecting groups will be on a page that wants to react to its changing value, you can simply link to the appropriate server-side action (in this case, group_select), and the rest is handled automatically.

The page object exposes two kinds of methods: those that require only JavaScript on the client, and those that require the Prototype library in order to execute. The JavaScript methods are as follows:

- alert(): Takes a message and renders a JavaScript alert() call

- redirect_to(): Takes a URL and passes it to window.location.href()

- call(): Takes a function name and a list of arguments and creates a local JavaScript call to the function, passing in the arguments

- assign(): Takes a variable name and a value and creates a local JavaScript code block to assign the value to the variable

- delay(): Takes a block and a number of seconds and creates a JavaScript timeout to wait that number of seconds before executing the block

The Prototype-dependent methods are as follows:

- replace_html(): Takes an element ID and a hash of options, uses Element.update() to replace the contents of the element

- remove(): Takes one or more IDs and uses Element.remove() to delete them from the DOM

- show(): Takes one or more IDs and uses Element.show() to make them visible

- hide(): Takes one or more IDs and uses Element.hide() to make the invisible

- toggle(): Takes one or more IDs and uses Element.toggle() to toggle their visible state

To get this feature right now, you'd have to be running what's called Edge Rails, which is the trunk of the SubVersion repository. It isn't part of any official release as of the time of writing, but it shows you the speed with which the Rails team is integrating Ajax directly into the framework and making it easier and easier to provide powerful client-side actions across your applications.

Chapter 14

Proxy-Based Ajax with DWR

One of the problems with pushing more business code into your web application's client-side JavaScript is that most of your application's logic is probably tied up back on the server, wrapped up inside of whatever server-side programming language you prefer—and unless you're some kind of freak, chances are that language is not server-side JavaScript. How, then, can you get at that logic from within your client-side JavaScript environment? You certainly could create a bunch of custom endpoints in your application to receive Ajax requests from web clients, but what a pain! Wouldn't it be nice if you could just call your server-side code from your client-side JavaScript?

Enter what we call *proxy-based Ajax*: frameworks that enable you to directly invoke arbitrary logic on the server side from your JavaScript code. More than allowing such calls to take place, these proxy frameworks make it seamless and natural to call your server-side code using JavaScript.

For example, consider this JavaScript code sample using DWR, a popular proxy framework:

```
Line 1    function submitOrder() {
    -         return Customer.submitOrder();
    -     }
```

Line 2 looks like any other line of JavaScript code. Call it, however, and the DWR framework will automatically search for an object named Customer in the server-side environment and invoke the submitOrder() method on that object, returning the value to the JavaScript environment.

This behavior has a few implications. First, unless you have a web application with only one customer, the customer object you interact with on the server side must be associated with the current web session. Many of the proxy frameworks do indeed support the notion of binding objects that you interact with to the user's browsing session, allowing for unique objects for each user.

Second, the proxy framework must also support some way to transfer values returned by server-side methods into some format that the JavaScript environment can understand.

As you can see with just this simple example, proxy-based Ajax is enormously useful stuff for allowing your web clients to take on a whole new level of complexity previously reserved for your server-side code.

14.1 DWR

Java developers are blessed to have an excellent proxy Ajax framework available: Direct Web Remoting (DWR). DWR differentiates itself from other proxy frameworks by offering much tighter integration with Java and in being much easier to set up out of the box.

DWR was written by Joe Walker of Getahead, a boutique software consultancy; you can download it at http://getahead.ltd.uk/dwr/. Happily, DWR breaks from the pack of most other frameworks we discuss in this book: it is fairly well documented.

Using DWR in your own Java web applications is a simple, three-step process:

1. Add the DWR servlet to your project.
2. Create a DWR-specific configuration file.
3. Add the DWR JavaScript to your HTML.

Let's discuss each of these steps.

Adding the DWR Servlet to Your Project

DWR is distributed in two different ways: as a JAR file and as a WAR file. The JAR file contains all the files necessary to use DWR in your own web application. The WAR file adds to the JAR file some examples demonstrating how to use DWR, including a template web.xml file you can copy for use in your own project. Our discussion of DWR will be based on the JAR distribution; if you'd like to follow along with

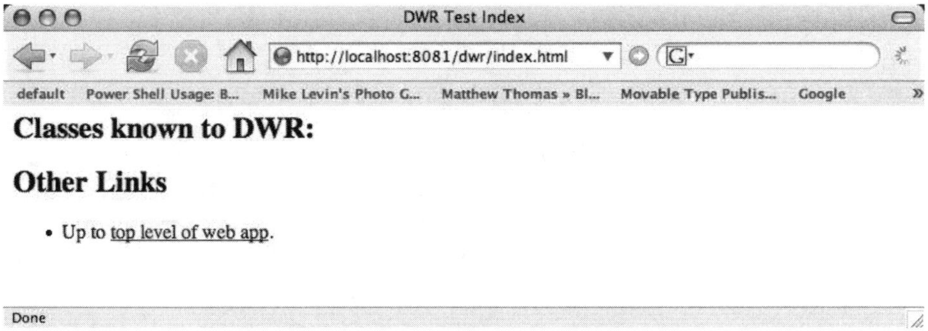

Figure 14.1: DWR Is Up and Running

the chapter as we discuss DWR, download that flavor. And if you do follow along, you should probably grab DWR version 1.0 to ensure the examples work properly.

Once you've got the JAR, place it in your web app's WEB-INF/lib directory, and add the following entries to your web.xml file:

```
<servlet>
  <servlet-name>dwr-invoker</servlet-name>
  <servlet-class>uk.ltd.getahead.dwr.DWRServlet</servlet-class>
  <init-param>
    <param-name>debug</param-name>
    <param-value>true</param-value>
  </init-param>
</servlet>
<servlet-mapping>
  <servlet-name>dwr-invoker</servlet-name>
  <url-pattern>/dwr/*</url-pattern>
</servlet-mapping>
```

Once you've added the DWR servlet to your web.xml file, you can deploy your application and access the DWR servlet. Test that it is installed correctly by visiting the page http://localhost[:port]/[webapp]/DWR/. You should see a very simple web page, shown in Figure 14.1. We'll talk about how to make that page more useful right now.

Create a DWR-Specific Configuration File

As we've mentioned, DWR lets you invoke methods on objects in your server-side environment. You have quite a few options for tweaking just how DWR permits such invocations. You can use DWR to allow

JavaScript code to create object instances (and persist them across requests by storing them in the session or application context), or you can integrate it with existing object instances or object management frameworks such as Spring.

Fortunately, the DWR folks had security on the mind and DWR imposes a few restrictions. First, you must explicitly expose those classes that DWR is authorized to interact with. You can even choose to restrict the methods on the class that may be invoked. Second, though DWR can convert any arbitrary JavaBean into a JavaScript object, by default it will convert only basic Java types into JavaScript types (primitives, primitive wrappers, String, Date and its java.sql subclasses, arrays containing these types, and Collection instances containing these types); you must explicitly declare which additional types DWR will attempt to convert when returning the result of a method invocation.

All of these options are controlled in the DWR configuration file, dwr.xml, which lives in your application's WEB-INF directory. Let's start our explanation of dwr.xml with a simple example:

```
<!DOCTYPE dwr PUBLIC "-//GetAhead Limited//DTD Direct Web Remoting 1.0//EN"
                     "http://www.getahead.ltd.uk/dwr/dwr10.dtd">
<dwr>
  <allow>
    <create creator="new" javascript="Validator">
      <param name="class" value="org.galbraiths.Validator"/>
    </create>
  </allow>
</dwr>
```

This is all the configuration we need to expose org.galbraiths.Validator and all of its methods for access from JavaScript code. The value of the javascript attribute, Validator, declares that the JavaScript proxy object that interacts with the server-side Validator class will also be named Validator. This class provides two methods that can validate certain types of data. For completeness, here's the source code to the class:

File 50

```java
package org.galbraiths;
public class Validator {
    private static final String[] CUSTOMER_IDS = { "123456", "654321" };

    public static String validateCustomerId(String customerId) {
        for (int i = 0; i < CUSTOMER_IDS.length; i++) {
            String id = CUSTOMER_IDS[i];
            if (customerId.equals(id)) return null;
        }
        return "Customer number is invalid";
    }
```

```
public static String validateTicketNumber(String ticketNumber) {
    if (ticketNumber.equals("")) return "Ticket number is required";

    try {
        Integer.parseInt(ticketNumber);
        return null;
    } catch (NumberFormatException e) {
        return "Ticket number must be a number";
    }
}
}
```

The important bit to take away from this code is that it has two methods, validateCustomerId() and validateTicketNumber(), that take strings and return null if the values are valid, and a string error message if the value is invalid.

Now we've added the DWR servlet to our application and we've configured DWR to expose our Validator class; the only thing left to do is create the JavaScript code that will use DWR to communicate with Validator.

Add the DWR JavaScript to your HTML

Now we've exposed Validator to DWR, so let's take another look at DWR's debug page. Visit http://localhost[:port]/[webapp]/DWR/ (if you're following along, you'll need to redeploy the application). You should now have a link named Validator on the resulting web page; click it, and you'll see a page that looks like Figure 14.2, on the next page.

This page is genuinely useful for a couple of reasons. First, it lists the exact lines of HTML you'll need to drop into your web page to use DWR:

```
<script type='text/javascript' src='/dwr/interface/Validator.js'></script>
<script type='text/javascript' src='/dwr/engine.js'></script>
```

These URLs won't actually exist in your project's file system, of course; because the URLs start with *dwr*, they'll be mapped to the DWR servlet, which will stream the JavaScript to your application at runtime.

Second, it actually lets you interact with the object you've exposed. It lists all of the exposed methods and allows you to directly enter an argument and execute the method; the results will be displayed next to the Execute button, as shown in Figure 14.3, on the following page.

It's now a fairly simple task to create a web page that can incorporate the DWR JavaScript to use the proxy-based Ajax approach. The following listing demonstrates a simple web page that we will use in the next few sections to incorporate DWR for Ajax validation of the customer ID and ticket number fields. The code appears on page 243.

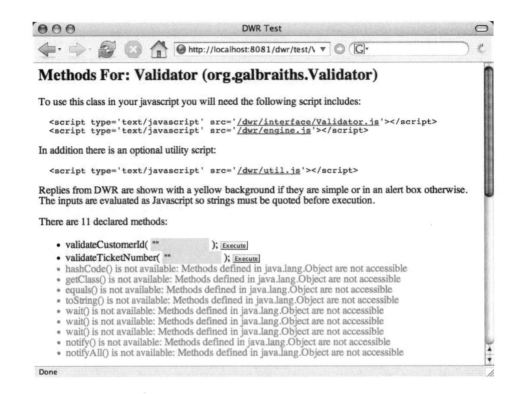

Figure 14.2: DWR EXPOSING THE VALIDATOR CLASS

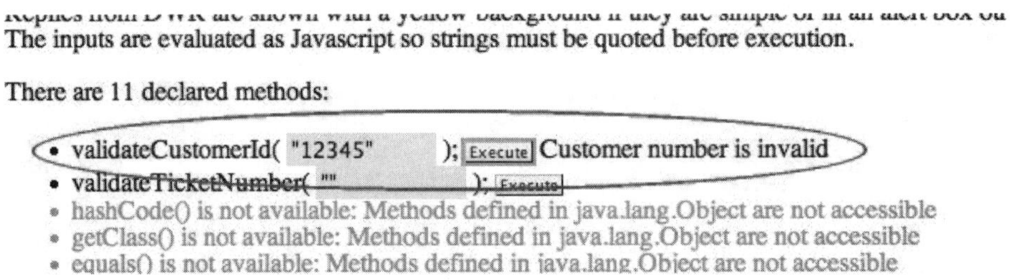

Figure 14.3: USING DWR TO INTERACT WITH THE VALIDATOR CLASS

File 47

```
<html>
  <head>
    <title>Form DWR Demo</title>
    <style type="text/css">
      .error {
        color: red;
      }
    </style>
  </head>
  <body>
    <h1>Data Entry Form</h1>
    <form method="post" action="/processForm">
      <table>
        <tr>
          <td>
            Customer Number:
          </td>
          <td>
            <input name="customerId" type="text" />
          </td>
          <td class="error" id="customerIdError"></td>
        </tr>
        <tr>
          <td>
            Ticket Number:
          </td>
          <td>
            <input name="ticketNumber" type="text" />
          </td>
          <td class="error" id="ticketNumberError"></td>
        </tr>
      </table>
      <input type="submit" value="Submit"/>
    </form>
  </body>
</html>
```

Adding DWR to the Web Page

To add DWR to the page, we'll paste the appropriate JavaScript into the web page's *<head>* tag, and we'll also write some simple JavaScript that will interact with the server-side *Validator* class:

File 48

```
Line 1    <head>
  -         <title>Form DWR Demo</title>
  -         <style type="text/css">
  -           .error {
  5             color: red;
  -           }
  -         </style>
```

```
     -      <script type="text/javascript" src="/dwr/interface/Validator.js"></script>
     -      <script type="text/javascript" src="/dwr/engine.js"></script>
    10      <script type="text/javascript">
     -        function validateCustomerId(value) {
     -          Validator.validateCustomerId(value, customerIdCallback);
     -        }
     -
    15        function customerIdCallback(returnValue) {
     -          document.getElementById("customerIdError").innerHTML = returnValue;
     -        }
     -      </script>
     -    </head>
```

Doesn't the method call on line 12 look like a normal Java invocation? DWR makes it pretty natural to use Java code in JavaScript. But, why do we pass in two arguments? Doesn't the Java method take just one?

It does; the second argument is a callback reference. Because Ajax (and DWR) is asynchronous, we have to provide a function to be invoked when the response to our request is received. That callback function, in this case customerIdCallback(), will be passed the returned content of the response as a string.

Now all we need to do is add a hook that will invoke our validateCustomerId() function at some point. Let's invoke the function whenever the customer ID input field loses focus; the HTML to wire this functionality together looks like this:

File 48

```
<input name="customerId" type="text"
       onblur="validateCustomerId(this.value)" />
```

Figure 14.4, on the facing page shows the finished product in action; after the customer ID field loses focus, DWR will pass its value to our Validator class on the server, which will return either null (which translates to an empty string in JavaScript) or an error message. In this case, an error message is displayed because we didn't enter an appropriate customer ID number.

DWR Configuration Details

We mentioned earlier that you can configure DWR to expose only a subset of the methods available in a class; let's discuss how to do that.

Returning to dwr.xml, we exposed the Validator class thusly:

File 46

```
<create creator="new" javascript="Validator">
  <param name="class" value="org.galbraiths.Validator"/>
</create>
```

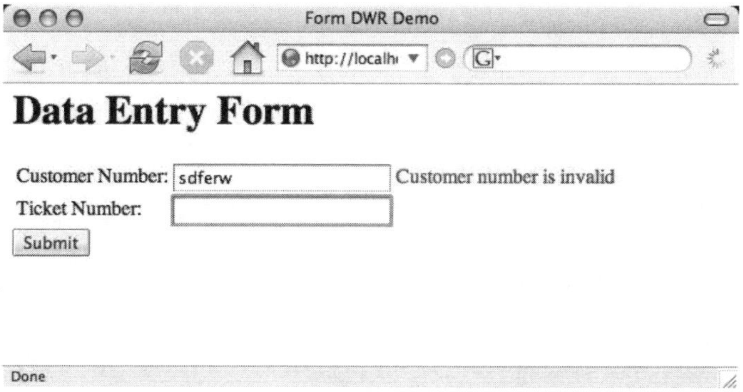

Figure 14.4: DWR INTEGRATED WITH THE WEB PAGE

As should be clear by now, this definition causes all of Validator's methods to be exposed. To refine the set of exposed methods, DWR gives you two choices: exclude all methods by default and explicitly *include* those methods you want exposed or the opposite—include all methods except for those you explicitly *exclude*. Using either is quite simple:

File 45

```
Line 1    <create creator="new" javascript="Validator">
   -        <param name="class" value="org.galbraiths.Validator"/>
   -        <include method="validateCustomerId"/>
   -      </create>
   5
   -      <create creator="new" javascript="Ledger">
   -        <param name="class" value="org.galbraiths.Ledger"/>
   -        <exclude method="revealSensitiveFinancialInfo"/>
   -        <auth method="cheatEmployeesOutOfMoney" role="boss"/>
  10      </create>
```

You can't mix and match your include/exclude strategy; thus, the presence of an *<include>* element on line 3 causes the include mechanism to be used for Validator, just as *<exclude>* on line 8 causes the exclude mechanism to be used for Ledger.

Line 9 illustrates another interesting DWR feature: integration with JAAS. Because DWR is designed for use within a servlet container, it can take advantage of the authentication services, specified by the Java Authentication and Authorization Service (JAAS), that servlet containers provide. In this case, we specify that only those users who have been authenticated and been granted the "boss" role can invoke the method cheatEmployeesOutOfMoney().

Method Overloading

Java supports the useful notion of *method overloading*. This feature allows you to define multiple methods with the same name but different arguments, such as foo(String bar) and foo(String bar, String baz).

JavaScript, however, does *not* support method overloading, primarily because the arguments JavaScript passes to a function are variable in length. That is, you can pass a function an unlimited number of arguments; those arguments defined when you declare a function simply assign the passed arguments to variables with those names:

```
function myFunction(foo) {
    // writing foo above is a shortcut for
    // writing this JavaScript code:
    foo = arguments[0];
}

function callMyFunction() {
    // I can pass as many arguments as I like
    // to the functions I invoke
    myFunction(1, 2, 3, 4, 5);
}
```

If you declare two functions with the same name in JavaScript, the most recent definition will overwrite the previous definition.

This means when using DWR, you need to be especially careful to avoid exposing overloaded methods. Because DWR's configuration file gives you no mechanism to specify the complete signature of the methods you expose, the result is that DWR will expose the first method it finds with the name you've specified. Java reflection does not specify the order in which it discovers methods, so with overloaded methods, you can't predict which method it will expose.

Variable Scopes

When you expose a class in the dwr.xml configuration file, DWR will create an instance of that class whenever the JavaScript proxy attempts to interact with it. Actually, that's not entirely true. When you expose static methods, DWR will invoke static methods on the class itself without bothering with instances. The first time DWR is used to invoke an *instance* method, it will instantiate the class.

This raises some interesting questions:

- How does DWR instantiate the class?
- Once instantiated, what's the life cycle of the instance?

Good questions; let's address them.

DWR and Object Instantiation

DWR delegates the creation of a class to a *creator* object, and of course, DWR can be extended with your own custom creators. Out of the box, DWR ships with creators that directly instantiate objects, integrate with Spring, and allow you to create objects using script code in the dwr.xml configuration file.

The type of creator you use is defined in the dwr.xml file as the creator= attribute of the <*create*> element:

File 46

```
<!DOCTYPE dwr PUBLIC
        "-//GetAhead Limited//DTD Direct Web Remoting 1.0//EN"
        "http://www.getahead.ltd.uk/dwr/dwr10.dtd">
<dwr>
  <allow>
    <create creator="new" javascript="Validator">
      <param name="class" value="org.galbraiths.Validator"/>
    </create>
  </allow>
</dwr>
```

In this code listing, the new creator is used, which directly instantiates objects.

The DWR documentation does a good job of defining all the different types of creators available, how to extend them, and so forth; we won't repeat that material here. See http://getahead.ltd.uk/dwr/server/dwrxml/creators for all of those details.

Object Life Cycles with DWR

As you probably expect, DWR integrates with the standard notion of object life cycles in a web application: session, application, request, and page scopes. You can specify the scope by adding a scope= attribute to the <*create*> element:

```
<create creator="new" javascript="Validator" scope="session">
  <param name="class" value="org.galbraiths.Validator"/>
  <include method="validateCustomerId"/>
</create>
```

If you specify session, application, or request scope, DWR will search for an instance in each of the objects controlling these scopes under a fairly mangled key it creates. If it fails to find an instance, it will create a new instance using the appropriate creator and place the instance in the appropriate scope.

While you might be tempted to place an instance into one of these scopes yourself for DWR to find or to access the instance that DWR creates, that's not a good idea. We've read the DWR source code and could tell you the scheme DWR uses to generate the instance keys, but we'd rather not tempt you.

However, DWR *does* provide two mechanisms for passing references for various servlet objects (such as the HttpSession) to your code. First, you can use uk.ltd.getahead.dwr.ExecutionContext, a DWR-specific class, in your own code. ExecutionContext is a singleton that uses a ThreadLocal variable to return the appropriate instances of the servlet objects, as in the following:

```
HttpSession session = ExecutionContext.get().getSession();
```

The second mechanism is interesting. If you expose a method that has any one of certain servlet API classes as a parameter, DWR's JavaScript proxy objects will ignore that argument and DWR will instead inject the appropriate servlet API instance into the invocation. These classes are: HttpServletRequest, HttpServletResponse, HttpSession, ServletConfig, and ServletContext.

For more information on interacting with servlet objects with DWR, see http://getahead.ltd.uk/dwr/server/javaapi.

Remoting Arbitrary Objects with DWR

We explained earlier that, out of the box, DWR is able to remote a limited set of Java types: primitive types and wrappers, String, Date (and the java.sql Date subclasses), arrays, collections, BigNumber, and various XML DOM formats (W3C DOM, DOM4J, JDOM, and XOM).

However, with a minor configuration tweak, DWR will happily remote any JavaBean across the wire, creating an equivalent JavaScript object with properties for each of the JavaBean getters and setters.

Up to now, this hasn't been an issue because our Validator class simply returned strings. Now, let us consider a new scenario with a method that will return a custom type to JavaScript. Let's start with a different class:

File 49

```java
package org.galbraiths;

import java.util.Date;

public class CustomType {
    private String name;
    private int number;
    private Date date;

    public CustomType() {
        name = "John Doe";
        number = 42;
        date = new Date();
    }

    public CustomType retrieve() {
        return new CustomType();
    }

    public String getName() {
        return name;
    }

    public void setName(String name) {
        this.name = name;
    }

    public int getNumber() {
        return number;
    }

    public void setNumber(int number) {
        this.number = number;
    }
```

```
public Date getDate() {
    return date;
}

public void setDate(Date date) {
    this.date = date;
}
}
```

We expose the retrieve() method to DWR, which returns an instance of
CustomType. In order to permit DWR to convert the CustomType instance
to a JavaScript object, we'll have to add a <converter> to the configuration file:

File 44

```
Line 1    <!DOCTYPE dwr PUBLIC
    -            "-//GetAhead Limited//DTD Direct Web Remoting 1.0//EN"
    -            "http://www.getahead.ltd.uk/dwr/dwr10.dtd">
    -    <dwr>
    5      <allow>
    -        <create creator="new" javascript="Validator">
    -          <param name="class" value="org.galbraiths.Validator"/>
    -        </create>
    -
    10       <create creator="new" javascript="CustomType">
    -          <param name="class" value="org.galbraiths.CustomType"/>
    -        </create>
    -
    -        <convert converter="bean" match="org.galbraiths.*"/>
    15     </allow>
    -    </dwr>
```

Line 14 shows this new converter entry. The converter= attribute indicates which converter mechanism will be used to convert the custom
type to JavaScript; in this case, we'll use DWR's built-in bean converter.
There are other built-in converters, but they're all predefined for you—
you generally don't need to worry about configuring them.

The match= attribute signifies which classes this converter is authorized
to convert. In this case, it's anything in the org.galbraiths package.

Now that we've got DWR configured to remote this type, let's create a
simple web page that demonstrate how easy it is to interact with this
object:

File 43

```
Line 1    <html>
    -      <head>
    -        <script type="text/javascript" src="/dwr/interface/CustomType.js"></scri
    -        <script type="text/javascript" src="/dwr/engine.js"></script>
    5        <script type="text/javascript" src="/dwr/util.js"></script>
```

```
 -      <script type="text/javascript">
 -        function getCustomType() {
 -          CustomType.retrieve(function(customType) {
 -            DWRUtil.setValue("name", customType.name);
10             DWRUtil.setValue("number", customType.number);
 -            DWRUtil.setValue("date", customType.date);
 -          });
 -        }
 -      </script>
15    </head>
 -    <body>
 -      <table>
 -        <tr>
 -          <td>Name:</td>
20           <td id="name"></td>
 -        </tr>
 -        <tr>
 -          <td>Number:</td>
 -          <td id="number"></td>
25         </tr>
 -        <tr>
 -          <td>Date:</td>
 -          <td id="date"></td>
 -        </tr>
30       </table>
 -       <button onclick="getCustomType()">Custom Type</button>
 -     </body>
 -   </html>
```

To save space, rather than define a callback function the traditional way, on line 8 we use an anonymous function to make the DOM manipulations to display the properties of the returned object.

Note also the new JavaScript we're using on line 5. This lets us use DWRUtil on line 9. Among other things, it has a handy setValue() function that will either use the value or innerHTML property, depending on whether the element referenced by ID is an input field or not.

The resulting web page looks something like the rendering depicted in Figure 14.5, on the next page.

Of course, you can create your own converters if you have custom requirements for converting your objects into JavaScript. You can find more information at http://getahead.ltd.uk/dwr/server/dwrxml/converters.

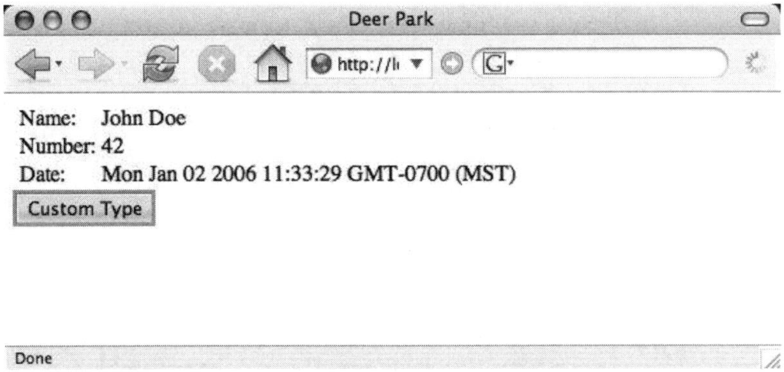

Figure 14.5: DWR REMOTING A CUSTOM TYPE

14.2 Conclusion

DWR is significant because it abstracts the underlying Ajax complexity and hides it behind a facade that is almost indistinguishable from direct Java object invocation. This makes the client-side code look familiar and, more important, straightforward to the developers on your team. DWR is the Ajax framework of choice for Spring development (see http://getahead.ltd.uk/dwr/server/spring), and Spring is a rapidly growing open-source alternative for building J2EE applications.

DWR is a wonderful starting point for Java web application developers because it exposes the server-side logic in an intuitive way to the client-side code. However, DWR currently offers little to no help in using the returned data in interesting ways in the UI. It is strictly about remoting; to achieve cool UI effects, you will need to write your own JavaScript or utilize another JavaScript framework, such as Script.aculo.us. It makes the data retrieval relatively simple, though, allowing your developers to focus their mental energy on the harder UI code.

Chapter 15

ASP.NET and Atlas

When we started writing this book, the idea was to cover two versions of Ajax for .NET: the open-source Ajax.NET toolkit from Michael Schwarz and the official Microsoft release for ASP.NET 2.0 called Atlas. While we were writing the book, though, the Ajax.NET project has been discontinued as a stand-alone effort and has been consumed by the commercial project called BorgWorX. We've tried hard to make sure that everything we originally wrote about Ajax.NET is still accurate now that it is BorgWorX, but we urge readers to check for themselves (at http://www.borgworx.net).

ASP.NET is a complex web development platform. It easily rivals anything to be had on the Java side, both in terms of complexity and in terms of features. ASP.NET grew out Microsoft's desire to make developing web applications feel as much like developing Visual Basic GUI applications as possible. To that end, ASP.NET is based around a visual design environment, self-contained server-side controls with HTML rendering capabilities, a custom state management solution, and the idea of *post back*—HTML forms continuously posting back to a server-side action as events are triggered on the GUI.

ASP.NET has long had Ajax-style interaction on certain components. Because Microsoft essentially invented XMLHttpRequest in its MSXML ActiveX libraries, it's had access to the asynchronous callback feature for a long time. ASP.NET has shipped with data and table controls that use MSXML since before the term Ajax was even coined.

As the movement has grown, though, the need for a more generalized, feature-rich, and, perhaps above all, extensible framework for doing Ajax has grown alongside. We need a real toolkit, as opposed to just a feature set for a couple of components. The first solution to hit the market was Ajax.NET, an open-source framework out of Germany. Then,

Microsoft announced it would release an official product called Atlas. We'll take a brief look at each.

15.1 BorgWorX

BorgWorX is based on a remoting framework similar to DWR. It creates server-side functions and client-side proxies to them that can be called from JavaScript. The client-side proxies transparently use XHR to invoke a broker on the server whose job it is to fire the server-side function, harvest the results, and return them as the XHR response.

To get this to work, you need the BorgWorX assembly available to your project. This means installing the file ajax.dll in the \ref folder within your project space and then adding it as a reference to the project.

Next, you need to configure a broker. The server-side broker is known as Ajax.PageHandlerFactory. This class extends HttpHandler, the ASP.NET base class that can be configured to receive requests targeted at specific URLs. To install this particular HttpHandler, you need to modify your project's web.config file:

```
<configuration>
  <system.web>
    <httpHandlers>
      <add verb="POST,GET" path="ajax/*.ashx"
           type="Ajax.PageHandlerFactory, Ajax" />
    </httpHandlers>
  </system.web>
</configuration>
```

Note that the handler is configured to listen for requests whose URLa ends in *.ashx. You will not create any URLs that utilize this extension; they will be generated for you by the framework later.

After configuring the handler, you have to identify the method(s) that you want to expose to your client side. The methods of any class can be used, but typically you would use methods of the current page class. Declaring a server-side method as Ajax accessible is simple; decorate it with the [AjaxMethod] attribute:

```
[AjaxMethod]
public string get_city_and_state(string zip)
{
  string results = "";
  // look up zip code
  return results;
}
```

You have now told the framework that you expect this method to be callable from JavaScript. What does it mean to be callable, though? It means that your JavaScript code can directly call get_city_and_state() and receive a string value as a result via an asynchronous callback to the server.

The results are returned, unsurprisingly, using JSON (see Chapter 10, *JSON and JSON-RPC*, on page 189). BorgWorX automatically translates many values into JSON data: integers, strings, doubles, booleans, DateTime, DataSets, DataTables, and arrays. In addition, any class that is designated as [Serialiazable] is a candidate. If your type isn't represented here, you can create a custom implementation of IAjaxObjectConverter to hook into the serialization chain and convert arbitrary types to JSON yourself.

The client-side JavaScript will parse the returned JSON as idiomatic JavaScript notation to provide access to the features of the returned value. If the value is a primitive type (integer, boolean, etc.), then there is no real JSON serialization, just a direct value returned in the response.

To create the client-side proxies for use by your JavaScript, you must tell the ASP.NET page to include at least two JavaScript blocks. The first is the core library of code that wraps the use of XHR, and the second is the JavaScript that serves as the proxy to a given server type's data. Neither of these JavaScript blocks is a *file*, but is instead generated for you by the PageHandlerFactory you installed at the beginning of this section. To create the JavaScript blocks, you have to tell BorgWorX which types to worry about:

```
public class AddressPage : System.Web.UI.Page{
   private void Page_Load(object sender, EventArgs e){
      Ajax.Utility.RegisterTypeForAjax(typeof(AddressPage));
   }
}
```

All this code does is inject links to the appropriate JavaScript blocks into the rendered HTML page. The HTML would now contain:

```
<script language="javascript" src="ajax/common.ashx">
</script>
<script language="javascript" src="ajax/CRMApp.AddressPage,CRMApp.ashx">
</script>
```

Our PageHandlerFactory is configured to intercept any URLs ending in .ashx. The handler then constructs and returns the JavaScript code that proxies any methods of the target type marked with the [AjaxMethod] attribute.

To use our new proxy, we simply make the method call and use it as needed:

```
function retrieve_data() {
  result = get_city_and_state(document.getElementById('zip').value);
  results = result.split(',');
  document.getElementById('city').value = results[0];
  document.getElementById('state').value = results[1];
}
```

That's it. This straightforward framework makes it simple to expose all kinds of server-side functionality to the client, and with its extensible type conversion feature, it is easy to return all kinds of complex data to the client. This framework is pretty much the totality of Ajax.NET as it existed as a stand-alone project. With the acquisition by BorgWorX, the framework has been expanded to include a host of UI components that utilize these underpinnings to update their own data. With these components, you don't even have to worry about writing the JavaScript; they generate their own supporting client code, and the Ajax just happens for you. Check out the BorgWorX feature road map online[1] for a complete list of available components.

15.2 Atlas

Microsoft has, of course, seen the dawning of the Ajax movement and has decided that it cannot afford to be left behind. Microsoft should have had a leg up on everyone else in the marketplace on Ajax. They've had two advantages for years: MXSML (and its XMLHTTP object, the precursor to XMLHttpRequest), and a custom extension of CSS for Internet Explorer that allows you to associate *behaviors* with CSS classes or IDs. These behaviors are just event bindings written as custom CSS syntax, but they give you the ability to bind to events without using JavaScript at all.

However, even with these advantages, Microsoft didn't really understand the power of what it had until the same time the rest of us did: right about when Jesse James Garrett released his white paper and Google released Google Maps as a beta. Microsoft has since been on fire to make Ajax part of its ASP.NET 2.0 plans.

---

[1] http://www.jobline.cc/BorgWorX/default.aspx/BorgWorX/RoadMap.html

Our dear readers, we have to be honest with you. We aren't big fans of the resulting framework. Our fervent hope is that when finally realized, most of what we're about to show you is hidden beneath Visual Studio wizardry and you don't know it is there. Our fear is that developers will have to code against this framework, and it will simply sour them on the taste of Web 2.0.

Handlers and Modules

As with BorgWorX, Atlas requires you to install server-side handlers to intercept certain URLs in order to treat them as Ajax calls. For Atlas, you need an HttpHandler to intercept the calls to designated server-side functions and a HttpModule to deal with Ajax call state. Here is web.config with the registered components:

```
<system.web>

  <httpHandlers>
    <remove verb="*"
            path="*.asmx"/>
    <add verb="*"
         path="*.asmx"
         type="Microsoft.Web.Services.ScriptHandlerFactory"
         validate="false"/>
  </httpHandlers>

  <httpModules>
    <add name="AtlasModule"
         type="Microsoft.Web.Services.ScriptModule" />
  </httpModules>

</system.web>
```

Note that the default strategy for enabling server-side calls is to override the default handling of Microsoft's web services format, ..asmx. By removing the default handling of the web services and replacing it with the ScriptHandlerFactory, it enables the web services to interact with JavaScript on the client.

To be able to call the web service from JavaScript on your page, you have to import a JavaScript block that exposes the proxy objects. To do this, you need to use a custom HTML tag library provided for you by the Atlas project. To import it, add the following to web.config:

```
<pages>
  <controls>
    <add namespace="Microsoft.Web.UI"
         assembly="Microsoft.Web.Atlas"
         tagPrefix="atlas" />
  </controls>
</pages>
```

Next, create the web service class that has the method you want to export:

```
public class GetCRMData : System.Web.Services.WebService
{
  [WebMethod]
  public string GetCityState(string zip)
  {
    // look up city and state
    return results;
  }
}
```

Where you want to asynchronously call this service in the .aspx page, use the new tag library's custom tags to import the JavaScript proxy:

```
<atlas:ScriptManager ID="scriptManager"
                     runat="server"
                     EnableScriptComponents="false" >
  <Services>
    <atlas:ServiceReference Path="GetCRMData.asmx" />
  </Services>
</atlas:ScriptManager>
```

Finally, call the proxy in JavaScript and utilize the returned results. The data passed back from the server is just JSON. Yes, you read that correctly. Microsoft uses JSON as the wire format for data transmission in Atlas. Why? Isn't Microsoft a devotee of XML? Yes. The decision is even stranger when you look at the implementation suggestions for Atlas (as re-created here). Microsoft would have you remove the standard handling of [WebMethod]s (which normally emit and consume XML in the form of SOAP) and transparently replace that with JSON.

Don't get us wrong; we love that Microsoft has chosen to go with JSON for its data transport layer. It means Microsoft has chosen to run with an emerging standard built by the community rather than come up with a unique solution. Kudos, guys! We're just a little confused by the conflation of standard [WebMethod]s and JSON emission.

The good news here is that Atlas also provides a way to customize the serialization of server-side objects and data into the JSON output format. You can create custom subclasses of JavaScriptObjectSerializer and JavaScriptObjectDeserializer to perform custom serialization on your types.

The proxy methods expose the parameters of the server-side method and provide two more parameters at the end of the list: a callback function for when the call returns and a second for when the call times out. The registered completion handler takes a parameter called result that is just the harvested response from the XHR request.

```
function getCityState() {
  zip = $('zip').value;
  getData = CRMApp.GetCRMData.GetCityState(zip, ShowData, ShowTimeOut);
}

function ShowData(result) {
  results = result.split(',');
  $('city').value = results[0];
  $('state').value = results[1];
}

function ShowTimeOut(result) {
  alert("Your method timed out!");
}
```

Note the use of the CRMApp.GetCRMData.GetCityState namespace in the getCityState() function. This leads us to our next topic, JavaScript "improvements."

JavaScript "Improvements"

If you visit the Atlas tutorial pages on MSDN, you will be treated to an example of what English professors call *unintended irony*. Microsoft has introduced a client-side library to change some of how we write JavaScript. The heading for the section is *Making JavaScript Easier*. We'll let our readers be the judge of the accuracy of the statement.

The three new features that the libraries included with Atlas add to JavaScript are namespaces, inheritance, and the ability to define, then implement, and finally consume interfaces. This sounds eminently reasonable until you realize that JavaScript already has a notion of inheritance, one that matches its definition as a typeless object-oriented language, and that one does not need an interface in a dynamically typed language. Regardless of these two facts, here are the JavaScript samples posted on the ASP.NET Atlas page demonstrating how JavaScript is made easier.

This is their suggested improvement to allow for namespaces and inheritance:

```
// namespaces
Type.registerNamespace("Demo");

Demo.Person = function(firstName, lastName, alias)
{
    var _firstName = firstName;
    var _lastName = lastName;

    this.getFirstName = function() {
        return _firstName;
    }
    ...
}


Type.registerClass('Demo.Person', null, Web.IDisposable);

// inheritance
Type.registerNamespace("Demo");

Demo.Person = function(firstName, lastName, emailAddress) {
    var _firstName = firstName;
    var _lastName = lastName;
    var _emailAddress = emailAddress;

    this.getFirstName = function() {
        return _firstName;
    }
    ...
```

```
    this.dispose = function() {
        alert('bye ' + this.getName());
    }
}

Type.registerClass('Demo.Person', null, Web.IDisposable);
...

Demo.Person.prototype.toString = function() {
    return this.getName() + ' (' + this.getEmailAddress() + ')';
}


Demo.Employee = function(firstName, lastName, emailAddress, team, title) {

    Demo.Employee.initializeBase(this, [firstName, lastName, emailAddress]);

    var _team = team;
    var _title = title;

    this.getTeam = function() {
        return _team;
    }
    this.setTeam = function(team) {
        _team = team;
    }
    ...

}

Type.registerClass('Demo.Employee', Demo.Person);

Demo.Employee.prototype.toString = function() {
    return Demo.Employee.callBaseMethod(this, 'toString') +
            '\r\n' + this.getTitle() + '\r\n' + this.getTeam();
}
```

This example pretty cleanly demonstrates turning JavaScript into C#
(or Java). Atlas introduces the Type object which allows you to specify
classes and their superclasses. Atlas then makes sure that functions
from the bases are inherited by the subclasses. Notice the use of the
callBaseMethod() call at the end of that code sample; this is the explicit
way that a subclass can make use of its base class functionality.

JavaScript is actually built around the concept of "prototype" inheritance, meaning that an object essentially copies the functionality of its
prototype at the time of implementation. To extend a class, one need
only append new functionality to the prototype before instantiating the

new class based on it. The downside is that it takes effort to extend an inheritance chain more than one generation; it is not impossible, but it requires work on the part of the programmer. The Atlas code simply requires you to register your classes through their framework as above. But now you have a completely new way to manage your class hierarchies that actually competes against the default behavior of JavaScript (which is the same complaint registered against the inheritance models built into Prototype and MochiKit, as well).

Next, and perhaps most puzzling, is the introduction of interfaces.

```
// interfaces
Type.registerNamespace("Demo.Animals");

Demo.Animals.IPet = function() {
    this.getFriendlyName = Function.abstractMethod;
}

Type.registerInterface('Demo.Animals.IPet');

Demo.Animals.Animal = function(name) {
    var _name = name;
    this.getName = function() {
        return _name;
    }
}

Type.registerAbstractClass('Demo.Animals.Animal');

Demo.Animals.Animal.prototype.toStringCustom = function() {
    return this.getName();
}

Demo.Animals.Animal.prototype.speak = Function.abstractMethod;

Demo.Animals.Pet = function(name, friendlyName) {
    Demo.Animals.Pet.initializeBase(this, [name]);
    var _friendlyName = friendlyName;
    this.getFriendlyName = function() {
        return _friendlyName;
    }
}

Type.registerAbstractClass('Demo.Animals.Pet', Demo.Animals.Animal,
                           Demo.Animals.IPet);

Demo.Animals.Cat = function(friendlyName) {
    Demo.Animals.Cat.initializeBase(this, ['Cat', friendlyName]);
}
```

```
Type.registerClass('Demo.Animals.Cat', Demo.Animals.Pet);

Demo.Animals.Cat.prototype.speak = function() {
    alert('meow');
}

Demo.Animals.Cat.prototype.toStringCustom = function() {
    return 'Pet ' + Demo.Animals.Cat.callBaseMethod(this, 'toStringCustom');
}

Demo.Animals.Felix = function() {
    Demo.Animals.Felix.initializeBase(this, ['Felix']);
}

Type.registerClass('Demo.Animals.Felix', Demo.Animals.Cat);

Demo.Animals.Felix.prototype.toStringCustom = function() {
    return Demo.Animals.Felix.callBaseMethod(this, 'toStringCustom') +
                    ' ... its Felix!';
}

Demo.Animals.Dog = function(friendlyName) {
    Demo.Animals.Dog.initializeBase(this, ['Dog', friendlyName]);
}

Type.registerClass('Demo.Animals.Dog', Demo.Animals.Pet);

Demo.Animals.Dog.prototype.speak = function() {
    alert('woof');
}

Demo.Animals.Tiger = function() {
    Demo.Animals.Tiger.initializeBase(this, ['Tiger']);
}

Type.registerClass('Demo.Animals.Tiger', Demo.Animals.Animal);

Demo.Animals.Tiger.prototype.speak = function() {
    alert('grrr');
}
```

We don't mean to beat a dead Cat here, but there is essentially no need whatsoever for an interface in a dynamically typed language. Interfaces are lightweight constructs that allow compilers to know about the published API of a type without the actual runtime executable code being required. They are tools for circumventing the restrictions of strong typing; they allow the compiler to bind to the definitions of the method of a class but allow the programmer to substitute different images of the code at runtime.

In a dynamically typed language, you simply implement the methods that you want to expose on the types you create. Called *duck typing*, it means that you don't have to make promises you don't want to keep. In fact, it means you don't have to make promises at all. You create a type and attach behaviors to it that make sense for that type. You can then pass instances of it to any methods that want to use those features. Since there is no compiler to whose needs you must attend, there is no compelling reason to predefine the expected behavior of a type.

While the previous code may supply ample benefits to the underlying framework, you would be hard-pressed to find any programmers working with JavaScript who would consider writing it this way. It flies in the face of the purpose of JavaScript and essentially feels like a continuation of the decade-long argument that scripting languages aren't real languages. It does not make JavaScript any clearer, more concise, or even more powerful (except possibly in the case of namespaces). This brings us back to a point we made at the beginning of this section: if the previous JavaScript example is simply the emitted artifact of some code generator in your toolkit, then it is reasonable. But it is burdensome if viewed as a necessary syntax extension to idiomatic JavaScript for programmers who must work directly in the language.

Components

The last major piece of Atlas is the suite of components that render controls automatically into the HTML document and rig up all the Ajax callbacks to make those components completely self-contained. This is where Atlas shines, because the integration with Visual Studio makes the components a compelling feature for developers who are used to using visual tools to create web pages.

As we write this, the component library is still being scoped out and developed. The building blocks are in place: the Atlas development kit ships with three major components you can use to build on:

- *UpdatePanel*: Essentially renders a *<div>* with a collection of server-side event callbacks autowired and to which you can assign one or more triggers (the Atlas term for a JavaScript event binding)

- *ScriptManager*: Lets you specify the external JavaScript files to include in your page (including both default, autogenerated files and your own custom files) as well as specify the proxies you want to use in this page (contained in a collection called Services)

- *TimerControl*: Does what its name says...establishes a JavaScript single-shot countdown or interval timer to trigger events. Those events can be client-side effects or server callbacks.

On top of the components themselves, there are also what Atlas calls *control extenders*. These are essentially Ajax behaviors that can be attached to any existing ASP.NET controls to supply callbacks on trigger events. They include autocomplete and drag-and-drop behaviors that can be attached to the properties of various server controls.

As Atlas grows and matures, we can expect these building blocks to grow into a complete suite of self-contained Ajax components that will simply require the user to drop them on their ASP.NET form and check a few boxes in the properties list. For now, though, you have to use these pieces to build up your control library yourself.

This collection of components will make or break Atlas. ASP.NET developers will use the Atlas framework in droves, regardless of complexity of the client-side JavaScript, *as long as that complexity is completely hidden beneath the toolset*. So watch the emerging documentation to see both how compelling the components really are and how well they hide the underlying implementation details.

15.3 Conclusion

We really like what we see from both the BorgWorX project and from Microsoft's Atlas framework in its support for the visual web developers who make up the bulk of the ASP.NET web development community. The component suites being created, and the strategies they use for providing self-contained, highly dynamic behavior, will help bring Ajax to the mainstream corporate web application development teams that are using the .NET platform. We also think that the remoting schemes, particularly BorgWorX's straightforward JSON framework with specialized callback methods on the server, are both simple and robust enough for most use cases.

We are somewhat disappointed with what we see as overengineering in the Atlas framework. From the decision to overload the expected behavior of web service methods to mostly needless additions to JavaScript, we see a lot of complexity for its own sake and hope, as the platform matures, that some of that is reduced or eliminated.

Chapter 16

Ajax in the Future and Beyond

So far in this book, we've talked about what people believe Ajax is today. The frameworks that we've covered have been built upon widely available mechanisms and platforms, largely JavaScript, XML, and XHR. These tools are available on every modern browser, thereby making them idea carriers for this new technology movement.

This chapter covers what's coming next. Here, we'll examine new standards and specs that are written and exist and will shape the future of web applications but might not yet be widely available on all platforms. We'll look at new tools that largely break down into two camps: tools for working more efficiently with structured data (and communicating it more efficiently between tiers) and tools for advanced UI effects and control.

On the data side, we'll take a peek at E4X, a strategy for giving developers direct access to structured data from within JavaScript itself. On the UI side, we'll look at the *<canvas>* tag and Scalable Vector Graphics (SVG). We'll see what they provide for our UI, and where each is available today.

16.1 Data Manipulation

So far, we've talked about two general strategies for moving data from the server down to the client. (We've really just used the standard HTML post mechanism, or the query string for GET requests, for pushing data up from the client). We've seen examples of sending custom-formatted data (usually a string of comma-separated values) as well as using the more formal, but flexible, XML notation.

In Chapter 10, *JSON and JSON-RPC*, on page 189, we examined JSON and JSON-RPC, a pure JavaScript notation for sending and manipulating structured data. This is great for teams that eschew sending complex XML packets down to the client tier because the tools for manipulating that data are complex and cumbersome. Using DOM parsing and navigation tools, XPath or XSLT in JavaScript is certainly possible but not exactly straightforward and far from easy. Instead, they stick with JSON and its inherent speed and simplicity.

However, the capabilities inherent in XML for data transfer (hierarchical data, ordered access, namespaces, etc.) are too powerful to be ignored for larger applications that have to shove a lot of data down the pipe. What we need are syntactically minimal tools for accessing and manipulating this kind of data, something that almost looks like the rest of JavaScript and that doesn't involve us jumping through too many hoops. Enter E4X.

E4X

What if your server-side framework is already adept at spitting out XML? After all, XML has dominated the data transfer space since the late '90s. Everything seems to have the ability to serialize to XML, and XML parsing libraries are ubiquitous. XML also has advanced features, such as namespaces that make it a more robust data representation format than, for instance, JSON.

What is needed is a way to interact with XML as though it were a normal JavaScript object, instead of as a DOM document through a custom library. E4X, originally conceptualized by BEA and standardized as ECMA-357,[1] is an extension to JavaScript that supports a more natural way to use XML in script.

Imagine, then, that your server is returning name and address data as XML:

```
<addresses>
  <address>
    <name>DOE, JANE</name>
    <street>111 Appian Way</street>
    <city>Atlanta</city>
    <state>GA</state>
    <zip>11111</zip>
  </address>
```

---

[1] http://www.ecma-international.org/publications/standards/Ecma-357.htm

```
  <address>
    <name>DOE, JOHN</name>
    <street>222 Something Street</street>
    <city>San Diego</city>
    <state>CA</state>
    <zip>22222</zip>
  </address>
  <address>
    <name>MCKENZIE, DOUG</name>
    <street>333 Maple Leaf Avenue</street>
    <city>Toronto</city>
    <state>ON</state>
    <zip>L4Z 1X2</zip>
  </address>
</addresses>
```

Instead of loading it up through a parser, using E4X, we can simply assign this to a JavaScript variable and begin navigating the document using the E4X notation:

```
var xml = new XML(xhr.responseText);
var num_addresses = xml.address.length(); // == 3
for(i=0; i < xml.address.length(); i++)
{
  new Insertion.Bottom('names', xml.address[i].name);
}

// alternatively, use .. notation to collect
// just the <name> elements
var names = xml..name;
for(i=0; i < names.length(); i++)
{
  new Insertion.Bottom('names', names[i]);
}
```

E4X essentially does for XML what JSON does for JavaScript data structures: parses the data and creates a series of nested JavaScript objects whose property names match the names of the data structure's element, providing direct access to the underlying values. E4X has the extra capability of collecting subsets of data based on element name, through the .. notation we saw previously. Its usage is essentially identical to XPath's //, meaning it finds all elements of that name at any depth in the hierarchy and creates a list out of them.

XML has another distinction over JSON (and structures like it). In addition to nesting data, XML allows you to use element attributes as another vector of data storage. Attributes, you'll recall, are unordered lists of data associated with a single element, whereas nested elements are ordered. Let's modify our previously returned data to include some attributes:

```
<addresses>
  <address id="1" country="US">
    <name>DOE, JANE</name>
    <street>111 Appian Way</street>
    <city>Atlanta</city>
    <state>GA</state>
    <zip>11111</zip>
  </address>
  <address id="2" country="US">
    <name>DOE, JOHN</name>
    <street>222 Something Street</street>
    <city>San Diego</city>
    <state>CA</state>
    <zip>22222</zip>
  </address>
  <address id="3" country="Canada">
    <name>MCKENZIE, DOUG</name>
    <street>333 Maple Leaf Avenue</street>
    <city>Toronto</city>
    <state>ON</state>
    <zip>L4Z 1X2</zip>
  </address>
</addresses>
```

We access attributes using the @ notation in our JavaScript:

```
var xml = new XML(xhr.responseText);
for(i=0;i<xml.address.length();i++)
{
  if(xml.address[i].@country == 'US')
  {
    // treat as a US state
  }
  else
  {
    // treat as Canadian province.
  }
}
```

You can likewise grab the entire list of attributes from any single element using the @* notation, as in xml.address[0].@*.

E4X isn't only about reading data. You can use it to add and edit data, as well. Editing is simple: just set the value of a property to a new value, and that's it. Adding is also extremely easy:

```
var xml = new XML(xhr.responseText);
xml.address += <address id="4" country="UK">
                 <name>WITHERSPOON, NIGEL</name>
                 <street>333 Trafalgar Square</street>...
               </address>
```

On top of all that, E4X offers a *builder* strategy for constructing XML documents. Using dynamic properties (the ability to refer to a nonexistent property of an object without generating an exception), E4X allows you to create this addresses list like so:

```
var xml = <addresses/>;
xml.address[0].@id = 1;
xml.address[0].@country = "US";
xml.address[0].name = "DOE, JANE";
// ...
xml.address[1].@id = 2;
// ...
xml.address[2].zip = "L4X 2Z1";
```

The E4X specification also includes support for namespaces and qualified names, as you would expect any XML library to do. In short, you get the full expressive power of XML for data transport but a direct and not-too-verbose syntax for reading, editing, and writing XML data inside your JavaScript.

We see E4X as the perfect storm of XML and client-side scripting. So many server-side frameworks are already spitting XML out of all their sockets that it will be easier in the long run to start consuming it using E4X than to change those servers to emit the customized JSON syntax. JSON is still faster than E4X because XML parsing will be slower overall than evaluating JSON, but the benefits of consuming standard XML cannot be ignored.

16.2 UI Manipulation

In this book, we've looked at how to transfer data from the server to the client. The other half of the equation is: what do we do with it once it arrives? Looking at the Ajax techniques we've covered in this book so far, the options would appear to be as follows:

- Pull values from the data, and assign them into form fields.
- Create or append new chunks of HTML inside the DOM.
- Apply CSS-based effects to pieces of the DOM.

Without being an absolutely amazing CSS and DOM guru, it would be difficult if not impossible to use incoming data to draw interesting pictures. Images tend to have to be generated on the server and imported through the old standby <*img*> tag. Charts, graphs, icons, and images of all types need to exist on the server for import into the UI.

But this is Ajax! This is the world where we suck data asynchronously down to the client! This is where the client side is in charge of the view! Surely, there must be a way around this. Of course there is. Several technologies exist today that let you consume raw data and turn it into graphical representations on the client side. You can do it (and have been able to for years now) with both Java applets and Flash movies. Both of these technologies can create graphics live in the browser; both, however, require an external browser plug-in to work. We've talked about Flash elsewhere in this book, and won't rehash that now except to say that just about everything we said about Flash applies to Java applets as well (except the part about most Flash being pretty).

It would be interesting to have native browser features that let us create graphics on the client tier. There are two emerging strategies for allowing this: the <canvas> element and Scalable Vector Graphics (SVG).

Canvas

Apple originally released the nonstandard <canvas> tag as part of the WebKit package for Safari. Since then, it has been rolled into a recommendation by the Web Hypertext Application Technology Working Group (WHATWG, http://www.whatwg.org) and implemented in Mozilla, Firefox and Opera, with third-party support for the tag in IE.

To quote the WHATWG specification, <canvas> is "a resolution-dependent bitmap canvas, which can be used for rendering graphs, game graphics, or other visual images on the fly." Its history is controversial, to say the least, because it competes with the already-standardized SVG specification (which we'll look at in a minute) and because it lacks certain key features. The one most often cited is that artifacts rendered inside a <canvas> cannot be manipulated or even identified from script once rendered; they are extra-DOM artifacts.

Regardless, the <canvas> tag gives developers a place to draw, and a syntax for drawing, entirely client-side graphics. Again, let's go to an example. You've got a server that returns data about how different people answer a given survey question, broken down by party affiliation. Here's the data, rendered as XML by our server:

```
<percs>
  <perc id="democrats">.44</perc>
  <perc id="republicans">.46</perc>
  <perc id="independents">.08</perc>
</percs>
```

We would capture this value as the result of an XHR callback, parse it into a local variable, and pass that into a function that could draw the results. Before we can draw it, though, there has to be a target to draw into. This would be an instance of the *<canvas>* tag. Here's an HTML page with canvas ready to go:

```
<html>
  <head>
    <!-- we'll fill this in in a sec -->
  </head>
  <body>
    <canvas id="canvas" width="300" height="300"></canvas>

  </body>
</html>
```

When using *<canvas>*, you are urged to fill in the element itself with the alternate data for display by browsers that do not support the tag. If the browser doesn't support the tag, whatever exists between the opening and closing tags will be rendered instead, kind of like the alt attribute on *<img>*.

Next, we'll write a draw() function that will take our returned data and draw a quick graph into the *<canvas>*. We'll feed it the XML as an E4X variable and use E4X's matching syntax to pull out individual values. To draw on a *<canvas>*, you have to retrieve a drawing context. The standard context provided is the 2d context, for drawing simple 2d bitmaps. Individual vendors are allowed to supply their own, custom contexts using vendor-specific prefixes (such as moz-3d). We'll use the 2d context to draw a simple bar graph.

We'll simply create a bar for each of the three percentages, in different colors, based on the geometry of the *<canvas>*. Since it is 300px tall, we need to apply each percentage to 300 to get the height of the bar. We'll use the fillRect() method of the context to create the bar. This method takes four parameters: X coordinate of the first vertex, Y coordinate of the first vertex, width, and height. Before calling fillRect() we have to tell the *<canvas>* how to fill in the rectangle, so we first call fillStyle():

```
function draw(vals) {
  var canvas = document.getElementById("canvas");
  var ctx = canvas.getContext("2d");

  var dem = vals.perc.(@id=="democrats");
  var rep = vals.perc.(@id=="republicans");
  var ind = vals.perc.(@id=="independents");
```

Do you think Elvis currently lives in a bunker beneath the White House?

Figure 16.1: USING CANVAS TAG TO DRAW GRAPHS

```
ctx.fillStyle = "rgb(0,0,200)";
ctx.fillRect (10, 300-(300*dem), 20, 300*dem);

ctx.fillStyle = "rgb(200,0,0)";
ctx.fillRect(40, 300-(300*rep), 20, 300*rep);

ctx.fillStyle = "rgb(0,200,0)";
ctx.fillRect(70, 300-(300*ind), 20, 300*ind);

ctx.fillStyle = "rgb(0,0,0)";

// draw black lines down left and along bottom for axes
ctx.fillRect(0,0,1,300);
ctx.fillRect(0,299,300,1);
}
```

Figure 16.1 show the resulting page rendered in Firefox 1.5 on OS X.

Obviously, you can do considerably more complex types of image rendering in the <canvas>. You can draw elliptical objects, draw areas using lines and curves, carve sections using object intersections, pretty much anything you can do in any other bitmap-rendering technology. In addition, you can use live transforms, zooming, alpha transparency, and animations to create games, windowing frameworks, etc.

The power of canvas to revolutionize web application development is not yet fully understood, but gradually the revelation is dawning. We can't point you to any websites that put canvas to any particularly interesting business use. But we can discuss a few demos on the Web that showcase some of what's possible.

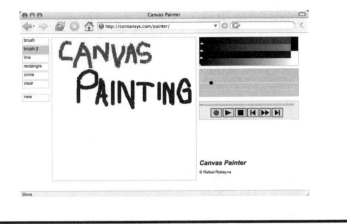

Figure 16.2: NOW YOU CAN PAINT ON THE WEB!

Canvas Demos

Rafael Robayna has put together the painting program shown in Figure 16.2 using canvas. Canvas Painter[2] allows you to use two different brushes and a few basic shapes to draw images. It also records the drawing process, letting you play back your drawing session.

What's interesting is how much (or rather, how little) code is behind the Canvas Painter demo. All of the functionality you see in the demo is provided by 726 lines of easy-to-understand, well-formatted JavaScript code (including whitespace), plus some boilerplate HTML/CSS. You might also find it interesting to know that the JavaScript that responds to user input to draw shapes, lines, etc., is implemented in only 185 lines; the remainder is concerned with drawing the various widgets (e.g., the color chooser on the right) and for recording what you draw.

If we offered an award for most visually twisted canvas demo in the fewest lines of code, it would probably go to Anne van Kesteren. Anne implemented what is probably a famous drawing in canvas, as shown in Figure 16.3, on the following page. When you look at this shape online,[3] it feels like the colors are shifting gradually—but they aren't. Neat.

The entirety of Anne's demo is as follows:

---

[2]http://caimansys.com/painter
[3]http://annevankesteren.nl/test/html/canvas/demo/002

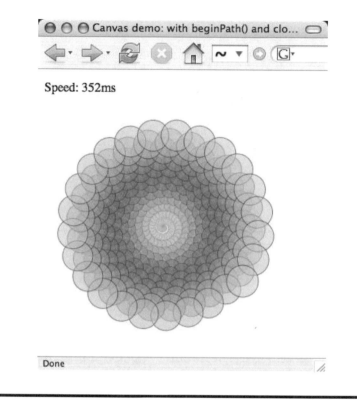

Figure 16.3: Are those colors shifting?

```
<!DOCTYPE html>
<title>Canvas demo: with beginPath() and closePath()</title>
<p>Speed:</p>
<canvas width="300" height="300">Your browser does not support canvas.</canvas>
<script>
 function drawStuff() {
  var phi = 1.61803399;
  var canvas = document.getElementsByTagName("canvas")[0];
  if(canvas.getContext){
   var ctx = canvas.getContext("2d");
   ctx.save();
   ctx.translate(canvas.width / 2.0, canvas.height / 2.0);
   var i = 0;
   var then = new Date();
   for (var i = 0; i < 300; i++){
    var theta = (i * phi * Math.PI * 0.05);
    var r = 0.4 * i;
    var xc = r * Math.cos(theta);
    var yc = r * Math.sin(theta);
    var rho = (i / 150.0) * Math.PI;
```

```
    var alpha = (i + 50) / 700;
    var red = Math.floor(192.0 + (63.0 * Math.sin(rho)));
    var green = Math.floor(192.0 + (63.0 * Math.cos(rho)));
    var blue = Math.floor(Math.sqrt(red));
    ctx.beginPath();
    ctx.fillStyle = "rgba(" + red + ", " + green + ", " +
                            blue + ", " + (1.0 - alpha) + ")";
    ctx.arc(xc, yc, alpha * 40.0, 0, 2 * Math.PI, 0);
    ctx.fill();
    ctx.arc(xc, yc, alpha * 40.0, 0, 2 * Math.PI, 0);
    ctx.strokeStyle = "rgba(0, 0, 0, " + alpha + ")";
    ctx.stroke();
    ctx.closePath();
   }
   var now = new Date();
   document.getElementsByTagName('p')[0].textContent += " "+(now-then)+"ms";
   ctx.restore();
  }
 }
 drawStuff();
</script>
```

The final demo we want to show you foreshadows the games that will eventually arrive using canvas. It's an implementation of a 3D shooter engine (without the shooting) in canvas, as shown in Figure 16.4, on the next page, Benjamin Joffe, as mentioned in the figure, is attempting a port of Doom to JavaScript/canvas (we wish him luck).

You should visit the demo[4] and check out how smooth the animation is as you use the keyboard to move around and jump. While this demo is just a little toy, our bet is that in three to four years, we're going to see some very impressive games of this genre emerge.

A simple painting program, a random shape, and the beginnings of a 3D shooter game; they are not much on the surface, but these represent a new evolutionary path that will lead us to an entirely new genre of web applications that are far more complex and visually impressive than anything we've seen before—and Ajax will power those applications, feeding them the data they need to render the interface.

IE Holds Back the Web, Yet Again

The biggest drawback to <canvas> is the lack of support in Internet Explorer. With a dominant market share, IE is the limbo bar for most

---

[4]http://www.abrahamjoffe.com.au/ben/canvascape/

Figure 16.4: WHERE ARE THE MONSTERS?

corporate applications. If an application doesn't work in IE, it can't be used, so even though it is dead simple to draw complex charts and graphs completely on the client side using the <canvas> tag in Mozilla, Firefox, Safari, and Opera, the lack of IE support will make it hard for <canvas> to become mainstream. There are interesting projects at work to make something for IE that works (see Emil Eklund's work,[5] which creates a tag that sits on top of IE's VML support), but we think Microsoft needs to go ahead and implement this one so everybody can join the party.

---

[5]http://me.eae.net/archive/2005/12/29/canvas-in-ie/

SVG

That brings us to SVG. SVG has all the benefits of *<canvas>*: it is a client-rendered image technology that can be scripted in the browser for animations. It has the same major drawback as *<canvas>*, too, in that it has no native support in Internet Explorer. (IE supports an older specification called VML, as we saw in the previous section). But SVG has two major distinctions:

- SVG is XML. SVG images are just valid XML snippets, with all the inherent goodness (and badness) that implies.

- SVG can be embedded directly in a page (in XHTML-conformant browsers) or linked through a variety of elements like *<object>* or *<embed>*.

A third major distinction isn't as much about the SVG technology itself as it is about browsers. Some browsers natively support SVG, just like *<canvas>*. These browsers are Firefox 1.5, Safari (latest builds), and Camino. For other browsers, notably IE, there is not much concrete information available about plans to add native SVG support. However, you need not worry: Adobe has released an IE-compatible SVG viewer plug-in that does the trick (http://www.adobe.com/svg/main.html). This makes SVG a reasonable, cross-browser rendering option today.

Let's revisit at our graphic example, this time using embedded SVG instead of *<canvas>*. Remember, for this to work, your browser must support rendering XHTML. (We rendered using Firefox 1.5.) First, we have to define our page as XHTML by adding a namespace to the *<HTML>* tag:

```
<html xmlns="http://www.w3.org/1999/xhtml">

</html>
```

Next, let's create the basis of our SVG graph. By default, it will render the x and y axes and three bars, one for each of our data points. We're going to set the bars to a height of 0 for now, since we want to fill the data in from the results of an Ajax call later. Also, we are using a 300x300 space for the chart, so all calculations are based on the upper-left coordinate being (0,0) and not wanting to exceed (300,300).

```
<div id="chart">
  <svg xmlns="http://www.w3.org/2000/svg"
       xmlns:xlink="http://www.w3.org/1999/xlink"
       version="1.1" baseProfile="full">
    <g fill-opacity="0.7" stroke="black" stroke-width="0.1cm">
```

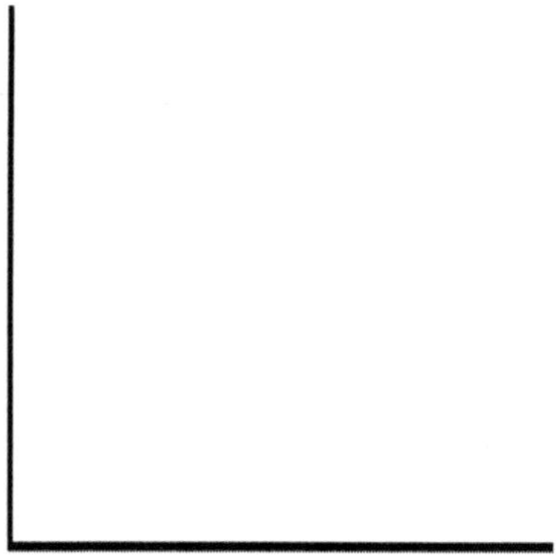

Figure 16.5: Empty SVG chart.

```
        <rect id="yaxis" x="0" y="0" width="1" height="300"
                        fill="black"/>
        <rect id="xaxis" x="0" y="300" width="300" height="1"
                        fill="black"/>
        <rect id="dem" x="10" y="10" width="20" height="0"
                        fill="blue" stroke="blue"/>
        <rect id="rep" x="40" y="10" width="20" height="0"
                        fill="red" stroke="red"/>
        <rect id="ind" x="70" y="10" width="20" height="0"
                        fill="green" stroke="green"/>
      </g>
    </svg>
  </div>
```

Figure 16.5, shows the rendering of this empty chart.

Since the embedded SVG graphic is just another part of the XHTML document, we can write JavaScript that interacts directly with any named element, just like with HTML. So, let's write a function that takes our three data points and adjusts the y coordinate and height of the three bars based on the data. We are using the old DOM-style document.getElementById(); method, although if you are using Prototype, you could also use $().

```
<script type="text/javascript">
        function change_chart(dem, rep, ind) {
                var demr = document.getElementById('dem');
                var repr = document.getElementById('rep');
                var indr = document.getElementById('ind');
```

2. Do you believe the black helicopters are coming to take away your tinfoil hat?

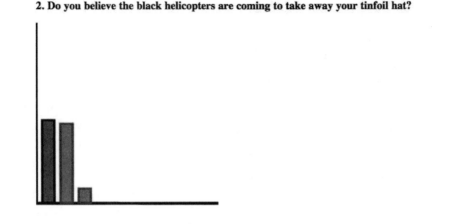

Figure 16.6: Simple SVG chart.

```
        demr.setAttribute('height', 300*dem);
        demr.setAttribute('y', 300-(300*dem));

        repr.setAttribute('height', 300*rep);
        repr.setAttribute('y', 300-(300*rep));

        indr.setAttribute('height', 300*ind);
        indr.setAttribute('y', 300-(300*ind));
    }
</script>
```

Since the *y* coordinate and height properties are just XML attributes, we can use our JavaScript DOM manipulation to adjust them on the fly. All that remains is setting up some kind of Ajax call to retrieve the data and, upon completion, to pass the data into our change_chart() function. This exercise is left to the reader.

Assuming that the resulting data is as follows:

- Democrats: .46
- Republicans: .44
- Independents: .08

then Figure 16.6 shows the final rendered chart.

While it is enormously appealing to be able to embed SVG graphics directly into the page like this, many browsers are not XHTML compliant yet so this technique won't work. The good and bad news is that the page won't throw any errors; it just won't show the SVG graphics. Users expecting the page to do anything of value for them might be left a tad confused.

The other option, then, is to link to SVG documents through another DOM element. You might think that the *<img>* tag is an ideal candidate; it has a src attribute that can point to URLs, and it is meant for displaying graphics. Unfortunately, this is not currently supported in any major release of any browser. Instead, you should use either the *<embed>* element or the *<object>* element.

For a full treatment of how and why each tag is useful, see the SVG wiki, specifically the page on embedding SVG in HTML.[6] Briefly, the prevailing wisdom is that you should wrap an *<object>* tag around an *<embed>* tag. Let's look at our charting example from this perspective.

In this case, instead of having an Ajax callback that retrieves our three data points, the Ajax method will return the SVG document itself. Since SVG is simply valid XML, the server need only craft a document and send it back as content-type: text/xml. We'll make the URL for this callback take the following form: http://myserver.com/get-svg-graph?question=2.

To create a linked element that renders this data, we would add the following to our page:

```
<object data="http://myserver.com/get-svg-graph?question=2"
        type="image/svg+xml"
        width="300" height="300">
  <embed src="http://myserver.com/get-svg-graph?question=2"
        type="image/svg+xml"
        width="300" height="300" />
</object>
```

Any browser that understands the *<object>* tag (and that means most modern browsers) will render the data as described by the attributes of the tag and *completely ignore* the enclosed *<embed>*. Conversely, browsers that don't understand *<object>* (namely, Netscape Navigator 2.x and 3.x) will ignore the surrounding *<object>* tag and render the *<embed>* instead.

---

[6]http://www.svg-whiz.com/wiki/index.php?title=SVG_and_HTML

SVG versus Canvas

As we've described, the major difference between SVG and canvas is that while SVG exposes all of its paths for manipulation in real-time using Ajaxian techniques, canvas is a painting surface that exposes no references to what is drawn on it. But, that doesn't mean you can't create interactive effects with canvas.

http://rig.vlad1.com/~vladimir/canvas/cdemo1.html is an example (Firefox 1.5 only) of using familiar mouseover listeners to create interactivity by redrawing the canvas as the user moves the mouse over certain portions. So while SVG makes interacting with graphics very easy, it's certainly possible with canvas.

16.3   Predictions

We've discussed many times that Ajax is based on technologies that are, frankly, not new. That's why Canvas, SVG, and E4X excite us. They show true innovation on the part of the browser providers—innovation the web development community hasn't experienced since Microsoft achieved dominance in browser market share. While we're not yet aware of any websites that put these technologies to any practical use, we hope what we've shown you gives you a taste of what is surely inevitable in the coming months.

And where does it go from here? Predicting the future is a task folks much smarter and better connected than us consistently do wrong. Having said that, a number of developments on the horizon, while still uncertain, are more probable than apocryphal. In the next few sections, we'd like to discuss a few of these possible futures.

Browser Local Storage Capabilities

One of the use cases that desktop applications handle much better than Ajax is an offline mode, the ability to cache data locally and provide some reasonable subset of functionality. While a number of hacks permit JavaScript applications to access the local file system, such as using proprietary browser APIs or Flash, there's room for tremendous improvement in this area.

The Firefox team is already discussing plans for implementing some form of browser storage capability. We believe this will come soon in the future and that Safari will quickly follow suit. Such a feature should address both the storage of arbitrary data as well as make it simple for a page to reliably store itself for offline use.

We expect a true, robust, and reliable offline storage API in the browsers to be an important and significant step in expanding the possibilities for Ajax applications.

Offline Storage with Dojo Today

As we mentioned earlier, the Dojo toolkit provides a local storage API today by wrapping whatever capabilities the browser provides. The nice benefit of using this API is that when browsers do introduce local storage capabilities, Dojo will wrap those abilities allowing you to continue using the same basic API.

More on Dojo

While we're on the subject of Dojo, have we mentioned how much we like it? We think Dojo, of all the existing JavaScript toolkits, has the most potential to break away from the pack and become a dominant player in the space. In fact, we feel so good about Dojo that we believe it will become obviously more popular than any other Ajax framework.

We believe a popular, stable, and widely used Dojo will do a great deal to remove much of the confusion in the Ajax space currently and gloss over many of the limitations of current JavaScript implementations. We further believe you'd be well advised to track Dojo closely in the coming months as its capabilities blossom.

Flash Apollo

We respect Flash's abilities. It's a very capable platform that offers some powerful features on top of what they claim is the most widely deployed piece of software in history—the Flash plug-in. Plagued by weird editing tools and slow performance in the past, the latest version of Flash offers some exciting possibilities.

Some of these interesting features include an Eclipse-based editing environment, a just-in-time JavaScript compiler, and hardware accelerated graphics (by layering on top of accelerated graphics APIs in the operating system). Flash is, in many ways, the JavaScript/SVG environment done right.

What's very interesting is that Adobe, the creator of Flash, has plans to create a version of Flash that targets desktop application development. This initiative is code-named Apollo. This environment therefore targets the same developers that Java and .NET are fighting over today, and unlike those environments, it can provide a web-hosted environment that's much more ubiquitous than any other programming platform.

When Apollo comes out and the next-generation Flash 8.5 platform we've described has reached 90%+ penetration (which Adobe claims will take a little more than a year after its release), Flash will be a very interesting platform that web developers will find familiar and that can be used broadly to accomplish great results. This could have a significant impact on the future of Ajax.

Compiled JavaScript

Ajax applications can retrieve data, draw graphics, and provide all kinds of rich dynamic effects. But there's one big problem: they're slow. In all of the current browsers, JavaScript is interpreted, and as such, is slow. Adobe Flash is doing a great job of demonstrating how the type of just-in-time (JIT) compilation of interpreted JavaScript can yield enormous benefits (just as Smalltalk, Java, and other interpreted languages have also used JIT to great effect).

We feel that it's only a matter of time before one of the major browsers provides a JIT JavaScript compilation environment, which would in turn free web pages that use JavaScript to run orders of magnitude faster than currently.

Let's be clear, however. For an application that uses JavaScript as simple glue—an event handler here, an Ajax request there—JIT compilation is not likely to yield perceptible results. But JIT compilation will open new doors for Ajax applications to be able to take on much more complex tasks than they are presently capable of tackling. For interesting case studies, just take a look at the reports of JIT compilation on the performance of Flash applications.

W3C's New Life

For years, the W3C has been the undisputed shepherd of web standards. HTML 4, XML, XHTML, and CSS (and more) all came from this venerable standards body. But times have changed. The WHATWG is now driving the next generation of web standards, and it's not entirely clear that the W3C will play any significant role in defining new web standards.

But that hasn't stopped the W3C from moving forward with its own standardization efforts. After failing to see its own Ajax-style standards catch on, the W3C is spinning up a number of new efforts intended to codify Ajax technologies into W3C standards and even an entirely new language for the creation of dynamic web-based applications.

It's hard to know whether these W3C efforts will ever produce officially approved specifications, and even harder to guess whether they will ever be implemented in browsers (well, except for perhaps Amaya, the W3C's own browser which is used by exactly no one). One thing that is for sure: it will be interesting to track these efforts to see what the eventual outcome will be.

16.4 Conclusion

Throughout this book, we've been extolling the virtues of this thing called Ajax. We've talked about how it is transforming the way we view web applications by providing us with asynchronous data retrieval and fancy UI effects. The future of Ajax, though, is about the disappearance of Ajax. If this technology is to succeed, it needs to be hidden underneath a framework that takes care of the dirty work for you.

The web frameworks of the future will seamlessly integrate standard HTML rendering with complex graphical output, all on the client side. They will communicate data from the server to the client using structured data in the form of XML or JSON. And, almost assuredly, they will hide 95% of the client-side JavaScript and server-side communication layers from you. Ajax will be *how these frameworks work*, not what you do while you are at work.

Index

Facets of Ruby Series

Now that you're a Ruby programmer, you'll want the definitive book on the Ruby language. Learn how to use Ruby to write exciting new applications. And if you're thinking of using Ruby to create Web applications, you really need to look at Ruby on Rails.

Programming Ruby (The PickAxe)

• The definitive guide for Ruby programmers. • Up-to-date and expanded for Ruby version 1.8. • Complete documentation of all the built-in classes, modules, and methods. • Complete descriptions of all ninety-eight standard libraries. • 200+ pages of new content in this edition. • Learn more about Ruby's web tools, unit testing, and programming philosophy.

Programming Ruby: The Pragmatic Programmer's Guide, 2nd Edition
Dave Thomas with Chad Fowler and Andy Hunt
(864 pages) ISBN: 0-9745140-5-5. $44.95

Agile Web Development with Rails

• The definitive guide for Rails developers. • Tutorial introduction, and in-depth reference. • All the scoop on ActiveRecord, ActionPack, and ActionView. • Special *David Says...* content by the inventor of Rails. • Chapters on testing, web services, Ajax, security, e-mail, deployment, and more.

Agile Web Development with Rails
Dave Thomas and David Heinemeier Hansson, with Leon Breedt, Mike Clark, Thomas Fuchs, and Andreas Schwarz
(560 pages) ISBN: 0-9745140-0-X. $34.95

The Pragmatic Bookshelf

The Pragmatic Bookshelf features books written by developers for developers. The titles continue the well-known Pragmatic Programmer style, and continue to garner awards and rave reviews. As development gets more and more difficult, the Pragmatic Programmers will be there with more titles and products to help programmers stay on top of their game.

Visit Us Online

Pragmatic Ajax
pragmaticprogrammer.com/titles/ajax
Source code from this book, errata, and other resources. Come give us feedback, too!

Register for Updates
pragmaticprogrammer.com/updates
Be notified when updates and new books become available.

Join the Community
pragmaticprogrammer.com/community
Read our weblogs, join our online discussions, participate in our mailing list, interact with our wiki, and benefit from the experience of other Pragmatic Programmers.

New and Noteworthy
pragmaticprogrammer.com/news
Check out the latest pragmatic developments in the news.

Save on the PDF and other Ruby Books

Save more than 60% on the PDF version of this book. Owning the paper version of this book entitles you to purchase the PDF version for only $7.50 (regularly $20.00). That's a saving of more than 60%. The PDF is great for carrying around on your laptop. It's hyperlinked, has color, and is fully searchable. Buy it now at pragmaticprogrammer.com/coupon

See the preceding page for information on *Programming Ruby*, the book to own if you're a Ruby programmer and *Agile Web Development with Rails*, the essential guide for Web developers.

Contact Us

Phone Orders:	1-800-699-PROG (+1 919 847 3884)
Online Orders:	www.pragmaticprogrammer.com/catalog
Customer Service:	orders@pragmaticprogrammer.com
Non-English Versions:	translations@pragmaticprogrammer.com
Pragmatic Teaching:	academic@pragmaticprogrammer.com
Author Proposals:	proposals@pragmaticprogrammer.com